JUVENILE CRIME and JUSTICE

JUVENILE CRIME and JUSTICE

GENERAL EDITOR

William J. Chambliss
George Washington University

KEY ISSUES IN *Crime* AND PUNISHMENT

SAGE | reference

Los Angeles | London | New Delhi
Singapore | Washington DC

Los Angeles | London | New Delhi
Singapore | Washington DC

FOR INFORMATION:

SAGE Publications, Inc.
2455 Teller Road
Thousand Oaks, California 91320
E-mail: order@sagepub.com

SAGE Publications India Pvt. Ltd.
B 1/I 1 Mohan Cooperative Industrial Area
Mathura Road, New Delhi 110 044
India

SAGE Publications Ltd.
1 Oliver's Yard
55 City Road
London EC1Y 1SP
United Kingdom

SAGE Publications Asia-Pacific Pte. Ltd.
33 Pekin Street #02-01
Far East Square
Singapore 048763

Vice President and Publisher: Rolf A. Janke
Senior Editor: Jim Brace-Thompson
Project Editor: Tracy Buyan
Cover Designer: Candice Harman
Editorial Assistant: Michele Thompson
Reference Systems Manager: Leticia Gutierrez
Reference Systems Coordinator: Laura Notton

Golson Media
President and Editor: J. Geoffrey Golson
Author Manager: Lisbeth Rogers
Layout and Copy Editor: Stephanie Larson
Proofreader: Mary Le Rouge
Indexer: J S Editorial

Printed in the United States of America.

Library of Congress Cataloging-in-Publication Data

Key issues in crime and punishment / William Chambliss, general editor.

   v. cm.

   Contents: v. 1. Crime and criminal behavior — v. 2. Police and law enforcement — v. 3. Courts, law, and justice — v. 4. Corrections — 5. Juvenile crime and justice.

   Includes bibliographical references and index.

   ISBN 978-1-4129-7855-2 (v. 1 : cloth) — ISBN 978-1-4129-7859-0 (v. 2 : cloth) — ISBN 978-1-4129-7857-6 (v. 3 : cloth) — ISBN 978-1-4129-7856-9 (v. 4 : cloth) — ISBN 978-1-4129-7858-3 (v. 5 : cloth)

   1. Crime. 2. Law enforcement. 3. Criminal justice, Administration of. 4. Corrections. 5. Juvenile delinquency. I. Chambliss, William J.

   HV6025.K38 2011

   364—dc22   2010054579

11 12 13 14 15 10 9 8 7 6 5 4 3 2 1

Contents

Introduction

Juvenile Crime and Justice

In this volume, authors address various topics pertaining to juvenile crime and justice. while varying in their specific discussion topics, many of the articles share common links, which typify the points of contention in the juvenile criminal justice system. Each author presents arguments in favor of various programs, treatments, and punishments, counterbalancing them with opposing arguments. Issues are raised along the lines of three loosely connected themes: prevention, prosecution, and corrections.

Prevention policies range from youth curfews, as discussed by Yvonne Vissing, to alternative schools, as discussed by Anthony Petrosino and Claire Morgan. Proponents for prevention policies point to successful outcomes as examples of the positives of these programs. For example, a study of the 1997 juvenile curfew in Monrovia, California, claimed that there was a 32 percent drop in residential burglaries after the curfew went into effect. Prevention policies such as alternative schools, it is argued, can target youths who are considered "at risk" and give them individualized instruction to avoid later criminal offenses.

Critics of prevention policies question their overall effectiveness, arguing that these policies inevitably result in the unfair targeting of some youths, and often lead to an escalation rather than a reduction in delinquency. Juvenile curfews, for example, lead to more youths who are arrested and incarcerated for curfew violations. Thus the law creates the crime rather than curtailing what would otherwise not be a crime. Furthermore, it is argued that juveniles arrested for curfew violations often are put into contact with more serious offenders that can lead to further delinquency. Youths involved in alternative schools are similarly stigmatized by being labeled as outcasts and are isolated with other students who may be more delinquent and aggressive, thus escalating potential problems.

When confronting juveniles in the criminal justice system, there are a few factors that the authors take into account in regard to the prosecution of youths. For one, the legally responsible party must be confronted in relation to the dualism of mens rea (guilty mind) and actus reus (physical act). Susan Reid and Gilbert Geis examine these issues in their chapters *Age Of Responsibility* and *Parental Responsibility Laws,* respectively. Where and how juveniles go to trial are relevant to issues of juveniles in adult courts and legal representation for juveniles. Those in favor of legal representation of juveniles believe that it creates a fair environment that protects constitutional rights. And while those in favor of juveniles in adult courts use the idea of "adult crime, adult time" in their defense, opponents of legal representation cite this idea as problematic. "Youth are treated like adults," Patricia Campie and Linda Szymanski write, "even though adolescent development research clearly indicates that youth decision making and subsequent delinquent behaviors require a much different response than what is needed to prevent or reduce adult re-offending."

There is a plethora of arguments on the positive and negative effects of different juvenile corrections policies. Arguments related to juvenile corrections range from sentencing options to where juvenile offenders should be housed to the death penalty for juvenile offenders. Arguments for boot camps, group homes, and out-of-home placement focus on the capacities of these programs to rehabilitate juvenile offenders and act as an intervention process to avoid further offenses. However, opponents of these programs highlight their cost, possibilities for abuse and neglect, and haphazard selection processes.

Also important to discussions of juvenile crime and justice is the Juvenile Justice and Delinquency Prevention Act (JJDPA) of 1974. The JJDPA has affected and helped mold many of the processes described above. Juveniles who are prosecuted in the juvenile court system, for example, are kept out of sight and earshot of adult offenders. This is done to prevent the victimization of the juvenile offender by adult offenders. Curfews, as Vissings points out, have roots in the JJDPA. When the JJDPA issued deinstitutionalization mandates in 1974, curfews helped keep those who had recently been incarcerated for infractions and mental health problems off of the streets. The JJDPA has also made strides to address the overrepresentation of minority youths in the juvenile justice system through various amendments.

The Office of Juvenile Justice and Delinquency Prevention (OJJDP) is an institution, established out of the JJDPA, that has had a large impact on the ways in which juvenile crime and justice is handled in the criminal justice system. The office is responsible for creating a model boot camp protocol; providing data and databases that are used in many of the chapters in this volume; and funding research on various topics related to the prevention, prosecution, and correction of juvenile crime. While the creation of boot camps is contentious, as is evidenced in Campie's discussion, the research brought forth by the OJJDP addresses many crucial issues in this field. The creation of a Disproportionate Minority Confinement (DMC) Best Practices Database provides states with a fully searchable Website that details models shown to be affective in curbing DMC, as noted in the chapter *Racial Disparities* by Tommy Curry. The OJJDP also began the Due Process Advocacy Project in 1993, which helps provide youths with legal representation in court.

Juvenile crime and justice is a very sensitive subject with much to be discussed. These chapters sift through the leading arguments pertaining to important topics in this field. As with most issues in the study of criminal justice, the best response to the problem of juvenile delinquency and crime is a hot-button issue around which there is endless debate. Legislature like the JJDPA and institutions like the OJJDP are attempting to fashion a fair and just way to handle juvenile crime and justice, but as the authors point out, there is still much to be done. In the last analysis, the arguments will be settled by empirical research, but unfortunately there is a lack of sufficient research at present to allow for definitive conclusions on many of the most controversial issues in juvenile justice policy.

William J. Chambliss
General Editor

1

Age of Responsibility

Susan A. Reid
St. Thomas University, New Brunswick

There are a number of provisions in law that use a child's age to protect those under the age of majority, usually under 18 years of age, from activities that are available to adults, but are deemed harmful to children. Examples of such protections include age restrictions on the sale of alcohol and tobacco products, minimum age restrictions on employment, and in the case of criminal law, the right to be presumed to lack capacity to infringe penal law if the person is below a certain minimum age. When considering the issue of criminal responsibility and the age at which full responsibility for criminal actions occurs, there are a number of issues that must be addressed. First, the traditional notion of the dualism of mens rea (guilty mind) and actus reus (physical act) in order to seek a criminal conviction must be considered in the context of age. Historically the age at which a child was seen to understand "good" from "evil" or "right" from "wrong" was set at under the age of seven, with special rebuttal provisions for those young people between seven and 14 years of age. The minimum age of juvenile court has wide fluctuations around the world, and the setting of this age is based on questions about a child's capacity as well as the doctrine of best interests of the child. Another issue that must be considered is the question of whether or not the machinery of the formal criminal court is the most appropriate means of intervention with children and youths when they commit acts that might be deemed criminal. The final issue is the question of the child's rights as outlined in international human rights instruments, and in particular, the United Nations Convention on the Rights of the Child (UNCRC).

Arguments for raising the minimum age of criminal responsibility include the issue of autonomy and capacity, as well as the desire to ensure that the state acts in the best interests of the child. Further considerations include a desire to protect the young person from the deleterious effects of a formal criminal trial and more serious adult sanctions, which has been shown to increase the likelihood of further entrenchment in the criminal justice system and may lead to a life of crime. By way of contrast, there are some who argue that it is important to treat certain young offenders in the same manner as adult offenders, due to the nature of the crimes they have committed. This "adulteration" of juvenile justice, they argue, is in keeping with what has been seen as an increasing maturity of young people and the responsibility they bear for their actions. This focus on the political dimensions of naming and shaming young offenders is in keeping with the idea that they must be held accountable for the heinous nature of their criminal behavior.

The academic literature on the effects of labeling on young criminals is helpful in considering the trajectories leading to career criminals from an early involvement in the criminal court process. Similarly, the literature from psychology and physiology is useful regarding the developmental pathways and brain development of children and youths in terms of their mental capacity to form judgments and understand the nature and circumstances of the events that surround their criminal conduct.

The main issues to be resolved regarding the question of age and criminal responsibility is the balance required between society's historic ideological focus, which has been seen as the need to protect children, legally and socially; and society's right to be protected from the wrongdoings of its members through accountability and punishment.

The Legal Regulation of Childhood and Adolescence

The law that regulates criminal conduct is based on a binary system, looking to the state for the protection of children until such time as they cross the threshold, known as the *age of majority,* to adulthood. While there is variation in the upper age jurisdiction of the youth court throughout the world, the age of majority assumes that the individual has reached a period in their development wherein they can be seen as fully autonomous individuals who are responsible for their choices and actions and no longer require the protection of the state. The problem with this binary system, focusing on immature children and competent adults, means that there is no opportunity to include the evolving capacities of children as they mature during their adolescent years. Some have argued that the period of adolescence is virtually invisible in law and regulatory bodies. When provisions do exist with respect to increasing rights, responsibilities, and obligations for adolescents, they are framed within this binary stance. Adolescents are viewed as either dependent, vulnerable, incompetent, and in need of protection like their younger counterparts; or as maturing adults who are self-sufficient, responsible, and competent.

The cutoff age when a child is no longer a child is reached at the age of 18, considered the age of majority. Prior to the age of majority, children and youths receive protection from the state in the form of restrictions on their freedom and investment in their development with the intent that such policies will pay dividends in terms of the promotion of competent adults as productive members of society. Where there have been changes to this upper age of childhood, policies have been put in place to allow for changing capacities of young people based on the notion that social welfare and the welfare of the young person can both benefit through such a reclassification. One example is related to the age of consent for a minor to receive medical treatment. By lowering the age of consent, there is a benefit to the young person and to the larger community in the form of reduced health costs associated with pregnancy, sexually transmitted disease, and other social welfare costs. In the case of youth justice, however, the rationale for lowering the age is not focused on the promotion of the welfare of youths. Rather, treating a youth like an adult for the purposes of criminal responsibility is more of a reflection of societal values reflected in the adage, "adult crime equals adult time."

The "best interest of the child" doctrine, which was paramount under the parens patriae doctrine (state acts like a kindly parent), in most juvenile courts appears to be in direct opposition to an increasing trend throughout the world known as the "adulteration" of youth crime, which treats young people in the same manner as an adult criminal. There are now provisions in juvenile criminal statutes throughout the world that makes it easier to transfer youths who commit criminal offences to the adult system, either for adjudication or for punishment. There are also a number of juvenile justice statutes that undermine the principle of confidentiality in youth justice proceedings by increasing the number of opportunities to share information about the youth defendant with criminal justice, educational, and social service agencies, as well as the media. Such repressive policies toward young people as zero-tolerance policies, curfews, naming and shaming rituals, and the targeting of pre-criminal disorder and incivility through anti-social behavior orders have underscored this punitive stance toward young people. The provision of a lowered age of criminal responsibility means that a child before the courts on a criminal matter has every other legal provision and protection of childhood, except when it comes to criminal punishment.

History of Criminal Responsibility

The first construction of legal responsibility for crimes comes from Hebrew law, where it was clear that children and those who were insane were not obligated to compensate victims for their harmful acts. Greek philosophers such as Plato and Aristotle elaborated upon the early Hebrew interpretation of criminal responsibility, outlining the early conceptions of voluntary and involuntary acts. The notion of some element of free will in the commission of an act is the cornerstone of the responsibility of the individual. According to Aristotle, children were seen as being able to act voluntarily, but like animals and the insane, children did not possess the capacity for premeditation, and so could not be considered morally responsible for their acts.

In Roman law, there is a brief mention of the incapacity of children and the insane in legal matters around 450 B.C.E. in the Twelve Tables. The Lex Cornelia, which was passed under the rule of Sulla and was in operation until the time of Julius Caesar, included criminal remedies for what could be seen as injuries to a person, property, or reputation, provided that the individual had the necessary intent for committing a harmful act. Children were not required to compensate their victims by virtue of their age and capacity. The term *doli incapax* referred to children under the age of seven, and were seen to be incapable of evil intent. Puberty was seen to be reached at this time at the age of 14 in males and 12 in females. Children between seven and 14 years of age were considered accountable for their actions, but only if the proof of their intention to act was clear and certain. This became known as the *rebuttable presumption*. The term *intellegat se delinquere* refers to the idea that a child is only liable on a charge if he is approaching puberty, and so understands that he is committing a wrongdoing. In the 7th century B.C.E., the practice of mitigating punishment for children and the insane was found in restrictions on contractual and delictual (compensatory civil action) obligations.

The legal doctrine of mens rea (guilty mind) can be traced to the moral philosophy of these early writers. During the medieval period, there was a clear focus on the control and punishment of criminals based on theological writings. There are many accounts of children not having the ability to form intent in the same manner in which "fools" could not be held responsible, because of their inability to choose the "good" from the "evil" (*conisaunt de bien ne de mal*). This "good and evil" test was noted in a number of decided cases throughout the 14th, 15th, and 16th centuries. In early English law, a child under the age of seven was free of judgment, as they were seen to be legally incapable of committing a crime. Between seven and 12 years of age, the concept of *militia supplet aetatem*, which means malice makes up for age, was applied.

By the time of Elizabeth I (c.1581), there was a practice in place of excluding infants and the insane from criminal responsibility because they failed to possess the necessary mental capacity to form the intent to commit a crime. They were treated as "non-persons" due to their lack of understanding, intelligence, and moral discretion. During the 17th century, the "good and evil" test continued to be paramount in cases involving children. In cases of children above the age of 14 but under the age of 21, the "good and evil" test was used to determine whether such individuals should be subjected to capital punishment as would others of "full age." The *praesumptio juris* meant that after age 14, children were *doli capaces* (capable), unless it could be proven that the individual could not discern between good and evil.

The "good and evil" test continued to be the main test of criminal responsibility through the 18th and the early part of the 19th century, but with increasing years, the terms "right from wrong" were used synonymously with "good and evil." This practice in English law formed the principle of common law, and became incorporated into the criminal law throughout North America. In the development of law in the United States in the 19th century, the work of William Blackstone was particularly important. He was most well known for a series of commentaries for judges regarding the provisions around criminal responsibility and children, published in 1771 as *The Commentaries on the Laws of England*. Referring to the evolution of British law since the time of Edward III, he remarks that the capacity of "contracting guilt" is to be measured not so much in terms of years and days, but by "the strength of the delinquent's understanding of judgment." Blackstone's *Commentaries* became the model for understanding the rules of evidence and the protection of young people from criminal prosecution.

While there were provisions to treat children as competent between seven and 14 years of age, the courts were extremely hesitant to sentence a child under the age of 14 to death.

Human Rights and the Age of Responsibility

In 1985, the United Nations (UN) Standard Minimum Rules for the Administration of Youth Justice, known as the Beijing rules, recognized the special needs of young people and the promotion of diversion from court proceedings. Further, these standards underscored the principle that custody should be used as a last resort for children, and that all proceedings against young people should be anonymous in order to protect children from lifelong stigma and labeling. The UN Convention on the Rights of the Child (UNCRC) expanded on these rules in 1989. The UNCRC has been ratified in more than 190 countries, and reiterates that children have a right to be protected from degrading and cruel punishment, and to receive special treatment in the justice system.

Further, it states that children below a minimum age shall be presumed not to have the capacity to infringe the penal law. While not setting an actual age for criminal responsibility, the UNCRC suggests that the minimum age of criminal responsibility should be set in line with the developmental capacities of children to avoid the formality of adult judicial proceedings. International standards recommend that the age of criminal responsibility be based on emotional, mental, and intellectual maturity, and that it not be set too low. There is great variation around the world in terms of the minimum age jurisdiction, with the youngest age being six years of age in some parts of the United States to age 18 in some parts of South America.

Most Violated Treaty

While the UNCRC has laudable objectives in its principles and articles, and it is the most ratified of all human rights instruments, it is also perhaps the most violated of the human rights treaties. Breaching the provisions of the UNCRC does not lead to any formal sanction. In many cases, the UNCRC has not been incorporated into domestic law in countries that have ratified it. In other cases, countries have put in reservations around specific issues regarding juvenile justice to allow for alterations to the provisions in the case of housing youth offenders with adult offenders, and other key issues that may promote the best interests of the young person. Even such fundamental principles as children not being exposed to inhuman or degrading treatment or punishment can be liberally construed in light of the controversy over the age of criminal responsibility and the ability of state parties to bend these rules to provide for more invasive and punitive sanctions for youths under the age of 18.

Pro: Supporting Minimum Age of Criminal Responsibility

The *infantia* rule from the earliest recorded documents, supplemented with the *doli incapax* provisions, were recognized formally in the development of the juvenile justice system in the early 1900s. Utilizing the overriding philosophy of the welfare of the child, the doctrine of parens patriae became the main ideology of proceedings against young people who came before the court for both criminal and child welfare concerns. In subsequent years, the child welfare focus of the juvenile court would be underscored in what became the legal doctrine known as the "best interests of the child." These ideologies and practices became a part of the principles and guiding philosophy of the UNCRC.

Circumventing the Juvenile Justice System

Research on the negative effects of labeling produced by early intervention into the lives of young offenders has been consistent over the years to show that reduced criminal justice processing is a preferred method to prevent future criminality among young people. The deeper that young people penetrate the youth justice system, the more damaged they become, and the less likely they are to desist from offending. Diversion from the criminal justice system is a preferred option for youths, and a main justification for a separate system for juveniles in the first instance. Proponents put forth that the most effective diversionary strategy is to remove children from the reach of the youth justice system altogether by significantly raising the age of criminal responsibility.

The UN Committee on the Rights of the Child has recommended that age 12 be the absolute minimum age of criminal responsibility, and that state parties should work to continue to increase this age to a higher level. Some commentators have gone so far as to argue that the minimum age of criminal responsibility should be 18 years of age or the age of majority, and until that time, youths should be dealt with through a more social interventionist manner outside the formality of the criminal justice system entirely.

Moral and Cognitive Reasoning

In a review of the psychosocial literature, there is convincing evidence of changes in moral and cognitive reasoning throughout the adolescent period. Prior to the age of 10, there is a lack of capacity to make moral judgments based on an awareness of the impact of one's actions on others. Children up to the age of 13 lack moral independence from adults, and some research has shown that moral discernment continues to develop up until the age of 17. Both cognitive and moral development continues into the early 20s, and it has been argued that young adults should also enjoy some kind of privileged liability.

Research has shown that an adolescent's brain is not fully developed until the age of 25, and some have argued that in light of the age–crime relationship and the sharp decline in the commission of crime when a young person is in their early 20s, perhaps the juvenile court should increase the upper age limit to reflect this maturation process.

Actual Juvenile Crime Rates

There is a popular misconception, spread largely through the media, that a large proportion of crime in society is committed by teenagers, and that juvenile delinquency throughout the world is getting worse. In fact, juvenile crime rates remain more or less stable from year to year across the continents. While there has been evidence of a small minority of young offenders committing serious crime at an early age, there is no evidence to suggest that harsher punishments will reduce the likelihood of recidivism or enhance the likelihood of desistance from a life of crime. The research evidence on the most appropriate interventions for young people have been those that target criminogenic risks and needs, are based in the community and support family systems, and seek out alternatives to incarceration.

The UNCRC provides a set of guiding principles that recognize that young people who commit criminal offenses must take responsibility for their behavior. The key to such responsibility is not the imposition of adult penalties on young persons who are granted protection from exploitation and abuse in other areas of their lives, but to ensure that youths are held accountable and that programs and services are put in place to promote reintegration.

Con: Opposing Minimum Age of Criminal Responsibility

The idea that children are not capable of committing criminal acts is seen as preposterous to some, and there are a number of leading cases that have led to public outcry around the world. Perhaps the most notorious case was in 1993 in England, where two 10-year-old boys killed three-year-old Jamie Bulger. The idea that such a horrendous act would be settled with impunity left many to question the historical underpinnings of the juvenile justice system.

Excuse or Full Responsibility

Some commentators have argued that the application of a simplistic application of criminal law concepts to juvenile offenders has limited the options before the court to only two choices: excuse or full responsibility. In legal terms, *excuse* means complete exculpation, so that the young person is not accountable for the harm caused and should receive no punishment. The application of this type of excuse is only reserved for severe mental impairment or extraordinarily coercive circumstances. Policymakers and the public are aware that this is outside the realm of normal operations of the criminal court, and have increasingly come to reject the idea that adolescent offenders should be excused from all criminal liability. The age at which criminal responsibility is assigned is seen by such proponents as being the point of life when it is absolutely certain that the young person did not have any concept of "right" and "wrong." Some have argued that one way to ensure that youths are held accountable for their actions is to test each offender before the court on their level of competency to stand trial in the same manner as adults who may be experiencing mental illness. This would be an involved and complicated process, even with the provision of instruments and tools that measure levels of competence, and may further exacerbate the lengthy court process for the young person. If the minimum age of criminal responsibility was abandoned, all youths would be subject to a test of competency to stand trial.

Fallout From the Era of the "Child Savers"

The welfare ideology of the "best interests of the child" has been questioned in light of the fact that many of the cases that come before the youth court could be seen as emanating from adolescent behavior that would have formerly constituted a status offence. Status offences are those violations of rules that apply to children but do not apply to adults, and might include such things as running away from home, truancy from school, alcohol consumption, or purchasing cigarettes or pornographic material. The early juvenile court was not concerned about the nature of the offense that brought the young person to the attention of the authorities. The key to successful intervention with a young delinquent was the provision of guidance and assistance, so that the young person would be a healthy and well-functioning adult member of society.

Even though most juvenile justice statutes currently deal only with criminal behavior and avoid using such courts for status offenders, there are some who would argue that the spillover from the ideology of the child-saving era cannot be underestimated, and that such intervention may be in violation of their right to be free from interference. Arguments in favor of eliminating a minimum age of criminal responsibility would follow from the premise that youths should not receive additional treatment or punishment beyond what an adult would receive simply by virtue of the fact that they are youths. Those who argue that children are persons with full rights suggest that a minimum age of criminal responsibility can be used to justify this paternalistic approach to children based on their lack of competence to make decisions and have their voice heard on matters that affect them.

Essential to Intervene

There has also been a body of research that has pointed out the long-term consequences of avoiding intervention with children who exhibit antisocial behaviors. Developmental and life-course criminology outlines that persistent disruptive behavior at a young age is a risk factor for the development of criminal careers throughout life. Rather than excusing children for their antisocial behavior in criminal courts, some would argue that it is essential to intervene in a more intensive way with those young children who present with antisocial tendencies to avert a lifetime of criminality.

David Farrington, in his seminal work on the age-crime relationship, showed that the crime rate increases starting from the minimum age of criminal responsibility to reach a peak in the teenage years, and then declines quickly at first and then more slowly over time. Some have suggested that it is the possible specific deterrent effect on the individual offender as he or she approaches the age of majority that leads to their desistance. Other researchers have shown that as offenders age, they are likely to have more responsibilities in terms of work and family obligations, and their increased responsibilities lead to their desistance from crime. Rather than focusing efforts on the age at which offenders should be treated as adults, some policy analysts have suggested that a more useful intervention might be to enhance the opportunities for young people to find a spouse and a job.

Developing Guidelines for Age Limits

New Zealand has issued a set of guidelines for government departments and public bodies when determining age limits in law and policy. The aim of these guidelines is to make certain that youth ages are used effectively and consistently in the broader policy context, without discriminating unjustifiably or negatively. The first step in determining an age policy is to consider the purpose of the policy and whether it is necessary. Youth age policies can serve any one of the following purposes: protection, empowerment, determination of entitlements, and definitions of responsibilities. In designing a youth age policy, potential alternatives have been given before setting a particular age boundary.

In setting the appropriate age, the question is whether the age is consistent with other laws and whether or not it will serve the child's best interests. In addition, the policy must consider how the age selected will affect the young person's ability to participate in decisions that affect them and their broader participation in society. In providing a rationale for the selection of the age, it is imperative that the age limit does not discriminate against young people nor impede access to benefits or entitlements that they might otherwise receive.

The most important element in the design of a youth policy is consultation with young people themselves. Including young people in the decision-making process will lead to a better understanding of what young people see as in their best interests, and will increase the likelihood of respect for the law by the young people affected by the policy. The rationale and the implications for the age limit that is chosen should be explained clearly in all relevant documents and written in a manner that is easily understood by young people. Consulting with children and young people and actively encouraging their full participation in the development of relevant legislation will not only reflect their perspectives, experiences, and concerns, but will also allow for their input in balancing protection and participation in the decision-making process.

Perhaps if young people become more engaged in policy decisions and have real input into the policy development process, the age of responsibility will no longer take on the heated debate it has for the past few years.

See Also: 6. Death Penalty for Juvenile Offenders; 10. Juvenile Offenders in Adult Courts; 11. Juveniles in Adult Correctional Facilities.

Further Readings

Altstein, Howard, and Rita J. Simon. "Coming of Age: The World Over." *Gender Issues,* v.24 (2008).

Arts, Karin, and Vesselin Popovski, eds. *International Criminal Accountability and the Rights of Children.* Cambridge, UK: Cambridge University Press, 2006.

Bobek, Deborah, Jonathan Zaff, Yibing Li, and Richard M. Lerner. "Cognitive, Emotional and Behavioral Components of Civic Action: Toward an Integrated Measure of Civic Engagement." *Journal of Applied Developmental Psychology,* v.30 (2009).

Covell, Katherine, and Brian Howe. *A Question of Commitment: Children's Rights in Canada.* Waterloo, ON: Wilfrid Laurier Press, 2007.

DiIulio, John. "The Coming of the Super-Predators." *Weekly Standard* (November 27, 1995).

Farrington, David P. "Age and Crime." *Crime and Justice,* v.7 (1986).

Ferreira, Nuno. "Putting the Age of Criminal and Tort Liability Into Context: A Dialogue Between Law and Psychology." *International Journal of Children's Rights,* v.16/1 (December 2008).

Goldson, Barry. "Counterblast: 'Difficult to Understand or Defend': A Reasoned Case for Raising the Age of Criminal Responsibility." *The Howard Journal,* v.48/5 (December 2009).

Lansdown, Gerison. *The Evolving Capacities of the Child.* Florence, Italy: Unicef Innocenti Research Centre, 2005.

Loeber, Rolf, N. Wim Slot, Peter vander Laan, and Machteld Hoeve. *Tomorrow's Criminals: The Development of Child Delinquency and Effective Interventions.* Surrey, UK: Ashgate, 2008.

Margo, Julia. *Make Me a Criminal: Preventing Youth Crime.* London: Institute for Public Policy Research, 2008.

Muncie, John. "The Punitive Turn in Juvenile Justice: Cultures of Control and Rights Compliance in Western Europe and the USA." *Youth Justice*, v.8/2 (2008).

Muncie, John. "Repenalisation and Rights: Explorations in Comparative Youth Criminology." *The Howard Journal*, v.45/1 (February 2006).

Osgood, D. Wayne, Michael Foster, and Constance Flanagan, eds. *On Your Own Without a Net: The Transition to Adulthood for Vulnerable Populations*. Chicago: University of Chicago Press, 2005.

Petrosino, Anthony, Carolyn Turpin-Petrosino, and Sarah Guckenburg. *The Impact of Juvenile System Processing on Delinquency*. Oslo, Norway: Campbell Collaboration Group, 2009.

Platt, Anthony, and Bernard L. Diamond. "The Origins of the 'Right and Wrong' Test of Criminal Responsibility and Its Subsequent Development in the United States: An Historical Survey." *California Law Review*, v.54/3 (August 1966).

Scott, Elizabeth S., and Laurence Steinberg. *Rethinking Juvenile Justice*. Cambridge, MA: Harvard University Press (2008).

Serido, Joyce, Lynne M. Borden, and Daniel F. Perkins. "Moving Beyond Youth Voice." *Youth and Society*, v.20/10 (2009).

Smith, Roger. "Children's Rights and Youth Justice: 20 Years of No Progress." *Child Care in Practice*, v.16/1 (January 2010).

Steinberg, Laurence. "Risk Taking in Adolescence: New Perspectives From Brain and Behavioral Science." *Current Directions in Psychological Science*, v.16 (2007).

Tonge, Jonathan, and Andrew Mycock. "Citizenship and Political Engagement Among Young People: The Workings and Findings of the Youth Citizenship Commission." *Parliamentary Affairs*, v.63/1 (2010).

2

Alternative Schools

Anthony Petrosino
Claire Morgan
Learning Innovations at WestEd

P ublic schools must determine how to handle students who repeatedly experience educational failure, particularly those in danger of dropping out. In addition, schools have to handle students who are consistently disruptive and are in danger of being expelled, including those who have committed violent or delinquent acts. Educators refer to such students as "at-risk." Students who drop out of or are expelled from school are not only at risk for academic failure, but also face further problems through adolescence and adulthood, including encounters with the juvenile and adult justice systems. Dropouts are more likely, according to some researchers, to be arrested, abuse drugs, receive public assistance, remain unemployed, and spend time in prison. Research by Johanna Wald and Daniel Losen in 2003 indicated that nearly seven in 10 adult prisoners never completed high school. Some researchers call this the "school to prison pipeline," describing the frequency with which students who experience academic failure end up being incarcerated. Thus, finding effective interventions to interrupt this pipeline is a goal in the United States.

There are other incentives for schools to deal with at-risk students. Persistently disruptive students can pose a distraction to other youths in the classroom and make it difficult for teachers to fulfill their teaching obligations because they have to spend more time on behavior management issues.

Aggressive, delinquent, or violent youths can also be school crime and safety concerns and can lead to perceptions among students and staff that the building is unsafe. For example, a 2004 study cited by Christopher Schreck and J. Mitchell Miller, using national data, indicates that increases in overall school disorder and disruption are associated with increases in student fear of crime. Finding effective interventions, therefore, to help such at-risk students and reduce school safety and discipline problems is a goal of the educational community.

One intervention that has been used to deal with at-risk students in public school settings is the alternative school. Finding a clear definition of an *alternative school* (also sometimes referred to as *alternative programming* or *alternative education*) can be elusive, as any other option besides the traditional, public school setting could be considered an alternative. Some alternatives, such as language-immersion schools or magnet schools, do not focus on at-risk students who are not succeeding in the mainstream school setting, but rather provide parents with a choice to enroll their children in an alternative setting with unique educational experiences.

An alternative school is defined here as an educational setting designed to accommodate adolescents experiencing behavioral and academic problems in the mainstream educational setting, who would generally be considered at-risk for dropping out or expulsion. This includes schools that are providing students with a last chance before expulsion, and those that are attempting to remediate academic or behavioral problems, making success in the mainstream setting unlikely. Alternative schools are relevant to crime and punishment issues because of their possible impact on school safety, crime, and delinquency in the community, and because they address concerns about future offending by students who are expelled or drop out of school.

In an alternative school, educators separate youths experiencing persistent academic and behavioral problems in traditional schools into a specialized, alternative educational setting, where such students can continue toward an educational degree within an environment that is more conducive to handling the unique challenges they present. The range of alternative school programs and curricula is wide, but the basic premise of providing more focused attention and services for troubled students is the unifying theme. Alternative schools, which have a history going back to the establishment of the nation, select students based on a set of criteria, such as at-risk characteristics and special needs. Models or types of alternative schools vary, but their primary characteristic is specialization and semi-autonomous educational programs outside of the mainstream school system. Several advantages and disadvantages of alternative schools have been circulated, which have been investigated and discussed in the research evidence on alternative school effectiveness.

The History of Alternative Schools

Alternative schools have existed in the United States since its inception, and were designed to provide learning experiences for children that were not being adequately served by the mainstream public school. For example, private and religious schools were viewed as common alternatives to the public "common school" that had been developed in the 1800s. In an early example, Irish-Catholic parents, dissatisfied with the strong Protestant influence in 19th-century American public schools in the northeast, created private Catholic schools as an option their children's education.

The 1960s and 1970s

During the 1960s, as mainstream education and other institutions were increasingly challenged by critics, many alternative schools were established to provide parents with options for the education of their children other than the public school, which was often viewed as fostering social inequities and lacking creativity. For example, Freedom Schools were created to provide high-quality education to minority students who were often marginalized in the mainstream public school system. Other alternative schools, under the label of Free Schools or Open Schools, were designed to permit students to pursue their own intellectual curiosity without the inhibiting structure of traditional schooling. Such schools attracted parents who wanted a different learning approach for their children, and in the cultural context of the 1960s, also believed that the traditional public school education was counterproductive and stifled creativity and curiosity. Although many of these early schools did not last, they could be considered a precedent for today's alternative education models that emphasize innovative programming or strategies to attract students (for example, magnet or charter schools). In Europe, Democratic Schools that permit students to essentially determine their own education exist to provide similar options to parents.

During the 1970s, the main purpose for alternative schools shifted. Rather than being instituted to provide nontraditional educational alternatives for students, they were more frequently established for remedial purposes, particularly for youths considered at risk for academic failure or behavioral problems. For example, in 1978, Florida passed legislation urging that school districts provide alternative schools as remedies for students experiencing academic failure or behavioral problems. Through the early 1980s, the U.S. Office of Juvenile Justice and Delinquency Prevention (OJJDP), the U.S. Department of Justice agency charged with overseeing the federal government response to juvenile crime and justice issues, promoted the use of alternative schools as a delinquency-prevention strategy. Based on research showing strong connections between school performance and delinquency, OJJDP funded the implementation and evaluation of 17 different alternative-school projects across the nation through its Alternative Education Program.

The 1990s: Rising Worries of Violence

Since 1990, growing concerns about school violence and the pressures on educators to meet federal and state standards have escalated school and district efforts to move children who are not successful in traditional public settings into alternative schools. The 1994 Gun-Free School Act required states receiving federal funding to pass laws mandating one-year expulsions for any student bringing a firearm or explosive device to the school. Many states and school districts have expanded the list of offenses for which students can be expelled beyond the Gun-Free School Act, and have adopted zero-tolerance policies for drug possession and other offenses. For example, in San Diego, there are at least 23 separate offenses for which schools can automatically expel a student, including possession of alcohol, tobacco, or fireworks. However, even with such laws and policies in effect, most jurisdictions permit schools to allow offending students to attend alternative schools that provide such youths with one last opportunity to continue their education.

2000s: No Child Left Behind

The No Child Left Behind (NCLB) Act of 2001 is a federal law that set the educational conditions that states, school districts, and schools that receive federal funding must meet. NCLB increased the accountability of schools, districts, and states for student learning within their jurisdictions, including alternative schools, resulting in greater pressures on educators to show that students in such institutions were meeting desired academic standards as evidenced by their performance on annual standardized tests and graduation rates. Some alternative school administrators argued that the increased accountability provisions of NCLB were unfair to them, given that they were dealing with the students who had experienced consistent academic failure and were much more likely to do poorly on standardized academic tests and drop out from school. Others argued that students in alternative schools were not held to the same standards for academic performance.

Despite the controversy over meeting NCLB accountability standards, the number of alternative schools has grown since the 1990s. Some recent estimates now place the number of alternative schools in the United States at over 20,000, with nearly four in 10 districts in the nation having at least one alternative school. While local control of education in the United States may foster the development of larger numbers and more varied types of alternative-education programs, alternative schools are increasingly common internationally, operating in Canada and several European nations, including the United Kingdom.

Selecting Students for Alternative Schools

The process for determining which students in a mainstream public school will be referred to an alternative school setting varies across jurisdictions. Some districts and states target specific types of students. For example, students who are consistently truant, have been arrested for possessing a weapon or for other offenses, have been chronically disruptive, consistently experience failing grades, or evidence severe emotional problems are among those students whom educators may consider eligible for the alternative school setting. Teen parents or students experiencing special physical, medical, or other needs may also be considered eligible in some jurisdictions.

Some states and districts have strict policies and eligibility criteria for referring students to alternative schools, while other jurisdictions allow educators at the mainstream public school wide discretion, on a case-by-case basis, to determine whether a student should be referred. Some educators and researchers have argued for the development of a district screening system that would systematically identify youths early in their academic careers who are not doing well in the mainstream academic setting, and who would be good candidates for success in the alternative school setting.

Generally, the process by which a student enrolls in an alternative school is through referral and admission. The mainstream public school is the main referral point, but in some jurisdictions, parents may ask for placement or students can self-select into the alternative school. U.S. Department of Education data from 2007 to 2008 show that in over three-fourths of referrals, placement of a student in an alternative school was due, to a large or moderate extent, to the recommendation received from regular school staff. Some schools have established advisory boards to oversee the referral process at the public school. Most alternative schools have an admissions process by which they review every referral and make an admission decision. In those alternative schools considered to be a last chance before expulsion, students may be required by authorities to attend.

Ensuring that the alternative school has the appropriate balance of staff and students can present a challenge to administrators. In some jurisdictions, alternative schools have a small number of available spaces for incoming students, and it is not uncommon for referred and admitted students to be placed on a waiting list. In other jurisdictions, the alternative school may struggle to fill its available spaces if the district or the schools are not referring many students. The same U.S. Department of Education data indicates that insufficient space to provide admission for all referred students is the more significant problem.

Types of Alternative Schools

There are many types of alternative schools, but the main component is that they are specialized and semiautonomous educational programs taking place outside of the mainstream school system. In the United States, the type of alternative school is determined by individual states or school districts. The most common type has its own staff and a separate building where students spend 100 percent of their normal school day. However, another common approach that some districts have designed is called the "school within a school" approach, in which all students are educated in the same building, but the alternative school operates in a separate space within the facility. According to federal data, nearly four in 10 of all alternative schools are housed within a regular school. More than eight in 10 alternative schools involve high school students, but several now serve middle school youths. Although still comparatively very rare when compared to those serving middle school or high school youths, some alternative schools for elementary students do exist.

Some specialized alternative schools feature innovative programming in specific areas such as technology, including job training and job placement, and may involve young adults who have long ago dropped out or were expelled from mainstream schools. Some researchers have estimated that there are more than three million young persons who are not enrolled in school, do not have a diploma or General Equivalency Diploma (GED), and are unemployed. This is a group that is considered to be particularly at risk for further problems with the law, not to mention persistent unemployment, and alternative schools have been designed to meet their needs. For example, the School for Integrated Academics and Technology (SIATech) works in partnership with the U.S. Job Corps program, a vocational and educational program for disadvantaged urban youths 16–24 years of age, who have either dropped out or were not able to succeed in a traditional educational setting. The SIATech program, which is located on Job Corps sites in several cities across the United States, provides students with a specialized and supportive environment to complete their high school education.

Continuation High Schools and Private Examples

Another common alternative school example, particularly in California, is the continuation high school. These schools offer flexible programming to accommodate students who have dropped out of high school, no matter how many high school credits they have previously accumulated, and allow students to complete their high school education at their own pace. Continuation schools in California and other states may also include a number of other services, including work-study opportunities and job placement assistance. Continuation high schools also have been implemented in other nations. For example, in Denmark, continuation high schools are sometimes viewed as an alternative to sending a delinquent to a youth detention facility.

Although some alternative school programs are designed to improve the student's academic performance so that they can return to the mainstream school setting, other alternative school programs are designed for students to complete their education and graduate within the alternative school setting without ever returning to the mainstream educational setting. While most alternative schools are run by the local school district, private companies that are not part of the local structure may also implement and maintain an alternative school. In some developing countries, alternative schools are commonly run by agencies that are not part of the government, also referred to as nongovernmental organizations (NGOs). For example, NGOs run the REACH program, an alternative education program for at-risk youths in impoverished urban and rural areas of India.

Characteristics of Alternative Schools

Although program components vary across alternative schools, some common characteristics can be found across many of them. Alternative schools usually serve a small number of youths, both in terms of total enrollment and class size, promoting one-on-one interaction between staff and student, and providing opportunities for informal, personal, and mentoring relationships between students and staff to develop. The learning environment is often more personalized and flexible than the mainstream public school, and may use innovative strategies to reach disengaged learners. For example, there may be more opportunities for alternative school students to work at their own pace, including computer-based instruction, and to participate in self-directed, independent learning activities and internships. Scheduling may also be flexible, allowing students to continue to work or care for children while attending school part time. Some alternative schools involve the students in the decision making and rule setting, giving them a voice in the operation of the school. Most alternative schools make an effort to hire teachers and other staff members who have the skills and are committed to work with at-risk students. Some research suggests that an alternative school's success is based more on the kinds of teachers they can attract and keep than on the structure and curriculum of the school.

Alternative schools often partner with community and social service organizations to connect students with resources and learning opportunities outside of school. Such opportunities and services may include service learning, internships, vocational training and guidance, courses and counseling in areas such as life skills and anger management, and support for pregnant or parenting students.

Pro: Arguments in Support of Alternative Schools

Anecdotal and emerging research-based evidence suggests that alternative schools may provide a second chance for students who have experienced academic failure and behavioral problems in traditional school settings. If students at risk for dropping out, expulsion, or legal trouble are appropriately targeted, alternative schools provide an opportunity for educators to intervene in the lives of troubled youths, possibly setting such students on a more positive path. Proponents argue that without alternative schools, a number of at-risk youths alienated from the mainstream educational system would end up dropping out or being expelled, and also be more likely to get into trouble with the law.

Some proponents argue that providing a more supportive environment with individualized instruction and increased one-on-one interaction between students and staff, creating opportunities for personal relationships, could increase the bonds that a student has with school, and that such connectedness is an important factor in a student choosing positive education and life goals and avoiding negative behavior. Such students, who normally would have dropped out or been expelled, can now learn in a program that includes the type of supports that are specifically designed to meet their individual needs. Proponents further argue that effective alternative schools do increase attendance and graduation rates, and reduce truancy and dropout rates among at-risk students. Some community and police proponents of alternative schools argue that by keeping behaviorally troubled young people occupied in school, there is less opportunity for them to get into legal trouble, resulting in less delinquency in the neighborhood.

Proponents also advocate alternative schools as one option for increasing overall school safety and improving school culture. As chronically disruptive students are removed from classrooms in the mainstream school setting and placed into alternative schools, the environment for learning in the regular school improves. Teachers are better able to focus on their students without spending an inordinate amount of time dealing with a few problem youths, and the other students in the mainstream classroom are not consistently distracted by a small number of disruptive youths.

Con: Arguments in Opposition to Alternative Schools

Although research is necessary to establish these claims, some anecdotal evidence questions whether the alternative school represents a wise choice in dealing with at-risk students. Some of the opponents of alternative schools argue that such schools have become a "dumping ground" for at-risk youths, sometimes referred to as *pushouts,* that mainstream public school administrators and teachers no longer want to deal with. For example, the California Legislative Analyst's Office (LAO) determined in 2007 that the state's system for holding schools and districts accountable for student academic progress actually permitted educational administrators to use referrals to alternative schools as a way to avoid their responsibility for the progress of low-performing students. Compounding this problem, these critics argue, is that in many jurisdictions, minority youths or students with disabilities are more likely to be sent to alternative schools than troubled white youths without disabilities. Analyzing national data from a 2001 survey on public alternative schools and at-risk programs administered by the U.S. Department of Education, researchers R. R. Verdugo and B. C. Glenn determined that the percentage of minority students in a school district is a strong predictor of whether that district will have an alternative school. Some critics also charge that educators are using alternative schools as a punishment for students who create problems in the mainstream school, rather than using the alternative school as an opportunity to help at-risk students achieve positive goals.

Second, some have argued that placing a student into an alternative school leads to a stigma or negative labeling of the youth as a problem student, a troublemaker, or a "stupid kid." Labeling is particularly harmful when the student and other persons such as those within the family and community believe the label is valid. Thus, every subsequent action reinforces the label that the youth is a problem student, a troublemaker, or "dumb." Critics point out that when youths are stigmatized, they no longer see themselves as being capable of completing school or achieving positive goals. When other persons accept or reinforce the label, the youth may come under greater scrutiny by the police or the community for behavior that is typically overlooked in young persons of a similar age. Finally, the alternative school brings a number of at-risk students together, including those who are delinquent or aggressive, in a single place and time. Some researchers have argued that the negative influences of criminal peers—also termed *peer contagion* by criminologists—could encourage noncriminal students in a setting such as an alternative school to engage in delinquent conduct.

Do Alternative Schools Work?

Despite the large number of alternative schools for at-risk students in operation since the 1970s in the United States, there are comparatively few studies that document their effectiveness in reducing dropout or behavioral problems. Although alternative schooling is supported by some research evidence, more studies are needed to justify the allocation of resources to alternative-education programs. Additional studies testing their effectiveness would inform decision makers determining whether to open, close, or modify such schools. Moreover, they would also help to inform federal and state policymakers as to whether they should invest their funds in supporting the implementation and running of alternative schools.

Some research indicates that alternative schools can make a difference. For example, a randomized experiment conducted in the early 1990s in Flint, Michigan, assigned entering middle school students who were behind grade level to an alternative middle school or the regular middle school system. The alternative school provided students with intensive psychological and academic services. In a 36-month followup, only three percent of the alternative middle school students had dropped out of school, compared to 17 percent of the regular middle school students.

In 1995, researchers at Michigan State University conducted a meta-analysis (a method for statistically synthesizing the results of prior studies) to assess the effectiveness of alternative education programs by examining the evaluations that were reported up through the early 1990s. This synthesis of research did report a small overall positive effect on school performance, attitudes toward school, and self-esteem among students; however, no effect on delinquency was reported. It is evidence like this that has led some organizations, such as the National Dropout Prevention Center, to conclude that alternative schools are an effective or promising strategy. Nonetheless, some of the evaluations that have been reported on alternative schools have been hindered by methodological problems.

Methodological Problems in the Research

First, many of the research studies completed to date do not take enough steps to isolate the impact of the alternative school on student outcomes, for example, by comparing results for alternative school students to carefully created groups of similar students that did not attend the alternative school. For example, the Department of Education's What Works Clearinghouse (WWC) was initiated to take stock of the research evidence behind a particular educational policy or program. For its 2009 report, WWC reviewed nearly 30 studies of a program titled YouthBuild, which offers job training and educational opportunities, generally within an alternative schools structure for youths 16–24 years of age who have dropped out of school. Not one of the 30 studies met the WWC criteria for acceptable evaluation evidence, most often due to the lack of a credible comparison group.

Second, because alternative schools deal with at-risk students, usually those youths who present a number of academic and behavioral challenges to completing their education, it would not be fair to compare their performance to the mainstream public school population. Thus, identifying a group of students being handled outside of the alternative school that is very similar to the alternative group population is a challenge for researchers.

Finally, some studies focus only on short-term results, such as the students' attitudes and grades in the first few months after they begin attending the alternative school. Although these results are important, more studies are needed to determine if alternative schools have longer-term effects on graduation rates, as well as later delinquency and employment outcomes.

The number of rigorous studies that have examined the impact of alternative schools on crime and delinquency is even more infrequent and less definitive than those studies that have investigated academic performance. For example, under OJJDP's earlier Alternative Education Program, several studies examined the impact of alternative schools on delinquency. Although some of the 17 projects resulted in increased attendance and better academic performance, only two of the projects reported being able to reduce subsequent delinquency on the part of their students. Thus, according to these sources, the jury is out on whether alternative schools work to reduce school and behavioral problems among youths.

Apart from the question of effectiveness, some research indicates that students who attend alternative schools are very satisfied with their experience. It is not clear whether this is due to the small enrollment and class sizes, the personal relationships with staff or other students, or other factors. However, such student satisfaction is important, although it sometimes does not translate into changed behavior on the part of the youths who attend alternative schools. Interviews and focus groups conducted at three alternative schools in a large U.S. southeastern city in the 2000s, for instance, indicated that Latino youths appreciated the caring and support of the smaller community. Studies also have generally reported that parents are satisfied with the alternative schools their children attend.

Public Opinion

Overall public opinion, however, is somewhat mixed regarding the benefits of alternative education. As indicated in the 2009 Center for Evaluation and Education Policy (CEEP) article "Alternative Schools: What's in a Name?" although some in the public see alternative schools as providing innovative and specialized programming options to traditional public education, other citizens view them merely as rehabilitation centers for problem youths. These varying perceptions of alternative schools may be due to differing degrees of educational quality among schools, including how well the school is funded, the qualifications of the staff, the supportiveness of the school climate, and the type of instruction and curricula being offered to the students.

❖

See Also: 3. At-Risk Youths; 7. Group Homes; 8. Juvenile Detention Facilities; 14. Parental Responsibility Laws; 15. Racial Disparities; 17. School Violence.

Further Readings

Aron, L. "An Overview of Alternative Education." Urban Institute. http://www.urban.org/UploadedPDF/411283_alternative_education.pdf (Accessed September 2010).

Aron, L. Y., and J. M. Zweig. "Educational Alternatives for Vulnerable Youth: Student Needs, Program Types, and Research Directions." (2003). Urban Institute. http://www.urbaninstitute.org/UploadedPDF/410898_vulnerable_youth.pdf (Accessed January 2010).

Brackett, A., and S. Guckenburg. *Preliminary Formative Evaluation Report: The School for Integrated Academics and Technologies, "Voices of SIATech Stakeholders."* Woburn, MA: Learning Innovations at WestEd, 2007.

Cable, K. E., J. A. Plucker, and T. E. Spradlin. "Alternative Schools: What's in a Name?" *Education Policy Brief,* v.7/4 (Winter 2009). Center for Evaluation and Education Policy. http://ceep.indiana.edu/projects/PDF/PB_V7N4_Winter_2009_EPB.pdf (Accessed January 2010).

California Legislative Analyst's Office. *Improving Alternative Education in California.* Sacramento: California Legislative Analyst's Office, 2007.

Carver, P. R., and L. Lewis. *Alternative Schools and Programs for Public School Students at Risk of Educational Failure: 2007–08.* Washington, DC: U.S. Department of Education, 2010.

Cox, S. "An Assessment of an Alternative Education Program for At-Risk Delinquent Youth." *Journal of Research in Crime and Delinquency,* v.36 (1999).

Cox, S., W. S. Davidson, and T. S. Bynum. "A Meta-Analytic Assessment of Delinquency-Related Outcomes of Alternative Education Programs." *Crime and Delinquency,* v.41/2 (1995).

de Velasco, J. R., G. Austin, D. Dixon, J. Johnson, M. McLaughlin, and L. Perez. "Alternative Education Options: A Descriptive Study of California Continuation High Schools." (2008). Stanford University, California Alternative Education Research Project. http://www.wested.org/online_pubs/AEOIssueBrief-4-08.pdf (Accessed January 2010).

Dynarski, M., and P. Gleason. "How Can We Help? Lessons From Federal Drop-Out Prevention Programs. Policy Brief." (1999). Mathematica

Policy Research, Inc. http://www.mathematica-mpr.com/PDFs/Howhelp
.pdf (Accessed January 2010).

Erase Initiative, Applied Research Center. *Profiled and Punished: How San Diego Schools Undermine Latino and African-American Student Achievement*. Oakland, CA: Erase Initiative, 2002.

Fairbrother, A. "They Might Need a Little Extra Hand, You Know. Latino Students in At-Risk Programs." *Urban Education,* v.43/5 (2008).

Lange, C. M., and S. J. Sletten. "Alternative Education: A Brief History and Research Synthesis." (2002). National Association of State Directors of Special Education. http://www.eric.ed.gov/ERICDocs/data/ericdocs2sql /content_storage_01/0000019b/80/19/e4/5c.pdf (Accessed January 2010).

National Economic and Social Rights Initiative. *Alternative Schools and Pushout: A Research and Advocacy Guide.* New York: National Economic and Social Rights Initiative, 2007.

Paglin, C., and J. Fager. "Alternative Schools: Approaches for Students at Risk." (1997). Northwest Regional Educational Laboratory. http:// www.eric.ed.gov/ERICDocs/data/ericdocs2sql/content_storage_01 /0000019b/80/17/98/4c.pdf (Accessed January 2010).

Schreck, C., and J. M. Miller. "Sources of Fear of Crime at School: What Is the Relative Contribution of Disorder, Individual Characteristics, and School Security?" *Journal of School Violence*, v.2/4 (2004).

U.S. Department of Education, What Works Clearinghouse. *YouthBuild Intervention Report.* Washington, DC: U.S. Department of Education, 2009.

Verdugo, R. R., and B. C. Glenn. "Race and Alternative Schools." Orlando, FL: Paper presented at the annual meeting of the Alternatives to Expulsion, Suspension, and Dropping Out of School Conference, February 16–18, 2006.

Wald, J., and D. J. Losen. "Defining and Redirecting a School-to-Prison Pipeline." *New Directions in Youth Development,* v.99 (Fall 2003).

3

At-Risk Youth

Lyndsay N. Boggess
University of South Florida

Travis W. Linnemann
Kansas State University

In 2009, there were an estimated 41.5 million youths between 10 and 19 years of age in the United States. Approximately 18 percent live in poverty; an estimated one child in every 25 is abused, neglected, or in danger of being maltreated; and seven percent have avoided school because of fear of attack or harm. Surrounded by negative circumstances, many of these youths will drop out of high school, end up behind bars, and be at risk of never becoming responsible adults.

There is growing concern that disadvantaged and undereducated youths will never develop into mature adults who successfully support themselves and raise children, sustain a long-term relationship, or profit from participation in the labor force. There is increasing fear that instead, children who are not provided for will get into trouble with the law, drop out of high school, become a parent at a young age, or become addicted to alcohol or drugs. However, addressing these concerns and helping high-risk youths requires understanding who these children are, what factors precede their involvement in risky behavior, and what sort of personalities, behaviors, or social backgrounds are indicative of negative outcomes in the future.

Defining the At-Risk Youth

One of the biggest challenges in helping youths today is accurately defining what it means for a youth to be at-risk. Though studies and programs abound, definitions and target populations differ greatly. The research literature often focuses on narrow categories of youths; those who are at risk of substance abuse, engaging in delinquent activities, or becoming a teenage parent, for example. Treatment programs, the educational community, and other preventative organizations often limit their definition of youths at risk to academic settings, such as youths at risk of dropping out of high school or finishing below potential. Such a constricted definition of *at-risk,* however, precludes those youths whose behaviors may be detrimental to their future but fall outside of the educational environment or the most common and pervasive negative outcomes; a broader consideration includes at-risk youths as those who are at an increased danger of not maturing into successful, responsible adults.

Predisposing Factors

Being viewed as (or labeled as) at-risk generally stems from certain predisposing or antecedent factors that originate with individual youth demographics or personality characteristics, as well as the familial and social context. These factors are the unseen motivations for behaviors that are used to distinguish youths who are at risk. These behaviors, such as truancy from school or aggression toward animals or peers, are measurable and can potentially lead to negative outcomes such as dropping out of high school or being arrested; outcomes that limit the ability of the youth to transition successfully into adulthood.

Predisposing factors are certain adverse circumstances, conditions, or characteristics that occur prior to antisocial or problem behavior. Factors that predispose youths to high-risk behaviors are generally classified within four categories: demographic characteristics, personality traits, familial contexts, and social contexts. Often, these factors overlap in their effects, and can influence a wide range of negative outcomes in youths, including delinquency, early childbearing, eating disorders, substance abuse, or dropping out.

Demographic Factors

First, the demographic factors considered antecedents to high-risk behaviors include age, gender, and sometimes race or ethnicity. The evidence consistently reveals, and experts overwhelmingly agree, that the younger the problem behavior begins, the more likely it will continue to occur into adolescence and adulthood. This means that children who act out in kindergarten are at a high risk of future risky behaviors and negative outcomes as they grow older. Gender is also a consistent predictor of negative future outcomes. Males tend to be more involved in risk-taking behaviors than their female counterparts. The research, however, is inconsistent in explaining the mechanisms behind gender disparities. Researchers attribute the risky behaviors of boys to genetic or hormonal differences, psychological differences, or social conditions that encourage male aggression and discourage female aggression.

The relationship between race/ethnicity and risky behavior is more contentious; although research shows a larger portion of minority youths are labeled at-risk, this likely stems from a variety of social and familial factors that increase minority youths' vulnerability, but are independent of race or ethnicity (such as poverty or residence in an urban area). Likewise, children of immigrants experience elevated risks, not because of any inherent shortcomings in their race/ethnicity, but because of language barriers and difficulties, poverty, and discrimination.

Personality Traits

Second, characteristics of the youths' personality and lifestyle are also associated with future risky behavior and delinquency. How youths perceive education is one of the strongest correlates of future negative outcomes. That is, youths who do not perceive benefits from school nor expect high grades tend to have lesser commitment to their education and little participation in school events or activities. Similarly, having a negative outlook on life in general and low self-esteem are also predisposing factors to negative outcomes. On the other hand, high religiosity, high self-esteem, positive perception of life options, and general good conduct are considered protective factors against engaging in high-risk behaviors.

Mental health status can also be an inciting factor for risky behavior. Youths who suffer from depression, anxiety, hyperactivity, or more serious psychiatric or personality disorders are more likely to engage in antisocial or problematic behavior in the future. Some work has suggested that youths with congenital abnormalities, in efforts to fit in with mainstream youths, may be particularly prone to engage in risky behavior, but little research has explored this relationship.

Outwardly, who the youth associates with and how he or she relates to peers are critical antecedents to high-risk behavior. That is, children whose peers are rebellious, engage in drug or tobacco use, have little interest in academics, or have dropped out of high school, are themselves at an increased likelihood of becoming involved in similar behaviors. Furthermore, how the youth responds to peer pressure is a key factor in determining who gets in trouble. Youths who have little resistance to peer influences, who feel a strong need for their friends' approval, and who favor their peers' opinions over their parents,' are especially inclined toward participation in high-risk behavior.

Familial Contexts

Third, the family environment is often considered one of the most influential antecedents to risky behavior—or on the contrary, one of the most important protective factors from engaging in high-risk activities. Low socioeconomic status is consistently linked to youths' quality of life; youths from households with limited means to provide private school educations, tutors, and socialization opportunities such as music lessons or team sport participation are more likely to engage in high-risk behaviors. As of 2008, there were 14 million children in families whose income fell below the federal poverty level ($22,050 annually for a family of four); many more black and Latino families are impoverished than non-Latino whites. Youths who come from single-parent households are especially vulnerable to negative outcomes in the future.

Within single-parent homes, children have fewer opportunities for positive social bonding with their parent, usually because parental work obligations take them away from home. Single parents typically have a lower income than dual-earner households and, simply because of the single-parent structure, there are fewer role models available to encourage positive behaviors. The 2008 American Community Survey reveals that nearly one-third of all households with children are single-parent households. Single-parent and poor households generally move often, a factor that further predisposes youths to interrupted education and disrupted friendship networks.

More important than family structure, however, is the quality of the relationship between the youth and his or her parent(s), the management style of the parent(s), and the parents' own involvement in high-risk, dangerous, or illegal behavior. Children of parents who are not supportive or communicative, who are not involved in their child's life, and who are physically or emotionally unavailable are much more likely to engage high-risk behaviors. Parental management style is also useful in predicting delinquent or problematic behavior. Youths who come from unsupportive homes at either end of the extreme—that are either overly restrictive and authoritarian or who are seriously neglectful—tend to fare worse in future undertakings, although some research has shown that children raised in authoritarian environments tend to have higher grades. Home environments that expose children to aggression, abuse, and violence or alcohol and drug abuse are likely to encourage similar behaviors in youths. Abused and neglected children are twice as likely to have a juvenile criminal record as children who are not maltreated. Similarly, girls with a teenage mother or whose unwed sisters are young mothers are also predisposed to early childbearing. Some research also suggests that heredity may play a role in acting out, substance dependency, and alcoholism.

Social Context

The fourth category of predisposing factors include the larger social context surrounding the youth; in particular, the community and the school environments. Children who live in densely populated urban communities that are plagued by high violence and high poverty are at a greater risk of failing to become successful adults. Children from such communities may perceive that they have limited options for the future or may become involved in violence, as an offender or a victim. School quality is strongly associated with neighborhood conditions; lower-quality schools are often located in minority-dominated areas and typically have high dropout rates, overcrowded classrooms, a larger proportion of low-achieving students, more violence, and a disjuncture between the racial and ethnic composition of the teachers and the student body, all of which are antecedents to negative outcomes as a teenager and into adulthood.

Influence of Violence and Conflicting Standards in Society

Finally, two additional broad-scale factors that do not fall into the four categories delineated above also facilitate problematic behavior in youths. One is the pervasiveness and prevalence of violence in American society. Almost all youths are exposed to violence in the media and in film, whether depicting fictional events or real-life brutality such as the school shootings in Littleton, Colorado, or the terrorist attacks of September 11, 2001. A second large issue affecting youth development is conflicting standards of behavior for young adults. One on hand, young adults are instructed to be mature and behave as a grownup would. The media and many advertisements encourage youths to be more adult in their sexual relationships, manner of dress, and physical appearance. But, on the other hand, people under the age of 18 have few rights, and most major decisions in their lives are dictated by their parents, so no matter how old or mature the youths appear outwardly, they are still treated as children. These two factors induce uncertainty and fear about the future and further compromise youths' abilities to cope with stress, peer pressure, and adolescent life, and put them further at risk of not maturing into responsible adults.

Not all youths who are predisposed to negative outcomes, however, are doomed. In fact, most youths from dysfunctional families, disadvantaged communities, and poor schools transition successfully into adulthood. Ultimately, it is a combination of the youth's personality factors and his or her ability or inability to cope with negative family, community, and school situations that can manifest as high-risk behaviors that lead to poor future outcomes. Fortunately, there are some observable behaviors that can help identify youths who may be having particular difficulties preparing for adult life.

Identifying the At-Risk Youth

Once a definition the of at-risk youth has been agreed upon, identifying which youths are at risk of not maturing into successful adults is another complex task. Focusing on behaviors too narrowly runs the risk of excluding many youths who are in fact in need of help, while too encompassing a classification may be ineffective in addressing individual youths' needs. A variety of youth behaviors, often in combination with other events or actions, may indicate that a youth is at risk of not successfully transitioning into adulthood. Some of the behaviors are considered less serious, such as a preoccupation with video games, the occasional cut class, or sip of alcohol, but established patterns of high-risk behavior are indicative of impediments to successful adulthood. At the other end of the spectrum, more serious behaviors such as not completing high school or being arrested are often considered negative outcomes in and of themselves; in this context, however, these more severe behaviors only worsen the likelihood of a youth making it as a responsible adult.

Problems at School and Home

Behaviors that indicate a child is at risk often occur at school. Students with excessive tardiness or absenteeism, that do not pay attention in class or complete work as assigned, who have poor or failing grades, verbal and language deficiencies, and low test scores may be at risk. Research on delinquent youths consistently finds that youths who get in trouble with the law generally have poor academic and communication skills, and youths who develop substance abuse problems generally report a history of truancy and acting out in school. Habitual truancy is one of the largest predictors of who will ultimately drop out of high school. A 2006 investigation, sponsored by the Bill and Melinda Gates Foundation, surveyed 450 dropouts and found that 43 percent of the dropouts stated they had missed too many days of school to catch up as a leading contributor to their dropping out. The survey also revealed that as students missed more and more classes, they were less inclined to return to school. Other warning signs of dropping out include youths who are academically behind their classmates, who have failed a grade, have been previously suspended or expelled, or youths who have friends who have also dropped out.

Youth actions at home are also indicative of the potential for future high-risk behavior. In particular, youths who are antisocial at home and avoid participating in family activities or spend a substantial amount of time alone, who disobey household rules or parental directives, and who are argumentative or uncommunicative with family members may signal future problems. Additionally, youths who do not regularly engage in physical exercise are at an increased risk of obesity and health problems as an adult.

Behavioral and Social Indications

Another means for identifying at-risk youths is monitoring their general behavioral characteristics. Youths who act out, are aggressive to other people and animals, display antisocial tendencies, or are particularly anxious or stressed may be at risk. Youths who are inactive and sedentary are at risk of health complications and isolating themselves, and youths who are self-conscious about their physical or public image may be at risk of developing poor eating habits or an eating disorder. Often, the predisposing factors lead to serious negative behaviors during young adulthood, which often translate into increasing difficulty transitioning to adulthood. For example, youths engaging in high-risk activities such as unprotected sex (often with multiple partners), running away, drug and alcohol use, eating disorders, cigarette smoking, or breaking the law are especially vulnerable to difficulties as adults.

Any particular problematic behavior can lead to a number of negative outcomes. For example, girls who have low grades, low expectations for education, and common absences are more likely to engage in early sexual intercourse or become a teenage mother. Low grades and poor attendance are also associated with drug and alcohol use and delinquency. Similarly, youths who engage in high-risk behaviors often engage in more than one activity. Research shows that many youths who are sexually active also use alcohol and/or marijuana; and teens who get in trouble with the law often have a history of cutting classes, driving recklessly, and using illegal drugs. A study by the National Alliance to Advance Adolescent Health in 2007 found that nearly 53 percent of high school students engage in two or more risky behaviors, and nearly a quarter are involved in four or more. What this means, however, is that despite a concise definition of *at-risk,* it is difficult to determine how many youths are actually considered at-risk.

Labeling the At-Risk Youth

Research warns that there is a potential problem in defining youths as at-risk. Pioneering research by Erwin Lemert in 1951 concluded that once a youth receives a negative label (such as at-risk, deviant, or criminal), the youth internalizes the label that reinforces his or her involvement in rule-breaking behavior. In 1963, Howard Becker described labeling theory in his book, *Outsiders: Studies in the Sociology of Deviance.* He referred to labeled youths as "outsiders" for being outside of (or apart from) the mainstream, law-abiding society that makes the rules and defines what is deviant. Becker emphasized that the initial behavior is relatively unimportant, but that negative labels reinforce unacceptable behavior and impact the youth later in life, ultimately leading to the perpetuation of criminality or deviance. In 1973, William Chambliss published an in-depth ethnographic study of the effect of labeling on youths' life chances. In his article, *The Saints and the Roughnecks,* Chambliss shows that lower-class youths who were labeled as delinquent and troublemakers were less likely to be successful as adults than middle-class youths who—though engaged in similar delinquent acts—were not labeled as deviants. Based on this work, identifying and labeling at-risk youths can be tenuous: Identifying at-risk youths prematurely can lead to a self-fulfilling prophecy and diminished life chances, but labeling can also lead to successful prevention and intervention strategies to help youths.

Prevalence

With a broad definition of *at-risk,* the precise number of at-risk youths is not known, but what is known are the prevalence rates of certain antecedent behaviors and negative outcomes. Listed below are some of the most severe and most common forms of youth high-risk behavior. The specific prevalence rates can be used to roughly estimate the pervasiveness of youths who may have trouble during adulthood.

High School Dropouts

U.S. Department of Education data from 2010 reveals that nationally, approximately 4.1 percent of all high school students fail to complete high school; with the greatest risks for high school senior (6.1 percent), African American (6.7 percent), Latino (6.0 percent), and Native American (7.3 percent) students. The Alliance for Excellent Education estimates that approximately 7,000 students drop out every school day, and nearly 44,000 youths a year will not graduate in New York City or Los Angeles. Youths who do not complete high school are in danger of continued problems during adulthood. For example, high school dropouts are more likely to be unemployed, live in poverty, or have children who also drop out than high school graduates. High school dropouts are 3.5 times as likely to be incarcerated as graduates, and dropouts earn significantly less income over the course of their lifetime: $260,000 less than a high school graduate and $1 million less than a comparable college graduate.

Sexual Promiscuity and Unprotected Sexual Intercourse

Surveys estimate that nearly half of all teens have had sex at least once by the time they are 19 years old. The Youth Risk Behavior Surveillance System (YRBSS) conducted by the Centers for Disease Control and Prevention (CDC) reveals that 11 percent of girls and 16 percent of boys have had four or more partners before they complete high school. The vast majority of youths in the YRBSS study did not use birth control pills or condoms the last time they had sex, even though research has found that a teen who does not use protection has a 90 percent chance of becoming pregnant within one year. 750,000 girls between 15 and 19 years of age become pregnant each year; 60 percent of these pregnancies result in births, and the rest end in abortion (27 percent) or miscarriage (14 percent).

In addition to pregnancy and early motherhood, promiscuous sexual activity can lead to sexually transmitted diseases (STDs). Nearly half of the STDs diagnosed annually are to youths 15–24 years old, and according to the YRBSS data, 89 percent of males and 85 percent of females have never been tested for HIV. Young mothers are also at an increased risk of premature births, health complications, lifelong welfare dependency, unstable marriages and high divorce rates, not attending college, and lower-status jobs. Children born to teenage mothers are also predisposed to future life problems: becoming teenage parents themselves, lower academic achievement, and behavioral and emotional problems. Male children born to teenage mothers are more likely to spend time incarcerated. Childhood sexual abuse is a common antecedent to risky sexual behavior as a teenager. Girls who have been sexually abused at home often report initiating sex with peers at a younger age, having more than one sexual partner, and not using contraceptives.

Crime and Delinquency

Youths at risk of not maturing into responsible adults are often involved with the criminal justice system. Youth violence is relatively pervasive, and one of the leading causes of death for youths 10–19 years of age is gun-related homicide. According to the Office of Juvenile Justice and Delinquency Prevention, the homicide arrest rate of youths 10–17 years of age was four per 100,000 youths in 2008. The overall violent crime arrest rate (for homicide, rape, robbery, and assault) was 288 per 100,000 youths in 2008. Surveys of high school seniors reveal that 10–15 percent have committed an act of serious violence in the past year. Serious violence, however, is much more rare than minor forms of delinquency; youth arrests for drug abuse violations, vandalism, liquor law violations, drunkenness, running away, and disorderly conduct are much more common. The property crime arrest rate for youths 10–17 years of age was 1,323 of 100,000 youths in 2008. Juveniles involved with the criminal justice system at a young age are at an increased likelihood of future involvement and at increased danger of not completing their schooling; 75 percent of prison inmates dropped out of high school. As with other types of risky behavior, male youths are significantly more likely to participate in violent behavior than females.

Drug and Alcohol Use and Abuse

Engaging in alcohol use is more common among young adults than illicit drugs or cigarettes: 74 percent of females and 71 percent of males have had at least one drink by the time they graduate from high school, and approximately 40 percent of youths had a drink within one month of the YRBSS survey was administered. In 2007, the U.S. Surgeon General warned that over three million teenagers are alcoholics. In addition to increasing depression, anxiety, and risk of cirrhosis of the liver, alcohol is strongly associated with risky sexual practices and the accidental death of teenagers (in automobile, firearm, or drowning accidents).

Although cigarette smoking among middle and high school students is currently at the lowest level in recent history, the National Institute on Drug Abuse (NIDA) estimates that approximately 20 percent of students still smoke regularly. Cigarette smoking can lead to negative health outcomes, including lung disease and cancer, heart disease, stroke, and nicotine addiction. Teenage cigarette smokers are likely involved in other high-risk behaviors, and some researchers argue that an early introduction to smoking leads to the increased likelihood of other illicit drug use.

Sizeable percentages of youths engage in illegal drug use; marijuana is the most common illicit drug, used by 21 percent of high school students in 2009. Approximately three percent of students use cocaine; 12 percent inhalants; seven percent ecstasy; and four percent methamphetamines. These rates represent decreases in the proportion of students using illegal drugs in the past 10 years. The use of prescription narcotics such as Vicodin and OxyContin, however, appears to be increasingly used for nonmedical reasons. Youths heavily involved in drug use and abuse run the risk of accidental overdose, becoming addicted, or getting in trouble with the law. Substance abuse problems can lead to trouble holding steady, gainful employment, as well as lower grades and decreased commitment to school. Drug-related problems can continue into adult life if left untreated.

Obesity and Other Health-Related Risks

Currently, there is much attention paid to the negative health-related outcomes of youths who are overweight, obese, or unhealthy. YRBSS data shows that many youths are sedentary and not involved in regular physical activity: Only 18 percent of students engage in at least an hour of physical activity daily, whereas 25 percent of students play video or computer games, and 33 percent watch television, for three hours or more on a daily basis. The same survey found that 12 percent of students are considered obese and nearly 16 percent are overweight. At the same time, students were also engaging in risky eating behaviors in order to lose weight. Nearly 11 percent of students reported going without food for 24 hours; five percent of students took diet pills, powders, or liquids; and four percent purged after eating in order to keep from gaining weight. Both overweight and underweight individuals run the risk of health problems in the future, and eating disorders in youths often stem from low self-esteem, social stigma, and a desire to fit in. These factors are also strongly related to other negative behaviors, including cigarette smoking, drug use, and promiscuous sexual relations.

Other High-Risk Behaviors

Youths often engage in other high-risk behaviors that can impede development into a mature, responsible adult. For example, many youths engage in behaviors that are linked to accidents or unintentional injury, such as riding a bicycle without a helmet (84 percent of youths) or not wearing a seat belt (10 percent). Youths who engage in such risky behavior are also likely to be more reckless in other activities as well. Unintentional injuries are the leading cause of death for 10–19-year-olds.

Prevention and Intervention Strategies

Strategies to help youths develop into responsible adults are varied. Some programs are designed to prevent youths from being at-risk in the first place, while other programs intervene after the fact. Furthermore, many programs aim to holistically target the antecedent factors that put youths at risk, while other strategies are more limited in scope. These single-component programs aim to reduce the influence of one predisposing facet, such as improving educational factors or bettering the child's physical welfare, or preventing one specific outcome (i.e., dropping out) rather than encompassing the broader range of predisposing factors and negative outcomes.

A primary debate about the most effective strategies to help youths develop into responsible adults focuses on the timing of assistance. Prevention strategies are often initiated early in the youth's life before any high-risk behaviors, whereas intervention strategies are more responsive and attempt to correct risky behavior before it worsens as the youth transitions into adulthood. Prevention strategies are typically more common, and there are several benefits, but there are also limitations to preventative mechanisms that intervention strategies can provide for.

Pro: Benefits of Prevention Strategies

Multidimensional prevention programs are often the most well-known and the most successful mechanisms for preventing high-risk behaviors in youths and for their long-term success in adulthood. These programs often work because they target the variety of predisposing factors present in youths' lives in order to prevent high-risk behaviors before they begin. Experts further argue that the most successful methods to ensure positive and successful youth development begin early. These early prevention strategies target the home and the school environments, and can be as simple as parents playing and reading with their children.

Programs such as Head Start are comprehensive initiatives that provide children with classroom-based preschool, transportation to and from school, and healthy meals twice a day, as well as focus on socializing and educating low-income children and their parents. The programs involve parents in program decision making, and educate parents on childrearing strategies, child development, and money management. Head Start programs have been shown to provide educational and health benefits for youths and economic rewards for the community. That is, children who graduate from Head Start programs are closer to national norms in reading, writing, and vocabulary than similarly disadvantaged children who did not attend the Head Start program; and parents involved in Head Start are more likely to read to their children. In addition, Head Start children are less likely to be obese, more likely to have received immunizations, and less likely to be charged with a crime. By reducing the welfare dependency of Head Start families and costs associated with crime and special education, while simultaneously increasing family stability, employment, and earnings, the benefit-cost ratio of Head Start has been estimated at $9 to $1.

Preventative programs similar to Head Start have shown long-term successes. The Perry Preschool Study, which examined African American youths from impoverished neighborhoods in the 1960s, found positive, long-term effects for participants who had received a special preschool program (a forerunner of the modern Head Start programs). Perry Preschool graduates were more likely to graduate from high school, earn higher salaries, own their own home, and wait until marriage to have a child, and were arrested less often than the youths who did not attend the special preschool program. In a 10-

year followup, the Yale Child Welfare Project, an in-home visitation program that provides parent training and prenatal care, shows that the program increased parental involvement and the children's' greater academic success.

Con: Drawbacks of Prevention Strategies

Despite the purported benefits of preventative measures that incorporate families, schools, and communities, there are some drawbacks to the method. To begin with, strategies such as Head Start focus on early prevention, but are ineffective at helping youths deal with problems that manifest later in life, such as substance abuse, gang membership, and sexual promiscuity. In fact, studies of youth violence suggest that most youths who become violent begin doing so in adolescence, not childhood. Therefore, prevention strategies to help youths plan for the future must account for the late onset of certain high-risk behaviors and intervene before the risky behavior translates into an unproductive and ineffective adulthood. More effective treatments for youths engaging in risky behaviors may be true intervention programs that occur after the initial presence of risky behavior, such as behavior management.

Several programs show promise in intervening with bullying, delinquency, and poor academic achievement. One, the School Transitional Environmental Program, or STEP, attempts to reduce the negative influence of stressful life events, particularly transitioning to a new school. The program employs strategies to reduce student anonymity and increase accountability. Evidence suggests that students who participate in STEP report feeling better adjusted to a new school, improved academic performance, and better equipped against substance abuse. Second, Functional Family Therapy (FFT) is a multicomponent intervention program that targets youths who show signs of delinquent behavior. FFT provides direct services by a variety of professionals to the youth and the family, focusing on preventing dropping out, increasing motivation to change and improve attitudes toward school and interpersonal relationships, and skills training. Third, the Intensive Protective Supervision Program intercedes between juvenile arrest and punishment. The program diverts arrestees from incarceration and instead provides proactive community supervision, and has been shown to reduce future delinquency.

An additional problem with multicomponent preventative methods is that collaborative efforts between multiple entities can be overly idealistic. From a pragmatic perspective, parents who have multiple jobs or are burdened by child care duties may simply be unable to participate because of time obligations, regardless of their desire to help their children. Studies of adjudicated youths show that less than half of the parents of seriously delinquent boys were ever helped. Though this critique is also applicable to some intervention methods, several intervening strategies that are school-based and less reliant on parental involvement still show signs of success. Other single-faceted, low-cost intervention techniques do not necessitate parental involvement, such as training in problem solving, thinking skills, and moral reasoning.

Finally, although the effectiveness of preventative programs is measured in terms of total youths who reach certain goals (such as graduating from high school), in actuality, the effects are vastly different based on gender, and sometimes, race or ethnicity. For example, although more of the Perry Preschool participants graduated from high school than nonparticipants, only 32 percent of the male students graduated from high school.

See Also: 2. Alternative Schools; 5. Curfews; 15. Racial Disparities; 20. Treatment and Rehabilitation.

Further Readings

Alliance for Excellent Education. "High School Dropouts in America." (February 2009). http://www.all4ed.org/files/GraduationRates_Fact Sheet.pdf (Accessed September 2010).

Becker, Howard S. *Outsiders: Studies in the Sociology of Deviance.* New York: The Free Press, 1963.

Biglan, Anthony, Patricia A. Brennan, Sharon L. Foster, and Harold D. Holder. *Helping Adolescents at Risk: Prevention of Multiple Problem Behaviors.* New York: Guilford Press, 2005.

Capuzzi, David, and Douglas Gross. *Youth at Risk: A Prevention Resource for Counselors, Teachers, and Parents.* Alexandria, VA: The American Counseling Association. 2006.

Chambliss, William. "The Saints and the Roughnecks." *Society* (November–December 2005).

Coleman, John, and Ann Hagell, eds. *Adolscence, Risk and Resilience: Against the Odds.* West Sussex, England: John Wiley and Sons, 2007.

Commission on Behavioral and Social Sciences and Education. "Losing Generations: Adolescents in High-Risk Settings." (1993). http://www.nap .edu/openbook.php?record_id=2113&page=1 (Accessed September 2010).

Dryfoos, Joy G. *Adolescence: Growing Up in America Today.* New York: Oxford University Press, 2007.

Dryfoos, Joy G. *Adolescents at Risk: Prevalence and Prevention.* New York: Oxford University Press, 1990.

Guttmacher Institute. "Facts on American Teens' Sexual and Reproductive Health." (January 2010). http://www.guttmacher.org/pubs/FB-ATSRH .html (Accessed September 2010).

Knoll, Crystal, and Melissa Sickmond. "Delinquency Cases in Juvenile Court, 2007." Washington, DC: U.S. Department of Justice, 2010.

Lemert, Erwin. *Social Pathology.* New York: McGraw-Hill, 1951.

Loeber, Rolf, and David P. Farrington, eds. *Child Delinquents: Development, Intervention, and Service Needs.* Thousand Oaks, CA: Sage, 2001.

National Center for Chronic Disease Prevention and Health Promotion. "Healthy Youth!" http://www.cdc.gov/HealthyYouth/index.htm (Accessed September 2010).

National Head Start Association. http://www.nhsa.org (Accessed September 2010).

Parks, Greg. "The High/Scope Perry Preschool Project." Washington, DC: U.S. Department of Justice, 2000.

Santelli, John, Nancy Brener, Richard Lowry, Amita Bhatt, and Laurie Zabin. "Multiple Sexual Partners Among U.S. Adolescents and Young Adults." *Family Planning Perspectives,* v.30/6 (November–December 2006).

Sedlak, A. J., J. Mettenburg, M. Basena, I. Petta, K. McPherson, A. Greene, and S. Li. *Fourth National Incidence Study of Child Abuse and Neglect.* Report to Congress, Executive Summary. Washington, DC: U.S. Department of Health and Human Services, 2010.

Stouthamer-Loeber, Magda, Rolf Loeber, and Christopher Thomas. "Caretakers Seeking Help for Boys With Disruptive Delinquent Behavior." *Comprehensive Mental Health Care,* v.2 (1992).

Thornberry, Terence P., David Huizinga, and Rolf Loeber. "The Cause and Correlates Studies: Findings and Policy Implications." *Juvenile Justice,* v.9/1 (September 2004).

U.S. Department of Health and Human Services. *Youth Violence: A Report of the Surgeon General.* Rockville, MD: U.S. Department of Health and Human Services, 2001.

Widom, Cathy Spatz. "Understanding Child Maltreatment and Juvenile Delinquency." Child Welfare League of America. 2003. http://www.cwla .org/programs/juvenilejustice/ucmjd03.pdf (Accessed September 2010).

4

Boot Camps

Patricia E. Campie
National Center for Juvenile Justice

As a response to 1990s tough-on-crime initiatives, juvenile boot camps were first modeled after adult boot camps for criminal offenders. Protocols were later developed, with varying results. Some residential camps featured an emphasis on treatment and skill building within a positive culture, while others placed an emphasis on military-like discipline. While boot camps are less expensive in the short run than incarceration, and maintain a high degree of public support as an appropriate punishment for youths and an effective way to keep communities safe, concerns have been raised over the way these camps are sometimes implemented. Studies examining whether boot camps actually affect youth recidivism have shown very little evidence of effectiveness; in some cases, these studies have even shown higher recidivism outcomes for youths who have been boot camp participants. Boot camps have even been caught up in serious controversies such as death and injury lawsuits. While the juvenile justice system in many jurisdictions has started to shift away from the use of boot camps as an intervention for youth offenders, the approach remains popular with the general public and is widely implemented in several states throughout the United States, mainly through the provision of private, fee-based services for parents. From the history of juvenile boot camps, current trends have emerged, as well as current thinking on the pros and cons of using the boot camp approach as an effective deterrent to juvenile crime.

History of Boot Camps

Juvenile boot camps became popular in the 1990s as a tough-on-crime response to what appeared to be a rising tide of violent crime among youths. These camps were modeled after the adult boot camps used for criminal offenders and featured military-like discipline and an emphasis on physical conditioning. Juvenile boot camps were initially conceived to be highly structured residential programs providing youths with up to 90 days of programming, sometimes followed by transitional supports back into the community, known as aftercare.

Office of Juvenile Justice and Delinquency Prevention Study

As the number of boot camp programs grew throughout the country during the 1990s, The Office of Juvenile Justice and Delinquency Prevention (OJJDP) created a model boot camp protocol in 1995 and funded three pilot sites to study to what degree, if any, the boot camp approach was an effective response to juvenile crime. Studies were conducted in Cleveland, Denver, and Mobile, Alabama, to examine the efficacy of the boot camp approach.

Recidivism outcomes were shown to be either weak in the intended direction or strong in the opposite direction, with one of the three sites so poorly administered that little reliable data could be generated for the study. A major limitation at each site was the manner in which aftercare services were implemented, with no site able to administer its aftercare process as intended. Some of these sites were either completely redesigned during the study period or were shut down entirely.

As the 1990s wound down, juvenile crime statistics started to show a steady decline in juvenile offending, which continued through FBI data released in 2008. Despite this statistical drop in the number of crimes committed by youths and the decreasing severity of violent crimes committed, public support and federal funding continued to support the implementation of juvenile boot camps. This was true in spite of the fact that the research was not yet in on whether or not boot camps were effective for reducing delinquency. The few studies that were beginning to accumulate suggested that boot camps had either no impact on recidivism or, in the case of the OJJDP study, may actually result in an increase recidivism among boot camp participants.

In 2001, a meta-analysis was conducted by researchers Doris MacKenzie, David Wilson, and Suzanne Kider to examine the overarching deterrent effects across boot camp programs to determine how well they deterred future offending. Twenty-nine quasi-experimental and experimental studies were used to evaluate programs that had the features of residential boot-camp environments. Recidivism rates of program participants were compared to equivalent groups of youths receiving a different correctional sanction. The study produced mixed results, mainly explained by the substantial variation among boot camp implementation processes and differing program content in each setting. In nine of these settings, boot camp participants exhibited lower recidivism rates than those from a comparison group of equivalent youths. In eight of the 29 studies, the comparison groups had lower recidivism than the boot camp groups. In the remaining 20 studies, no significant differences in re-offending rates between groups were found.

National Institute of Justice Analysis

The National Institute of Justice (NIJ) released a 10-year retrospective analysis of boot camps in 2003. This comprehensive study looked more generally at the practice of boot camps across both adult and juvenile implementations by reviewing studies that had previously been done on boot camps from the late 1980s through the end of the 1990s. Similar to the meta-analysis done by MacKenzie, Wilson, and Kider, the studies that were reviewed in the NIJ study were not conducted in similar manners, and the boot camps included in these studies were designed and implemented in very dissimilar ways. Overall, this retrospective analysis conducted by NIJ found no convincing evidence that boot camp programs reduce recidivism among adult or juvenile offenders. Like previous reports, the NIJ study found that

- participants reported positive, short-term changes in attitudes, behaviors, and problem-solving skills;
- participants' perceived gains in positive, short-term changes did not generally result in lowered recidivism upon completion of the boot camp program;
- those boot camp programs that did produce marginal impacts on reducing recidivism were unique in that they offered more treatment programming to participants; however, there were boot camps that included treatments that did not produce any recidivism benefits;
- boot camp costs were generally less expensive than the costs of providing standard incarceration;

- boot camp implementation models, including staff training, participant eligibility criteria, and engagement strategies varied greatly;
- effective aftercare and reentry practices were not strongly tied to the boot camp experience; and
- the disciplined setting in which therapeutic programming was made available created a sense of safety among participants, which translated into short-term improvements in participant attitudes.

The California Youth Authority (CYA) commissioned a study in 2002 to address the criticism that many boot camp studies were limited in their explanatory power because they had not utilized rigorous study designs. In response to these shortcomings, the CYA commissioned a boot camp research study using an experimental design and control and treatment group to explore the effectiveness of California's juvenile boot camps. The study was longitudinal in nature, following youths past their boot camp experience to look at long-term reoffending behavior. In 2006, followup arrest data were collected on study participants, and researchers found that there were no statistically significant differences between boot camp participants and youths in the control group with regard to average arrest frequency or time to first arrest after exiting the program.

Recent Trends

In Florida, one of the first states to respond in the 1990s with tough-on-crime juvenile policies sanctioning youth offenders as though they were adults, boot camps became part of the juvenile correctional system. Until 2006, Florida boasted the greatest number of juvenile boot camps than any other jurisdiction in the United States. Because of this, Florida juvenile boot camps presented a potentially rich source of research information to study the impacts of boot camps on youth outcomes.

In 2004, researchers from Yale University conducted a study on the effectiveness of Florida's correctional programs (including its boot camps) as part of a study looking at the relative cost-effectiveness difference between public and private correctional programming and facilities. At the time, all juvenile boot camps in Florida were run by county sheriff's departments, with oversight provided by state justice officials. Youths 14 to 18 years of age were eligible for participation in the camps, and were selected by county officials using a subjective standard related to how well the youths could tolerate rigorous physical activity and how much they could stand to benefit from a highly structured and disciplined environment. Study results determined that privately run boot camp facilities in the state resulted in statistically significant higher recidivism rates than publicly run correctional facilities. The study also found that the short-term cost savings of using a private boot camp provider over a public corrections option was not great enough to mitigate the long-term recidivism "cost" that resulted from youths participating in these programs.

Despite the fact that most research studies cannot confirm a definitive link between boot camp participation and deterrence from reoffending, many states still continue to use this form of intervention with delinquent youths. And, while boot camps are less expensive to implement in the short run than traditional youth placement alternatives (akin to incarceration), and public support for these programs is high, very serious concerns continue to mount over the way these camps are sometimes implemented. Some camps have been accused of using unnecessarily harsh and physically punitive sanctions, often against very minor, first-time offenders. Some of these incidents have even resulted in youth deaths, from which subsequent wrongful death suits have been filed, leading some states to reconsider whether they should continue to use this publicly popular youth delinquency intervention even when studies have failed to demonstrate their effectiveness.

Backlash at Boot Camps

In 2006, after several sensationalized news reports of juveniles in Florida being severely injured and killed while under juvenile boot camp supervision, there were public and political calls to shut down boot camp facilities. Added to these allegations was the sober news that Florida's juvenile justice system was reporting that up to 62 percent of graduates from the several boot camps around the state had been rearrested after release. The final blow to juvenile boot camps in Florida came after a 14-year-old boy died from having ammonia tablets pushed up his nose by boot camp program staff as punishment for minor misbehavior. Consequently, in May 2006, Governor Jeb Bush endorsed state legislative actions that effectively prohibited the use of juvenile boot camps as a consequence prescribed through the juvenile justice system in the state. Other states are following suit as the incidence of lethal restraint used against youths in boot camp settings continues to rise.

In February 2010, a Philadelphia family settled a $10.5 million wrongful death lawsuit against a boot camp in Tennessee, where their 17-year-old son was sent by the Philadelphia Department of Human Services, even though the department knew at the time that this boot camp had been reported to be a danger to youths. A family court judge ordered the boy to be placed at the boot camp to receive mental health treatment after he violated his probation by missing a court hearing, and then tested positive for marijuana use. During the civil court case brought by the youth's parents against the camp, video surveillance tapes showed a boot camp staff member on the ground strangling the young man after he refused to leave his room. The boot camp facility in Tennessee was operated by a Philadelphia-based, for-profit company, and city officials claimed they were sending youths to the Tennessee facility because no providers in Pennsylvania would agree to take these troubled youths. After the death of this 17-year-old, the Philadelphia Department of Human Services stopped sending youths to this facility (which continues to operate, but under a different name) and has now cut all of their out-of state placements by half in order to keep closer ties to, and oversight of, the settings in which these youths have been placed. It cost the city of Philadelphia more than $6 million to send 14 youths to the facility over the course of the three years prior to terminating its relationship with the Tennessee facility.

A Cottage Industry

The use of juvenile boot camps as a formal response to delinquent acts is declining as jurisdictions shift their scarce dollars toward evidence-based programs that are designed to address a youth's criminogenic needs, in the hopes of reducing recidivism. However, the boot camp industry remains a robust supplier of disciplinary services for parents who are dealing with troubled teens. The cost to send a youth to one of these programs may be as high as $10,000 for a 30-day program, with many programs extending offers of credit and payment plans to allow families to finance the cost of these services.

   A series of specialty, spinoff camps have also developed in the wake of boot camps losing their toehold in the juvenile justice system and moving into the private sector. Wilderness programs claim to offer a less militaristic approach to troubled teens, but still aim to provide youths with a physically demanding environment that stresses individual responsibility and character development. These programs are even more expensive than private boot camps, costing upwards of $18,000 to attend. Faith-based intervention has also become popular in recent years. The Christian outpatient treatment program Second Chance advertises their camp as focusing on "spiritual renewal resulting in inner transformation through a personal relationship with Jesus Christ," and describes their process to include positive techniques such as "point systems, phase levels, and rewards and consequences." They emphasize that there are treatment methods they refuse to use, which include such negative techniques as intimidation, psychotropic medication, mechanical restraints, and lockdown facilities.

Most recently, a new intervention known as Brat Camp has taken hold in the United States, patterned after a reality television show produced in the United Kingdom. The reality television show was so popular that it was renewed for three additional seasons, and similar shows have been created in the United States and Germany. The youths in these reality television shows tend to come from wealthier families and seem to typify normal teenage misbehavior rather than the serious or delinquent offending behavior that boot camps were originally created to counter. In actuality, however, these so-called brat camps offer the same type of setting and programming found in traditional wilderness camps, where youths need to take care of themselves, live in sparse accommodations, and are challenged by extreme levels of physical activity.

Since the majority of juvenile boot camps and wilderness camps act as private entities providing fee-for-service programming to justice agencies, social service organizations, and individual families, they are not under any sort of comprehensive government regulation. Consequently, there is no central clearinghouse of data on how many of these camps exist, what programmatic features they contain, how their staff are trained, or what outcomes they achieve.

Pro: Advantages of Juvenile Boot Camps

Completion Rates

Some boot camps report youth dropout rates as high as 50 percent. However, when juvenile boot camp programs are located in an area that is secure and away from a youth's normal neighborhood or home community, program completion rates tend to be quite high, ranging from 75–96 percent, as compared with a maximum of 80 percent program completion in most other settings where youths receive delinquency intervention programming.

Delinquency intervention programs that require youth attendance either due to a prescribed loss of freedom (secure confinement) or as a condition of probation tend to have higher completion rates than voluntary intervention programs, or those with no judicial enforcement consequence for failure to attend. In addition, intervention programs that successfully limit negative disruptions from peers and family members can have the effect of helping youths develop new relationships within the intervention program, which can also help boost program completion rates if those relationships are positive.

There has been little evidence to suggest that many boot camps typically contain these supportive environments. However, the idea of a boot camp setting as envisioned in the OJJDP program guidelines and offering a structured, active environment where supportive adults help youths learn new pro-social skills is the type of intervention setting that typically has the best chance of producing high completion rates and positive youth outcomes.

Competency Development-Educational Outcomes

Among those boot camps where program staff is documenting education outcomes, and youths are receiving educational supports, youths have shown positive gains in their reading, spelling, language, and math skills. The OJJDP-funded study conducted in Cleveland in the 1990s showed that these educational gains allowed youths to advance their work an entire grade level in each of these academic areas.

One of the more unique boot camp profiles comes from Texas, where a local public school partners with the county juvenile court and probation department to house a juvenile boot camp within the school. The Specialized Treatment and Rehabilitation program, known as STAR, was found to produce positive outcomes with regard to youth perceptions of teamwork and life skills, while still supporting youth educational needs in their home school. Negative findings from the study included greater recidivism effects, and for more serious offenses than the original offenses triggering boot camp participation in the STAR program. After the state of Florida outlawed the traditional boot camp model in 2006, that state adopted the STAR approach in its boot camp jurisdictions, intent on focusing more on educational and aftercare outcomes than on the military-like discipline that was blamed for several injuries and deaths among boot camp youths in that state.

Cost Savings Compared to Incarceration

When used as an alternative to juvenile correctional facilities, boot camps are more cost-effective due to the shortened length of stay, which is typically

90 days. For serious offenders, boot camps are more cost-effective if only a 90-day or shorter correctional sentence would be the alternative course of action. However, these short-term gains in terms of reduced cost are not realized in the long term, according to most studies that examine boot camp cost effectiveness.

Youth and Public Perceptions

In a study of more than 4,100 youths confined to boot camps or youth correctional facilities, researchers at the University of Maryland found that youths in boot camp environments reported feeling safer from peer conflicts as compared with youths in traditional correctional settings. Boot camp youths also reported their environments to be more structured, supportive, active, and controlled as compared to youths from the correctional setting. Youths in these correctional settings reported their environment to be less therapeutic and less focused on successful transition back to the community than youths in boot camp settings. However, in both the boot camp setting and the traditional correctional setting, all youths still reported higher than average levels of fear and conflict between themselves and staff supervising youth behavior.

Con: Disadvantages of Juvenile Boot Camps

A Flawed Theory of Change

Juvenile boot camps were created in the image of the military model that tries to break individuals down to build them up. The use of military service as a diversion alternative for adult offenders is no longer practiced in the United States. However, when juvenile boot camps were originally introduced in the 1980s, the idea garnered bipartisan support. More liberal voters like the idea of shorter sentences for youth offenders and in an environment other than traditional confinement. Conservatives liked the get-tough disciplinary approach used in the boot camp model, likening it to a military setting.

However, criminological research has failed to show any connection between a youth's delinquent behavior and the lack of military-like disciplinary practices in their lives. Instead, criminogenic factors affecting a youth's likelihood of offending have been identified as either static or dynamic. Static factors are those not impacted by any intervention or prevention program, such as age, gender, prior history of offending, or parental history of crime. Dynamic factors associated with youth crime involve peer relation-ships, academic engagement, family bonding, and individual-level factors such as moral reasoning and impulse control. Boot camps are not designed to impact any of the criminogenic factors identified with youth offending. Instead, boot camps may decrease the protective factors that keep youths from offending or re-offending by removing them from school and family and traumatizing youths through punishments that are disproportionately harsh.

Allegations of Abuse and Neglect

In a 2007 study conducted by the Government Accountability Office (GAO), investigators reported thousands of abuse allegations against youth boot camp and wilderness facilities. Of the 10 programs where teenagers died under dubious circumstances, five were still operating at the time of the GAO's study—often using a new name or in a different place.

A few of the more disturbing examples of the types of abuse and neglect that have occurred in juvenile boot camps as documented by the GAO include the following:

- A 15-year-old who died from a severed neck artery after being held face down in the dirt for 45 minutes.
- A 14-year-old at an Arizona boot camp who died of dehydration after being forced to sit in 113-degree desert heat as punishment for asking to go home. The program closed, and the director was sentenced to six years in prison for manslaughter.
- A case where boys at a boot camp were required to stand with bags over their head and a hangman's noose around their necks.

There is no central clearinghouse for reporting alleged abuses from par-ticipating in a boot camp or residential program for youths. When allega-tions arise, states may submit these reported incidents to a federal database, but this reporting is only on a voluntary basis.

Inconsistent Program Implementation

Because residential programs for youths are largely unregulated, boot camp programs can vary greatly in the way they select youths, train staff, and design their programming. These management inconsistencies can lead to substantial problems mixing repeat and first-time offenders together, creating issues with overuse of force during training exercises led by staff, and lack of structured activities that are effective for developing the pro-social, educational, or competency development skills youths may need to succeed.

Boot camp programs also suffer from poor aftercare planning, which is an essential component of successfully transitioning youths from court supervision so they can succeed in the community on their own. In the OJJDP study from 1995, this critical component was either poorly implemented or lacking altogether in those boot camps, and the results from that study showed how recidivism was actually worse for participants in two of the three boot camps studied, with the third site showing just slightly better recidivism outcomes as compared with a control group. Many boot camp settings are placed in remote locations where the military-like boot camp environment can be played out through wilderness exercises, ropes courses, survival tests, and the like. The isolation of these settings from other social, educational, and employment opportunities further complicate the process for ensuring that youths experience an appropriate and seamless transition from the boot camp environment to the community in which they live, work, and go to school.

Higher Overall Costs

Low-level and first-time offenders who are sent to boot camps end up costing jurisdictions more money in the short run than they would otherwise save from being on standard probation due to costs associated with the program, such as housing, staffing, meals, equipment, and transportation.

While short-term boot camps are more cost effective when used as an alternative to juvenile correctional facilities, these short-term reductions in cost are not realized in the long term, according to most studies that examine boot camp cost effectiveness. The long-term outcomes for boot camp participants have been shown to include new delinquent or criminal offenses, often more serious than the acts for which the boot camp program was prescribed. Because of this, the cost for each episode of providing boot camp to a youth might be less expensive than placing that youth in a state facility, but the successive costs of having this same youth continue to require the attention of the juvenile or criminal justice system eventually outweighs these short-term savings. If the boot camp program does not provide treatment services for mental health or substance-abuse needs, those needs will still need to be met (and paid for) after the youth exits the program. Research into collateral effects from a negative boot camp experience suggest that youths may require additional counseling or treatment for post-traumatic stress disorder after participating in a boot camp experience. These post-program costs, if added to the proximal cost of having a youth in the boot camp program, could be adding additional expense to what might already be an ineffective delinquency intervention.

Recidivism Rates

Although comprehensive studies have not been possible due to the lack of program fidelity at many boot camp programs, those studies that have been undertaken show that first-time and persistent offenders tend to have higher recidivism rates when they are mixed together in a boot camp environment once they are released back to the community.

Studies measuring the efficacy of boot camps continue to demonstrate little benefit, from either a recidivism or positive youth development perspective. Further, the litigation, investigation, and corrective action costs of responding to complaints over cases of excessive abuse and neglect increase the collateral costs of operating boot camps for the providers, as well as for the jurisdictions that must account for the safety and effectiveness of these court-sanctioned facilities.

In sum, juvenile boot camps are no longer the program of choice for juvenile justice agencies and courts, although they still are used in some jurisdictions and have created a cottage industry to serve parents looking for solutions to dealing with troubled teens. Modeled after the adult boot camps used for criminal offenders and featuring military-like discipline and an emphasis on physical conditioning, boot camp environments do not produce long-term savings or increased public safety, as studies have shown that recidivism rates for boot camp participants are often higher than for youths placed in other interventions, placed on probation, or sent to residential placement or juvenile corrections. Although short-term educational performance benefits have been shown in some boot camps that emphasize educational achievement activities, these results have been sporadic across the research literature. Further, while public support has continued to be strong for the use of these camps, highly publicized cases of alleged abuse and neglect, even resulting in death, have called into question the intimidation techniques often used at boot camps to instill discipline in unruly youths. As a result, boot camps have been prohibited from use in some jurisdictions, which are instead focusing their scarce economic resources on intervention programs with a strong evidence base, rooted in research on the static and dynamic criminogenic characteristics that best predict future offending behavior and support the development of youth competencies into adulthood.

See Also: 3. At-Risk Youth; 7. Group Homes; 8. Juvenile Detention
Facilities; 11. Juveniles in Adult Correctional Facilities;
13. Out-of-Home Placement; 20. Treatment and Rehabilitation.

Further Readings

Bayer, Patrick, and David Pozen. "The Effectiveness of Juvenile Correctional Facilities: Public Versus Private Management." Discussion Paper No. 863. New Haven, CT: Yale University, November 2004.

Bottcher, Jean. "Examining the Effectiveness of Boot Camps: A Randomized Experiment With a Long-Term Follow Up." *Journal of Research in Crime and Delinquency,* v.42/3 (2005).

Dilanian, Ken. "GAO Study Reveals Boot Camp Nightmare." *USA Today* (October 10, 2007).

Family Treatment Services. http://www.purposedrivencamp.com (Accessed February 2010).

Graham, Troy. "Family of Boy Strangled at Tennessee Center Settles Suit for $10.5 Million." *Philadelphia Inquirer* (February 12, 2010).

Latessa, Edward J., and Christopher Lowenkamp. "What Are Criminogenic Needs and Why Are They Important?" *For The Record* (Fourth Quarter, 2005).

MacKenzie, Doris, David Wilson, and Suzanne Kider. "Effects of Correctional Boot Camps on Offending." *Annals of the American Academy of Political and Social Science,* v.126/578 (2001).

Parent, Dale G. *Correctional Boot Camps: Lessons From a Decade of Research.* Washington, DC: National Institute of Justice, 2003.

Second Chance. http://www.2chance.org (Accessed September 2010).

Styve, Gaylene, et al. "Perceived Conditions of Confinement: A National Evaluation of Juvenile Boot Camps and Traditional Facilities." *Law and Human Behavior,* v.24/3 (2000).

Trulson, C., et al. "Social Control in a School Setting: Evaluating a School-Based Boot Camp." *Crime Delinquency,* v.47 (2001).

WJHG. "Boot Camps Abolished in Florida." http://www.wjhg.com/home/headlines/2905871.html (Accessed September 2010).

5

Curfews

Yvonne Vissing
Salem State College

Laws imposing juvenile curfews have become commonly used strategies for controlling juvenile crime, reducing youth victimization, and helping parents to supervise their children. The efficacy and legality of juvenile curfews are widely debated, and center on questions such as: If youths are unsupervised and on the street late at night, are they more inclined to get into trouble? Will restricting young people's right to be on the streets actually reduce the amount of youth violence, offenses, and delinquency? Are curfews a violation of young people's civil liberties? Advocates for juvenile curfews allege that curfews protect both youths and the public from violence and crime. If curfews reduce crime and protect youths, they argue that limiting young people's rights may be justified. Advocates also assert that the needs of the community outweigh the individual rights of minors. Critics disagree, and argue that curfew laws are a violation of juvenile's fundamental constitutional rights. Moreover, critics cite data that reports curfews simply are not effective in reducing crime. In 1997, an article by the Harvard Law Review Association confirmed these views, and found that juvenile curfews may also lead to antagonism between youths and law enforcement officials. Courts have provided mixed decisions on the juvenile curfew issue, leaving communities without guidance on whether they should use them or not. Data on the effectiveness of curfews has been mixed as well, adding to community confusion regarding their use.

Community leaders, law enforcement officials, and the general public tend to encourage the use of curfews. The appeal of curfews is simple and attractive: If youths stay home under the watchful eyes of their parents, then serious crime may not occur. Because people believe they are effective, as of July 2009, over 500 U.S. cities had juvenile curfews, including 78 of the 92 cities with populations greater than 180,000. It is estimated that at least 75 percent of U.S. cities impose some sort of evening curfew on youths. In most places, youths under the age of 18 are prohibited from being on the streets between 11 P.M. and 5 A.M. Around 100 cities also have daytime curfews to keep children off the streets during daytime hours when they are supposed to be in school. Other developed nations, such as Australia, Scotland, and Britain have also implemented juvenile curfews.

Reports vary significantly on the efficacy of juvenile curfews. Some imply that curfews are successful in reducing youth crime, other reports indicate that they do not cause crime to go down, some indicate they may actually increase crime, and many are inconclusive. Reports applauding the benefits of curfews are often more opinion than data-driven. Those with statistical analyses are often limited to selected time periods and specific types of crimes and areas, and do not compare jurisdictions that enforce curfews to those that do not. For example, a U.S. Conference of Mayors study of law enforcement authorities in 1,010 cities with populations of more than 30,000 found that only one-third of the cities responded to the survey. Of those, 88 percent claimed that curfews reduced youth crime, but provided no statistical analysis of the effect curfews have had on crime. Los Angeles conducted three studies between 1997 and 1998 on its Enhanced Curfew Enforcement Effort, and found differing results of curfews, rendering no clear conclusion on their efficacy. An Office of Juvenile Justice and Delinquency Prevention study in 1996 of seven cities where curfews were implemented indicated that comprehensive, community-based curfew programs helped to reduce juvenile delinquency and victimization, but the study did not present the necessary data to support that conclusion. The lack of quality data on the efficacy of curfews has fueled the debate on whether or not they should be used as a crime deterrent.

History of Curfews

Curfews began in England under the reign of Alfred the Great, who ordered villagers to put out their fires and go to bed when the town bell rang. The word comes from the French term *courfvrefeu,* meaning to "cover fire." William the

Conqueror used an 8:00 P.M. curfew in 1068. The United States implemented curfews before the Civil War and during emergencies. They are frequently imposed during wartime. The first youth curfew was enacted in Omaha, Nebraska, in 1880. In 1884, President Benjamin Harrison referred to curfews as the most important municipal regulation for protection of children from the vices of the street. Juvenile curfews become widespread around 1890, when crime was blamed on immigrant youths and poor parental supervision. During World War II, curfews were perceived as an effective control for parents who were busy helping with the war effort. Chicago, the nation's largest city with a curfew, passed curfew laws in 1955. By 1960, 60 of 110 cities with populations over 100,000 had curfews, and by the 1970s, juvenile curfews became commonplace. The Juvenile Justice and Delinquency Prevention Act of 1974 endorsed deinstitutionalization mandates for youths who had previously been incarcerated for infractions and mental health issues. Curfews helped alleviate community safety concerns of allowing troubled youths on the street.

1980s: Spike in Violence

During the late 1980s in the United States, data indicated a significant increase in the rates of youth violence. The increase was most striking in the area of youth homicide. This generated concern and fear, so federal, state, and local governments responded by instituting a new set of policies and practices to address the issue. This was evidenced by the stiffening of a variety of laws relating to juvenile justice. In 1988, a national panel on juvenile crime concluded that most juveniles commit crimes, but most are minor and not serious, despite what the public may think. They found that only four percent of crimes were violent (including rape, robbery, and aggravated assault) and only one-tenth of one percent was homicide.

When juvenile laws are stiffened, arrest rates increase exponentially. In the early 1990s, the arrest rate for minors in the District of Columbia was the highest in the nation; homicide rates were high, and between 1987 and 1995, the juvenile arrest rate for aggravated assault increased by 89.8 percent, for murder by 157 percent, and for carrying a dangerous weapon by 282.7 percent. Concerned with these frightening statistics, the D.C. Council adopted a juvenile curfew ordinance. In Atlanta during late 1990, heightened public concern resulted when 25 youths were shot in a drug-related incident. Both cities responded by enforcing curfews against youths, and sometimes their parents, whom they saw as having the legal responsibility for their children's misbehavior.

The juvenile crime rate rose in the late 1980s and peaked in 1994, but by 1999 had declined to rates similar to those prior to the increase. Regardless, public concern continued. In 1996, President Bill Clinton endorsed curfews to "keep children out of harm's way." Organizations like the U.S. Conference of Mayors and National League of Cities supported curfews as ways to protect youths and communities. In 1998, the Crime and Disorder Act was enacted to enable local authorities to establish curfews for younger children. The act was ignited by concern that society was escalating toward lawlessness and moral decline. It sent forth a message to youths who inappropriate behavior would not be tolerated. Curfews continue to be used in over 500 U.S. cities, even with declining juvenile crime rates.

Legality of Curfews

There is widespread sentiment that juvenile crime is out of control, so officials should do something that will both curb crime and prove that they are concerned leaders. Despite good intentions, juvenile curfew laws raise serious constitutional issues. Courts have not clarified the conditions under which curfews are constitutionally valid, and curfew laws have been challenged on a variety of constitutional grounds.

Pro-curfew advocates allege that teen curfews are necessary for crime prevention and the rights of the community outweigh the rights of children, while critics argue that minors have the same constitutional right as adults. The Supreme Court indicated in 1944 that the rights of minors are not equivalent to those of adults in *Prince v. Massachusetts*. It concluded that the state's authority over children's activities is broader than its authority over similar actions of adults. But in the 1967 case *In re Gault et al.*, the Court concluded that "the Fourteenth Amendment nor the Bill of Rights is for adults alone." The Court ruled in the 1976 case of *Missouri v. Danforth* that all people have full constitutional rights regardless of age. In the Court's opinion, constitutional rights do not mature, and become implemented only when one attains the state-defined age of majority. It has been argued that curfews are a violation of the Fifth Amendment's right to free movement and due process. Legal challenges to the constitutionality of curfew ordinances have been based on the First, Fourth, Fifth, Ninth, and Fourteenth Amendments to the Constitution.

In 1993, the Fifth Circuit Court upheld a Dallas juvenile curfew ordinance after the American Civil Liberties Union (ACLU) challenged the law. In *Qutb v. Strauss*, the U.S. Court of Appeals upheld the law, arguing that the ordinance was narrowly tailored and met a compelling state interest, the two conditions necessary for passing the "strict scrutiny" test of constitutional infringement. As a result, cities across the nation established curfew laws based on the Dallas model. Since that time, several cases have re-examined the constitutionality of juvenile curfew laws, such as the 1997 *Schleifer v. City of Charlottesville.* In *Hutchins v. District of Columbia,* the district court found curfews unconstitutional because they prohibited minors' rights to freedom of movement and interfered with parental rights to control their children. Rochester, New York, enacted a curfew in 2007, but the New York Court of Appeals later deemed it unconstitutional. The 1993 juvenile curfew law imposed in Lowell, Massachusetts, was recently found to be unconstitutional, violating the Declaration of Rights guarantee to all people with the fundamental right, irrespective of age, to move freely without police interference. To date, the U.S. Supreme Court has refused to hear appeals on the constitutionality of juvenile curfews, which leaves communities unsure what to do, since state and federal courts have issued conflicting decisions.

S. M. Horowitz conducted a review of U.S. juvenile curfew ordinances in an attempt to better understand the constitutional standards applied to juvenile curfew laws, and found that the 1989 ruling by the U.S. District Court for the District of Columbia invalidated the juvenile curfew law enacted by Washington, D.C. The 1989 curfew law was found to have violated the first amendment rights of young people to have freedom of speech and assemble. It also denied them equal protection promised in the Fifth Amendment. The Washington, D.C., law had argued that curfews could be upheld when there were sufficient state interests to justify the infringement of minors' fundamental rights, but the ruling was overturned since it "irrationally distinguished between juveniles and non-juveniles."

The question of whether it is possible to limit youth freedom while simultaneously supporting civil rights fuels debate. Both the United States and Australia are democratic countries that espouse support of civil liberties but implement curfews that limit human rights by prohibiting free movement throughout the community. Moreover, where curfews exist, police officers and courts vary significantly in how they enforce them. Penalties for curfew violations range from warnings, fines, criminal charges, community service, and counseling, to prosecution of parents. Critics question whether curfews actually dissuade youths from engaging in troublesome behavior. Most youths don't cause problems, while curfews may not deter the four percent of youths who are intent in engaging in serious crime.

Pro: Arguments in Support of Juvenile Curfews

Curfews have been widely regarded as an effective tool for reducing youth crime. By keeping youths at home, curfews are expected to reduce the incidence of crime, according to the Federal Bureau of Investigation. In addition, since juvenile perpetrators of crime often target other youths, curfews can reduce rates of youth victimization. Youths are subject to status offenses, such as truancy, loitering, running away, underage drinking, and disruptive behavior, and curfews are thought to help limit those types of problems, as well as violent offenses. Curfews also provide parents with a legitimate, legal basis for restricting how late children can be out.

By reducing the opportunity for youths to meet with others who could lead them astray or become accomplices in illegal activities, curfews promote decreased criminal and troublesome activities. By targeting evening hours, curfews are thought to limit temptations for troublesome or deviant behavior. Seven cities that are usually considered models for juvenile curfew efforts include: Dallas; Phoenix; Chicago; Jacksonville, Florida; Little Rock, Arkansas; New Orleans; and Denver. Each of these communities tout having comprehensive curfew programs that include at least one of the following: a dedicated curfew center or use of recreation centers or churches to receive juveniles who have been picked up by the police for violating the curfew; staffing of these centers with trained professionals or volunteers to work with youths; referrals to social services, counseling, and education for juveniles and their families; procedures for how to handle repeat offenders; recreation, job, antidrug, and antigang programs; and hotlines for crisis intervention.

Many communities that have instituted curfews have reported a decrease in juvenile crime, especially shortly after they were instituted. For instance, during the 1990s, Dallas reported that juvenile arrests decreased 14.6 percent and youth victimization dropped by 17.7 percent during curfew hours; during the same time frame, Phoenix and Little Rock both found about a 10 percent decrease in juvenile arrests, while New Orleans alleged a 27 percent reduction in youth crime after curfews were established. Other communities report success as well. After Monrovia, California, adopted a 1997 juvenile curfew, there was a 32 percent decline in residential burglaries. Evening curfews are sometimes reported to be associated with a reduction in fatal injury for youths, since youths are at home and not in situations where they could be the victims or perpetrators of violent crime. Similarly, during the 1990s in Dade County, Florida, medical trauma of children 5–16 years of age dropped after enforcement of the curfew law. In 1991, San Antonio, Texas, enacted a juvenile curfew for youths under the age of 16, and found that the victimization of youths dropped 84 percent; it was regarded as so successful that in 1993, a curfew for daylight hours was adopted as well. Because community leaders felt the evening-hours curfew was so effective, in 2006, the city of Dallas instituted daytime curfews in addition to the evening, alleging that no youths should be on the street between 9 A.M. and 2:30 P.M. during the weekdays when they should be in school. During the 1990s, many cities such as Detroit and Cincinnati instituted juvenile curfews, and reported decreased crime and increased arrests. The popularity of curfews has grown since 2000 because of the success touted by police officers, political representatives, and community leaders during the late 1990s.

Curfews enable communities to enforce stronger penalties for status offenses, thereby protecting youths from getting involved with more serious offenses. Curfew arrests of California youth rose fourfold between 1989 and 1997; in the same period in Long Beach, California, police officers attributed a downward trend in juvenile crime to antiloitering and juvenile curfew programs. Curfews are also thought to protect the general public from crime and violence. According to a national survey of police agencies, Andra Bannister, David Carter, and Joseph Schafer reported in 2001 that jurisdictions with curfew ordinances felt curfews were effective in controlling vandalism, graffiti, nighttime burglary, and auto theft. President Clinton promoted the use of juvenile curfews because he felt they would limit crime, sexual experimentation, drug use, and violence. Curfews are positively viewed by parents who wish to have more control over their children, and view curfews as an external source of support to enforce compliance with parental rules and regulations. Curfews can also be seen as a beneficial way to preserve parent-child relations by "blaming" the curfew law for when youths have to be home. Advocates for curfews feel their use is in the public's best interest, especially if they reduce the chance that youths can get into trouble. As one youth reported, "nothing good happens after midnight," indicating that even youths may be relieved for a reason to have to curtail their activities and go home.

Con: Arguments in Opposition to Juvenile Curfews

While public opinion may support the use of juvenile curfews, empirical studies indicate that they are not effective at reducing juvenile offending or victimization. Critics argue that they violate basic constitutional guarantees, lead to antagonism between noncriminal youth and law enforcement officials, and that they are inefficient ways to control crime. Data indicate that even the strongest curfew enforcement has no effect on youth crime or safety, no matter what the time period, jurisdiction, or type of crime measure studied. But perhaps the strongest criticism of juvenile curfew laws stems from viewing them as unconstitutional. Juvenile curfew ordinances are regarded as paternalistic and an invasion of personal liberty.

Critics argue that curfews are not needed, and may be a simplistic solution to reduce crime that actually has no demonstrable effect. Data indicate that the youth crime crisis has peaked and passed. Imposed on and off since the turn of the century, curfews tend to receive increased attention when there is a perceived need for more stringent efforts at social control. While there was a crime increase at one time, a reduction in youth crime has since occurred, therefore eliminating the need for more stringent reactions to curb crime rates that have already stabilized.

Juvenile Crime Rates and Types

Many juveniles do not comply with curfew laws and still do not get in trouble. Juveniles commit a small proportion of overall crime, and the vast majority of the crimes they do commit are status offenses; in fact, only four percent of youths are thought to engage in serious crime. Many status offenses that form the basis for curfew violations would not be crimes if committed by adults.

In addition, as most juvenile crime occurs at times when curfews are not even in effect, evening curfews may be ill-conceived since they are not necessarily the time period when most teens get into trouble or break the law. FBI data indicates that the hours between 2 P.M. and 8 P.M., the period between school dismissal and parents returning home from work, is the peak time for drug use and sales, sex, robberies, assaults, and other activities. This is also the time of day in which there is no curfew.

According to the National Council on Crime and Delinquency, curfew enforcement unnecessarily funnels large numbers of nondelinquent youths into the criminal justice system. Curfew crackdowns have shown little effect on crime over the long term. Because police resources are relatively limited, officers engaged in curfew enforcement are not available for other duties that may be more effective in controlling crime. Critics argue that police time may be more effective in reducing crime when spent on more serious and potentially violent conflicts. Curfew enforcement is regarded as inconsistent and discriminatory, with some youths being sent home while others get taken to jail, and inevitably involves officer discretion and selective enforcement. Often, police curfew enforcement efforts focus on low-income, minority neighborhoods to the exclusion of more affluent, white neighborhoods.

Curfew enforcement can result in counterproductive escalation of problems, such as added financial and emotional stress on parents and guardians, more conflicted interactions with their children, and the incarceration of youths who will then be exposed to more serious offenders. Studies indicate that while curfews may have a neutral effect for white, middle-class youths, they may actually escalate crime among Hispanic and Asian youths. Data indicate that while curfew laws are not inherently racist, discretion of law enforcement practices that are higher in nonwhite neighborhoods has resulted in arrest rates that may be over two-thirds as high for black youths compared to arrests in white neighborhoods. Ironically, curfews may create discriminatory practices and result in the very problems the curfews seek to avoid.

Evidence based on a large-scale study points to a more positive role of the streets in the lives of young people than is acknowledged in current discussions. Curfews do not offer a way forward: for young people, they reinforce a sense of powerlessness and alienation; and for adults, they establish a power hierarchy that alienates youths from their world. Juvenile curfews are not embraced enthusiastically by parents who learn that they would be fined or penalized if their children are out after hours. Throughout the curfew debate, there has been little attempt to incorporate the views of young people. Use of more inclusionary strategies that encourage the incorporation of young people into communities, empower their voices in environmental decision making, and challenge the hegemony of adulthood upon the landscape are regarded by those in opposition to juvenile curfews as potentially more successful in achieving community safety.

Flawed Data

Data problems obfuscate claims of curfew effectiveness. Methodologically, critics argue that reports indicating that curfews are effective frequently lack scientific rigor and are fraught with subjective data interpretation errors. There is little comprehensive data on the direct and indirect costs of such programs or the efficacy. Data on curfew ordinances is often context-specific and based on nonsystematic data, which dilutes the claims of their effectiveness. Some studies found that jurisdictions with curfews promoted the allegation that curfews lower crime rates, when in fact there may be spurious or intervening variables that actually account for the crime reduction. Some communities have experienced a reduction of all types of crime; therefore, when juvenile crime decreases, a more ecological explanation may be required, rather than attributing the reduction to curfews. Success figures cited from some communities do not reflect community-wide declines in all types of crime. Others base their success ratings on increased arrest figures instead of actual amount of crime. Many fail to use baseline data for accurate comparisons of their purported success. A systematic operationalization of what constitutes juvenile crime complicates the generalization of data findings. Mixing units of analyses and types of data may complicate and mask the actual relationship between curfews and crime. Rates of serious crime among youths are strongly correlated with those of adults around them, both by local area and over time. Abolishing curfew laws may be a crucial step to reducing youth crime and victimization, according to critics.

Data indicate that there may be more effective ways to reduce youth crime than the use of curfews. These rely on a supportive community infrastructure that can actively engage youths to pursue more positive actions. Protecting juveniles through noncriminal means when they commit status offenses may be in the best interests of both the community and youths. Comprehensive, community-based programs enacted by local governments may be more effective in reducing youth crime than curfews. Communities that offer a range of alternatives to curfews, such as youth recreation and education programs, counseling, volunteer and jobs programs, antidrug and antigang programs, or hotlines may provide greater prevention benefits. Such programs must be easily accessible, affordable, have supervision and enforcement support, and have proven to be effective services. These comprehensive programs help reduce juvenile delinquency and victimization without violating the legal rights of youths. Future policy and research should focus on the potential crime-reduction effects of prevention strategies that provide a comprehensive array of services, opportunities, and interventions. While this approach is likely to require a substantial infusion of public resources, the long-term benefits appear more promising than panacea approaches such as curfew and status policies.

❖

See Also: 1. Age of Responsibility; 3. At-Risk Youth; 9. Juvenile Gangs and Delinquency; 14. Parental Responsibility Laws; 15. Racial Disparities; 19. Serious and Violent Juvenile Offenders.

Further Readings

Adams, Kenneth. "Abolish Juvenile Curfews." *Criminology and Public Policy,* v.6/4 (November 2007).

Bannister, Andra, David Carter, and Joseph Schafer. "A National Police Survey on the Use of Juvenile Curfews." *Journal of Criminal Justice,* v.29/3 (May–June 2001).

Bilchik, Shay. "Curfew: An Answer to Juvenile Delinquency and Victimization." *Juvenile Justice Bulletin* (April 1996).

Budd, Jordan. "Juvenile Curfews: The Rights of Minors Versus the Rhetoric of Public Safety." *Human Rights,* v.26/22 (1999).

Center for Health Statistics. *Microcomputer Injury Surveillance System 1996.* Sacramento, CA: Department of Health Services, 1997.

Chen, Gregory. "Youth Curfews and the Trilogy of Parent, Child and State Relations." *New York University Law Review.* v.72/131 (April 1997).

Clinton, William Jefferson. "Remarks to the Women's International Convention of the Church of God in Christ in New Orleans, Louisiana." (May 30, 1996).

CNN. "Curfews Don't Cut Juvenile Crime." (1998). http://www.cnn.com /US/9806/10/teen.curfiew (Accessed September 2010).

Constitutional Rights Foundation. "Deliberating Democracy." Youth Curfews. Chicago, IL. http://www.deliberating.org/Lessons_Youth _Curfews.pdf. 2005 (Accessed September 2010).

Cook, Philip J., and John H. Laub. "The Unprecedented Epidemic of Youth Violence." In *Youth Violence,* edited by M. H. Moore and M. Tonry. Chicago: University of Chicago Press, 1998.

Criminal Justice Statistics Center. *California Criminal Justice Profile (1978–1998).* Sacramento: California Department of Justice, 1998.

Crowell, Anthony. "Minor Restrictions: The Challenge of Juvenile Curfews." *Public Management,* v.78 (1996).

Dallas Police Department. "Juvenile Curfew Ordinance." http://www .dallascityhall.com/committee_briefings/briefings0206/02172006 _Juvenile_Curfew.pdf (Accessed September 2010).

Dawson, John M., and Patrick A. Langan. *Murder in Families.* Washington, DC: Bureau of Justice Statistics, 1994.

Favro, Tony. "Youth Curfews Popular With American Cities, but Effectiveness and Legality Are Questioned." http://www.citymayors.com/society/usa-youth-curfews.html (Accessed September 2010).

Federal Bureau of Investigation. *Uniform Crime Reports for the United States, 1996*. Washington, DC: U.S. Department of Justice, 1997.

Fried, Carrie. "Juvenile Curfews: Are They an Effective and Constitutional Means of Combating Juvenile Violence?" *Behavioral Sciences and the Law*, v.19/1 (February 23, 2001).

Fritch, Eric J., Tory J. Caeti, and Robert W. Taylor. "Gang Suppression Through Saturation Patrol, Aggressive Curfew, and Truancy Enforcement: A Quasi-Experimental Test of the Dallas Anti-Gang Initiative." *Crime and Delinquency*, v.45 (1999).

Garrett, D., and D. Brewster. "Curfew: A New Look at an Old Tool." *Police Chief*, v.29/61 (December 1994).

Guobadia, Jessica DeWitt. "Massachusetts Supreme Judicial Court Finds Criminal Enforcement Provisions of Local Curfew Ordinance Unconstitutional." (October 2000). American Bar Association. http://www.abanet.org/crimjust/juvjust/newsletter/newsletteroct09.htm (Accessed September 2010).

Harvard Law Review Association. "Curfews May Be Ineffective and Discriminatory." In *Juvenile Crime: Opposing Viewpoints*, edited by D. Bender and B. Leone. San Diego, CA: Greenhaven Press. 1997.

Hemmens, Craig, and Kathleen Bennett. "Juvenile Curfews and the Courts: Judicial Response to a Not-So-New Crime Control Strategy." *Crime and Delinquency*, v.45/1 (1999).

Hirshel, J. David, Charles Dean, and Doris Dumond. "Juvenile Curfews and Race: A Cautionary Note." *Criminal Justice Policy Review*, v.12/3 (2001).

Jahn, Rich. "Analysis of U.S. Curfew Laws." National Youth Rights Association. http://www.youthrights.org/curfewana.php (Accessed September 2010).

Jones, Marshall Alan, and Robert Sigler. "Law Enforcement Partnership in Community Corrections: An Evaluation of Juvenile Offender Curfew Checks." *Journal of Criminal Justice*, v.30/3, (May–June 2002).

Justice Policy Institute. "Monrovia, California: A Case Study in Curfew Failure." (1999). http://www.cjcj.org/jpi/casestudy.html (Accessed September 2010).

Kizer, Scott. "Juvenile Curfew Laws: Is There a Standard?" *Drake University Law Review*, v.45/749 (1997).

Klein, Stephen P. "Declaration: *Harrahill v. Santoro*." February 9, 1998.

Kline, Patrick. "The Impact of Juvenile Curfew Laws." (2006). http://www
.econ.berkeley.edu/~pkline/papers/Youth%20curfews%20latest.pdf
(Accessed September 2010).

Lait, M. "Report Questions Teen Curfews." *Los Angeles Times* (February
10, 1998).

Levinthal, Dave. "Dallas City Council Enacts Daytime Juvenile Curfew."
http://cityhallblog.dallasnews.com/archives/2009/05/dalls-city-council
-enacts-dayt.html (Accessed September 2010).

Lundman, R. L. *Prevention and Control of Juvenile Delinquency*. New
York: Oxford Press. 1993.

Kim, Michelle Lersch, and Christine Sellers. "A Comparison of Curfew
and Noncurfew Violators Using a Self-Report Delinquency Survey."
American Journal of Criminal Justice, v.24/2 (March 2000).

Kline, Patrick. "The Impact of Juvenile Curfew Laws." (2009). http://
www.econ.berkeley.edu/~pkline/papers/Youth%20curfews%20latest
.pdf (Accessed September 2010).

Lersch, Kim Michelle, and Christine Sellers. "A Comparison of Curfew
and Noncurfew Violators Using a Self-Report Delinquency Survey."
American Journal of Criminal Justice, v.24 (2000).

Matthews, H., M. Limb, and M. Taylor. "Reclaiming the Street: The
Discourse of Curfew." *Environment and Planning,* v.31/10 (1999).

McCord, Joan, Cathy Spatz Widom, and Nancy A. Crowell. *Juvenile
Crime/Juvenile Justice*. Washington, DC: National Research Council
and Institute of Medicine, 2001.

McDowall, D., C. Loftin, and B. Wiersema. "The Impact of Youth Curfew
Laws on Juvenile Crime Rates." *Crime Delinquency,* v.46/1 (January 1,
2000).

Moak, Stacey, and Lisa Hutchinson Wallace. "Legal Changes in Juvenile
Justice." *Youth Violence and Juvenile Justice,* v.1/3 (2003).

National Center for Health Statistics. *U.S. Mortality Detail File 1985–95.*
Rockville, MD: Department of Health and Human Services, 1998.

Office of Juvenile Justice and Delinquency Prevention. "Curfew: An
Answer to Juvenile Delinquency and Victimization?" *Juvenile Justice
Bulletin* (1996).

Office of Juvenile Justice and Delinquency Prevention. "Juvenile Justice
Reform Initiatives in the States."(2009). http://ojjdp.ncjrs.gov/pubs
/reform/ch2_c.html (Accessed September 2010).

Public Agenda. *Kids These Days: What Americans Really Think About the
Next Generation*. New York: Farkas and Johnson, 1997.

Reynolds, K. Michael, Ruth Seydlitz, and Pamela Jenkins. "Do Juvenile Curfew Laws Work? A Time-Series Analysis of the New Orleans Law." *Justice Quarterly*, v.17 (2002).

Sasse, Benjamin. "Note: Curfew Laws, Freedom of Movement, and the Rights of Juveniles." *Case Western Reserve Law Review*, v.50 (Spring 2000).

Schiraldi, Vincent. "Curfew's Time Has Passed: System Is Not a Factor in Controlling Youth Crime, Statistics Show." (2002). http://www.cjcj.org/jpi/legal092899.html (Accessed September 2010).

Shepherd, Robert E., Jr. "The Proliferation of Juvenile Curfews." (2004). American Bar Association. http://www.abanet.org/crimjust/juvjus/cjcurfew.html (Accessed September 2010).

Sutphen, Richard D., and Janet Ford. "The Effectiveness and Enforcement of a Teen Curfew Law." *Journal of Sociology and Social Welfare*, v.28 (2001).

U.S. Conference of Mayors. *A Status Report on Youth Curfews in America's Cities: A 347-City Survey.* Washington, DC: U.S. Conference of Mayors, 1997.

6

Death Penalty for Juvenile Offenders

Megan C. Kurlychek
University at Albany

For as long as there have been records of written law, there have been records of the use of death as the ultimate penalty. Put most simply, the death penalty is the right of the governing authority to take one's life as punishment for the commission of a criminal offense. For example, in 18th century B.C.E., the Code of King Hammurabi of Babylon called for persons to be put to death for 25 specific crimes ranging from murder to theft. Perhaps most notably, the Draconian Code of Athens (7th century B.C.E.) deemed death the only punishment for all crimes. However, as societies have evolved and changed, so has the application of the death penalty, including restrictions upon the types of offenses and offenders that it can be applied to. One particular area of contention has been the application of this most severe punishment to children.

For example, in the 1st century C.E., King Aethelstand of England pronounced that a thief over the age of 12 could be sentenced to death; however, this law was later modified to increase the minimum age for execution to 16. Restricting the application of the death penalty to juveniles falls in line with the greater tradition of providing mitigated punishments to children for the commission of all crimes. For example, English common law deemed

73

all children under the age of seven incapable of mens rea (guilty mind) and therefore innocent of any offenses, and deemed children between 7–14 years of age as having reduced culpability for offenses committed. English common law also extended a form of clemency to youths all the way up to age 21, indicating that while youths between 14 and 21 years of age could be held fully responsible for their actions, the defense could argue for mitigated punishments based on their youthful status. While the exact age of adulthood varies across time and place, as does the level of mitigation offered, the basic trend remains.

Thus, any discussion of the application of the death penalty to juveniles must encompass two distinct realms: first, issues specific to the use of the death penalty in general, including the basic legal principles surrounding the application of the death penalty; and second, a discussion of the unique attributes and circumstance of children in society, including the application of these principles to the special circumstance of the execution of juveniles.

Death Penalty Implementation: Legal Principles

America's modern system of justice has roots that are most often directly traced to the writing of Cesare Beccaria's classic essay, *On Crimes and Punishment*. One of the primary ideologies that emerged from the doctrine was that a punishment should be proportional to the harm caused by a crime. Implicit in this approach is the notion that the most severe penalty, death, should be reserved for only the severest of crimes. Thus, the array of crimes for which the death penalty was deemed appropriate began to narrow. Another important consideration inherent to this school of thought is that the offender's responsibility or blameworthiness for the crime committed should also be considered in calculations of proportionality. In America, reform of the death penalty first began in Pennsylvania by Thomas Jefferson. Gaining the later support of Benjamin Franklin and William Bradford, Jefferson's efforts led Pennsylvania to become the first state to consider the culpability of the offender in the proportionality argument. As a result, in 1794, Pennsylvania repealed the use of the death penalty for all crimes except first-degree murder, which required the offender to have premeditated the crime. This notion of culpability for the offense committed takes on distinct importance when considering the application of the death penalty to juveniles, because juveniles have historically been deemed by societies as having diminished culpability for acts committed, and deserving of reduced or mitigated punishments.

Evolving Standards of Decency

A second, important legal concept applied to the arguments regarding the application of the death penalty to juveniles in America is the notion of "evolving standards of decency" as it applies to the interpretation of the Eighth Amendment. In 1958, the U.S. Supreme Court handed down the *Trop v. Dulles* decision, which, while not directly addressing the death penalty, addressed the meaning of the Eighth Amendment's prohibition of cruel and unusual punishments. In this decision, the Court specifically posits that interpretation of the Eighth Amendment requires consideration of the "evolving standards of decency that marked the progress of a maturing society." This means that interpretation of the Eighth Amendment is not static, but rather what is deemed as cruel and unusual punishment may change over time based on the progress of society. This particular argument has since been applied to several U.S. Supreme Court cases directed at the use of the death penalty.

Two of the most noted Supreme Court decisions regarding the death penalty in general were *Furman v. Georgia* (1972) and *Gregg v. Georgia* (1976). In the landmark *Furman* decision, the Court ruled Georgia's death penalty statute to be unconstitutional. In this decision, the Court did not reject the death penalty as unconstitutional, but rather its application. In order for the death penalty to be constitutional, the Court required that state death penalty statutes ensure the punishment was proportional to the crime, was not applied arbitrarily, did not offend society's sense of justice (which can be directly related to the evolving standards of decency noted in *Trop*), and be more effective than a less severe alternative. In response, states began to revise their death penalty statutes to meet these criteria. In the *Gregg* decision, the Court again allowed for the implementation of the death penalty under these new statutes.

Later, these three specific legal notions—considerations of the culpability of the offender, evaluation of the evolving standards of decency, and assessments of the actual application of the death penalty—were directly applied to arguments surrounding the use of the death penalty on juvenile offenders.

Application of Principles for Juveniles

The United States has a long history of reliance on the death penalty, specifically on the application of the death penalty to children. For example, in 1646, the Massachusetts Bay Colony passed the Stubborn Child Law, which called for the execution of "rebellious" or "stubborn" children who failed to obey their parents. While records indicate that the death penalty was not frequently used against children for such minor offenses as disobeying one's parent, historical records indicate that between 1642 and 1986, there were 281 offenders executed in the United States for offenses committed while under the age of 18. Despite the relative rarity of these events, and the noted historical tradition of extending leniency to children, it was not until the 1980s that the U.S. Supreme Court would specifically address the appropriateness of the death penalty for juvenile offenders.

Thompson v. Oklahoma

In the case of *Thompson v. Oklahoma* (1988), the specific question brought before the Supreme Court was whether or not the death penalty was cruel and unusual punishment when imposed on a minor who was under the age of 16 at the time of the offense. In this case, William Wayne Thompson, then 15, and three older accomplices had brutally murdered a man named Charles Keene. Mr. Keene had been married to Thompson's older sister and had been suspected of physically abusing her. The three older accomplices, all of whom were over 18, all convicted of murder and sentenced to death. The prosecutor requested a waiver hearing, at which time the juvenile court judge remanded the case to adult court. In adult court, Thompson was convicted of first-degree murder and sentenced to death. The defense appealed, and the case eventually made its way to the U.S. Supreme Court.

In drafting the decision of the plurality, Justice Stevens, joined by Justices Brennan, Marshall, and Blackmun, evaluated the meaning of cruel and unusual punishment according to the concept of evolving standards of decency that mark the progress of a maturing society. In doing so, the Court addressed issues of the age of maturity, existing laws, and the opinions of professional organizations. Toward the first end, the Court noted that while states draw the line between childhood and adulthood differently, there was almost unanimity among states in treating youths under the age of 16 as children. In their argument, the Court cited age restrictions on voting, driving, marrying without parental consent, and gambling. Most persuasive, they said, was the fact that no state set the maximum age for juvenile court jurisdiction at less than 16. In a concurrent line of reasoning, the Court inherently linked the progression of these laws with notions of offender culpability, noting that, "The reasons why juveniles are not trusted with the privileges and responsibilities of an adult also explain why their irresponsible conduct is not as morally reprehensible as that of an adult."

In addition, the Court specifically examined state and international law on the application of the death penalty. At the time, 37 states provided for capital punishment. Of those, 19 states had not set a minimum age, which was interpreted by the Court to mean that they simply had not addressed the issue. Of the 18 states that did set a minimum age, all set it at 16 or above. Finally, the Court also addressed several of the points from the *Furman* decision regarding arbitrary application and determination of a legitimate legal purpose. Regarding the former, the Court relied on Department of Justice Statistics to show that of the 1,393 persons sentenced to death between 1982 and 1986, only five were under the age of 16 at the time of the offense. Thus, the application of the death penalty to a minor of this tender age was unusual. Regarding the latter, the Court also shot down arguments regarding the proposed deterrent effect or purpose of imposing the death penalty on a juvenile under the age of 16, noting that youths under this age account for less than two percent of all such crimes; thus, applying this penalty to minors lacked the potential to reduce the prevalence of homicides.

In a vote of 5–3 (with Justice Kennedy abstaining), the Supreme Court deemed that the execution of an offender who was under the age of 16 at the time of the offense was unconstitutional, as it violated the Eighth Amendment's prohibition of cruel and unusual punishment.

Stanford v. Kentucky

Just one year later, the Supreme Court again addressed this topic. This time, the specific question was whether or not the death penalty was cruel and unusual punishment when applied to juveniles who were 16 or 17 years of age at the time of their offense. In *Stanford v. Kentucky* (1989), the Court failed to extend such clemency to juveniles who were 16 or 17 years of age at the time of offense, concluding that the execution of such offenders did not violate the Eighth Amendment's prohibition of cruel and unusual punishment.

Three of the justices who were on the plurality in the previous decision dissented in this case, based primarily on prior arguments of the reduced culpability of juveniles. The dissenting justices in the *Thompson* case (Scalia, Rhenquist, and White) were joined by Justices O'Conner and Kennedy to achieve the majority. In this decision, the Court again began with a discussion of the evolving standards of decency. However, the plurality used a somewhat different "mathematical" technique in counting state law, assuming that those 19 states that did not specifically set a minimum age for execution deemed it acceptable to execute a minor. The Court also used the point that of those states that did address the issue, some set the age at 16, some at 17, and some at 18, implying a "lack of national consensus" regarding the appropriateness of capital punishment for juveniles who were 16 and 17 years of age.

Finding no national consensus on the issue, and the statistics unconvincing, the Court rejected arguments of outside professional agencies and public opinion polls, saying that these were irrelevant to legal arguments and could not be relied upon to determine a national consensus. Thus, the Court did not find that the execution of an offender who was 16 or 17 at the time of the offense offended the evolving standards of decency. Perhaps most importantly for the current debate, however, in the final portions of the decision, the Court rejected the notion that no 16-year-old is adequately responsible for his or her actions or significantly deterred by the potential application of the death penalty. The Court maintained that even purely scientific evidence could not prove this fact. This argument was further elaborated by Justice O'Conner, who maintained that issues of the proportionality of the death penalty must be determined on an individual basis.

Roper v. Simmons

However, because the interpretation of the Eighth Amendment relies on evolving standards of decency, *Stanford* was not the final word on the issue. The Court again addressed this issue in *Roper v. Simmons* in 2005. In this case, 17-year-old Christopher Simmons was convicted of robbery and first degree murder in Missouri and sentenced to death. His lawyers appealed, claiming that the execution of a minor violated the evolving standards of decency. The Missouri Supreme Court agreed, and the state's appeal made it to U.S. Supreme Court in 2005. The question at hand was once again whether the execution of an offender who was 16 or 17 at the time of the offense violated the Eighth Amendment's prohibition against cruel and unusual punishment.

In evaluating this case, the Court returned to the notion of evolving standards of decency and searched for evidence of a national consensus against the death penalty for minors under the age of 18. At this point in time, the Court found that 30 states prohibited the juvenile death penalty, with 12 states specifically rejecting the death penalty altogether and 18 more pro-hibiting its use on juveniles. The Court also noted that since the time of the *Stanford* decision, five states that had previously allowed for the execution of 16- and 17-year-olds had amended state statutes to prohibit its use in these cases. Combined, these facts revealed a trend in the evolving standards of decency away from the execution of minors. The Court also noted that in the 20 states that permitted the imposition of the death penalty for 16- and 17-year-old offenders, only three states had actually imposed the death penalty on such an offender within the past 10 years, thus making its ap-plication rare and arbitrary.

Finally, in this case, more than any of the others, the Court turned to the notion of the culpability of a juvenile for acts committed. Noting that the death penalty in general is reserved for a very narrow category of only the most serious crimes and for those offenders seen as having extreme culpabil-ity, the Court posited that based on evolving scientific evidence, no juvenile could reasonably be assumed to fall into this class of offenders based on their reduced culpability. This notion of reduced culpability due to dimin-ished reasoning capacity was previously applied by the Court in the *Atkins v. Virginia* decision in 2002 to ban the death penalty for persons suffering from mental retardation.

The Court also addressed what it called the "stark reality" that the Unites States was the only country in the world that still supported the death penalty for juveniles in its legal doctrine. Although the United States not bound by the opinions of other nations, the Court laid heavy emphasis on the fact that the United Kingdom, upon which the U.S. laws were origi-nally modeled, abolished the death penalty for juveniles years before. The Court further noted that the execution of juvenile offenders violated sev-eral international treaties, including the United Nations Convention on the Rights of the Child (UNCRC) and the International Covenant on Civil and Political Rights. The Court interpreted such global rejection of the death penalty for juveniles as an even greater indicator of a "universal truth" that there are real and important differences between juveniles under the age of 18 and adult offenders.

Based on the *Simmons* decision, a sentence of death cannot be given to an offender who was under the age of 18 at the time of his or her offense. However, as indicated by the 5–4 vote in this decision, there is no consen-sus on the issue. The debate continues on, as evidenced by the primary arguments of those for, and against, the application of the death penalty to minors.

Pro: Support for Death Penalty for Juveniles

Those in favor of maintaining the death penalty for offenders who were under the age of 18 at the time of their offense maintain three basic premises: first, that the death penalty does serve a notable purpose of justice; second, that there are some 16- and 17-year-olds who are able to cognitively appreciate the full consequences of their actions; and third, given these two previous facts, it would be a miscarriage of justice to exempt those culpable and dangerous offenders from such penalty.

Justice and Maturity of Judgment

First, the death penalty removes an offender from society, which he is no longer able to harm. In addition, under a deterrence-based philosophy of justice, the punishment is intended to fit the crime. Thus, from the "an eye for an eye" viewpoint, proponents argue that the death penalty may be the only fitting punishment for crimes of premeditated murder, regardless of the age of the offender.

The second premise rests on the issue of maturity of judgment. This is important for both the deterrence and culpability arguments. If a juvenile is fully aware of his or her actions and the consequences, then the severity of punishment should serve as a deterrent and, moreover, the offender would be fully culpable for actions committed, and therefore deserving of punishment. While some arguments presented against using the death penalty for juveniles rely on scientific evidence regarding brain development and decision making, those in favor of the use of the death penalty on minors tend to discount the reliability of this evidence and its direct application to the act of murder. For example, much of the research on adolescent decision making focuses on risk-taking or impulsive behavior. Those in favor of the death penalty for juveniles proclaim that while juveniles surely are capable of being impulsive and making poor decisions, that murder, particularly premeditated murder, does not fall into this class of behaviors. That is, while a juvenile might be pressured by friends to drink while underage or engage in other types of risky behavior, such a youth is capable of understanding that murdering another person is inherently wrong.

When *Roper v. Simmons* came before the Supreme Court, Alabama, Delaware, Oklahoma, Texas, Utah, and Virginia all allowed for the execution of 16- and 17-year-old offenders. Together, these states submitted an amicus brief to the court detailing the specific cases of juvenile offenders on death row in Alabama, in an effort to show that some juveniles are indeed capable of premeditated murder and that they are as equally blameworthy as an 18-year-old who would commit such an offense. The primary premise of this argument is slightly different than that noted above, which states that all juveniles 16 years of age and older should be able to determine right from wrong in a life-or-death situation. Conversely, this argument is that while some, if not most, 16- and 17-year-olds may not be fully morally culpable, some clearly are. Therefore, supporters argue against a categorical ban on the implementation of the death penalty for offenders under the age of 18, preferring instead that the cases of 16- and 17-year-olds should be determined upon an individual basis to assess the level of the juvenile's culpability for the crime committed.

This sentiment is also expressed by Justice O'Conner in her dissent from the majority opinion in *Roper v. Simmons*. Moreover, the Supreme Court had previously set the precedent for such individualized assessments of culpability in capital punishment cases in the *Stanford v. Kentucky* (1989) and *Locket v. Ohio* (1978) decisions. In addition, in *Eddings v. Oklahoma* (1982), the Court required that age be allowed as a possible mitigating factor. That is, in cases involving the possible sentence of death, an individualized assessment of culpability must be determined, in which the defense can submit youthfulness as a mitigating factor. This approach resonates that of the English common law approach to offenders 14–21 years of age.

A Miscarriage of Justice

If some juveniles do have the maturity to be fully culpable for their actions, then this logically leads to the third point regarding the miscarriage of justice. For example, one case offered by the state of Alabama in the aforementioned amicus brief involved a 16-year-old who premeditated the murder of his father, his father's girlfriend, and the girlfriend's two young daughters. The juvenile planned and executed the crime with the assistance of three friends, at least one of whom was over the age of 18. The state of Alabama posits that for the 18-year-old participating in this crime to be subject to death, and the 16-year-old "mastermind" behind the crime not to be subject to the same penalty, would be "nonsensical." Put more simply, if this particular 16-year-old was fully capable of mens rea and therefore truly accountable for the crime committed, it would be a miscarriage of justice to sentence to death the older offender who is, at a minimum, not more culpable, and to extend clemency to the primary offender.

In addition to these arguments, Justice Scalia's dissent in *Roper v. Simmons* also outlines the nebulous nature of determining a national consensus and rejects the idea that the Supreme Court should be influenced by international policy. This argument centers not so much on the detriments or merits of executing juveniles, but rather on the Court's ability to determine an evolving standard of decency and to limit individual states' rights based on such a standard. For example, in the *Thompson* decision, those states outlawing the death penalty were "counted" in the states that determined it unfit for those under the age of 16. Yet, in the *Stanford* decision, states that banned the death penalty were not included in determining the consensus toward the execution of minors. Similarly, in some instances, states that allowed for the death penalty but did not set a minimum age were viewed as not having addressed the issue, while in other instances they have been viewed as directly supporting the execution of minors. This argument therefore rests not so much on the appropriateness or inappropriateness of subjecting juveniles to the death penalty, but rather to the federal government's right to restrict state laws on less-than-compelling evidence.

Con: Opposition to Death Penalty for Juveniles

The crux of the argument opposing the application of the death penalty to minors rests upon emerging scientific evidence on human cognitive development. Most often termed *maturity of judgment,* this notion specifically applies to the ability of youths to process information and make informed and rational decisions. There are three primary reasons that such a difference in decision making is important to the debate surrounding the death penalty. First, if a juvenile is not capable of properly assessing the consequences of an action, then the death penalty cannot serve a deterrent effect. Second, if a juvenile is not able to rationally calculate decisions but only to act impulsively, then mens rea cannot be fully determined. Third, because adolescence or youthfulness is a transient state through which the juvenile will ultimately exit, this lack of sufficient judgment is not a lifelong characteristic, but rather a temporary state that does not define who the adult will become.

Lack of a Deterrent Effect

All of these arguments are directly related to evolving medical research regarding adolescent brain development. While it has long been known that juveniles tend to be more impulsive than adults, medical science can now directly link this difference to brain development. Attributed primarily to the work of Dr. Jay Giedd of the National Institute for Mental Health, this research is based on the brain scans of healthy adolescents from the age of 10 to the early 20s. These images indicate that in the teenage brain, the prefrontal cortex is not yet fully developed. This is important because it is this specific portion of the brain that is believed to control reason and fore-thought. With the prefrontal cortex underdeveloped, then, teenage behavior is instead governed by the amygdale, or the emotional center of the brain. According to Dr. Ruben C. Gur, Director of the Brain Behavior Labora-tory at the University of Pennsylvania, this is germane to issues of criminal culpability because the prefrontal cortex is important in the control of ag-gression and other impulses. In other words, if the brain is not yet mature, then it only stands to reason that decision-making capabilities can also not be mature.

Another pertinent difference in thinking patterns that relates to deter-rence is the temporal focus of rational calculus. Research on adolescent de-cision making has shown than in addition to being impulsive and emotional, teens tend to focus much more on immediate temporal consequences instead of long-term outcomes. This is thought to be due both to the brain differ-ences noted above and to lack of life experience. For these reasons, then, the prospect or possibly of being subject to the death penalty is likely to have little impact on an adolescent's decision to partake in a crime.

Juvenile Impulsivity

In addition, the field of developmental psychology has found that a ju-venile's decision-making abilities are also much more susceptible to outside influence and peer pressure than that of an older adult. Developmental stud-ies by Lawrence Steinberg and Elizabeth Cauffman refer to such distinctions as "psychosocial" immaturity. According to this research, the differences between adolescent and adult decision making span three specific realms as follows: responsibility (the ability to make an independent, self-reliant decision); perspective (the ability to place this decision within a broader social and temporal focus); and temperance (the ability to control impulses). Combined, these disparities place adolescents at a clear decision-making disadvantage when compared to adults.

None of these differences diminish a juvenile's ability to carry out mali-cious and vicious crimes. Rather, they affect the juvenile's ability to understand his or her actions, to fully contemplate the consequences of such actions, or perhaps to even stop such actions from occurring even if he or she has obtained the moral state to determine right from wrong. For example, research has found that even juveniles who cognitively can report right from wrong in interview situations, may fail to act in manners consistent with these judgments in actual social situations, particularly in situations involving negative social influence.

The importance of these developmental differences does not relate to a juvenile's ability to act, but rather to understand and control such actions and to meet adult criteria of "blameworthiness" for actions committed. According to work by Elizabeth Scott and Thomas Grisso, in pure legal principles, accountability for an act means that a person must have committed the act voluntarily (not under the influence or pressure of others) and must be able to form reasonable expectations as to the potential consequences of the act. Based on the developmental literature, they conclude that juveniles are necessarily less culpable for acts than adult offenders.

Temporary Lack of Judgment

Finally, there is the consideration that this inability to reason is temporary; that is, adolescence is a transitory state through which everyone passes. For example, Terry Moffitt notes that many individuals who get into trouble as youths "age out" of crime as they mature. National statistics presented by the National Center for Juvenile Justice also confirm that less than 25 percent of all youths who come into contact with the juvenile justice system go on to commit crimes as adults. Thus, behavior as an adolescent is not necessarily predictive of internal character or who the individual will become as an adult. This particular point was of relevance to the Court in the *Simmons* decision, as they noted that the death penalty in society has been restricted and limited to only the worst class of offenders. Because a juvenile has not finished maturing and growing, the argument is that he or she simply cannot be deemed among this narrow class of offenders.

The arguments against the application of the death penalty to juveniles reach far beyond national borders as well, with those opposing its use spanning the globe. Amnesty International reports that since 1990, only six nations have executed a juvenile, including China, Iran, Pakistan, Nigeria, Saudi Arabia, and Yemen, and that no other industrialized society similar to the United States supports such executions in legal doctrine. Moreover, the execution of minors violates several international treaties, including UN-CRC and the International Covenant on Civil and Political Rights.

Conclusion

While there is historical precedence for the use of the death penalty against juveniles, there is also historical precedence for offering leniency to youthful offenders and reluctance to utilize this most severe of penalties against children. Modern arguments surrounding the issue center primarily on the evolving standards of decency in maturing societies, specifically as such standards relate to the culpability of a juvenile for his or her actions. Emerging social, scientific, and medical research indicate clear differences in the mental capacities of juveniles to make mature decisions, particularly when influenced by negative societal and environmental factors. Some proponents of the death penalty for minors contend that these differences in judgment should not extend to something as notably wrong as the commission of murder. Other proponents, however, accept that many if not most youths are incapable of such decision making, but maintain that some definitely are, and that decisions of the appropriateness of the death penalty for juveniles should be made on an individualized basis. However, in the *Simmons* decision, the U.S. Supreme Court specifically rejected this argument, noting that the differences between children and adults are too well known and documented to risk even one youth being put to death.

See Also: 1. Age of Responsibility; 10. Juvenile Offenders in Adult Courts; 18. Sentencing Options; 19. Serious and Violent Juvenile Offenders.

Further Readings

American Bar Association. "Cruel and Unusual Punishment: The Juvenile Death Penalty: Adolescence, Brain Development and Legal Culpability." (2004). http://www.abanet.org/crimjust/juvjust/Adolescence.pdf (Accessed September 2010).

Amnesty International. *On the Wrong Side of History: Children and the Death Penalty in the USA*. New York: Amnesty International USA Publications, 1998.

Amnesty International. *USA: The Death Penalty and Juvenile Offenders.* New York: Amnesty International USA Publications, 1991.

Atkins v. Virginia, 536 U.S. 304 (2002).

Bassham, G. "Rethinking the Emerging Jurisprudence of Juvenile Death." *Notre Dame Journal of Law, Ethics,and Public Policy,* v.5/2 (1991).

Brown, B. B., D. R. Clasen, and S. A. Eicher. "Perceptions of Peer Pressure, Peer Conformity Dispositions and Self-Reported Behavior Among Adolescents." *Developmental Psychology,* v.22 (1986).

Cauffman, E., and L. Steinberg. "(Im)Maturity of Judgment in Adolescence: Why Adolescents May Be Less Culpable Than Adults." *Behavioral Sciences and the Law,* v.18/6 (2000).

Dick, S. *Young Blood: Juvenile Justice and the Death Penalty.* Amherst, NY: Prometheus Books, 1995.

Eddings V. Oklahoma, 455. U.S. 104 (1982).

Furman v. State of Georgia, 408 U.S. 238 (1972).

Gardner, M., and L. Steinberg. "Peer Influence on Risk-Taking, Risk Preference, and Risky Decision-Making in Adolescence and Adulthood: An Experimental Study." *Developmental Psychology,* v.41 (2005).

Giedd, J., J. Blumenthal, N. Jeffries, F. Castellanos, H. Liu, A. Zijdenbos, T. Paus, A. Evans, and J. Rapoport. "Brain Development During Childhood and Adolescence: A Longitudinal MRI Study." *Nature Neuroscience,* v.2/10 (1999).

Gogtay, N., J. N. Giedd, L. Lusk, K. M. Hayashi, D. Greenstein, A. C. Vaituzis, T. F. Nugent, D. H. Herman, L. S. Clasen, A. W. Toga, J. L. Rapoport, and P. M. Thompson. "Dynamic Mapping of Human Cortical Development During Childhood Through Early Adulthood." *Proceedings of the National Academy of Sciences,* v.101/21 (May 25 2004).

Gregg v. State of Georgia, Proffitt v. Florida, Jurek v. Texas, Woodson v. North Carolina, and *Roberts v. Louisiana,* 428 U.S. 153 (1976).

Hale, R. L. *A Review of Juvenile Executions in America.* Lewiston, NY: Edwin Mellen Press, 1997.

Jackson, S. "Too Young to Die: Juveniles and the Death Penalty: A Better Alternative to Killing Our Children: Youth Empowerment." *New England Journal on Criminal and Civil Confinement,* v.22/2 (1996).

Lerner, R., and L. Steinberg, eds. *Handbook of Adolescent Psychology.* New York: Wiley, 2004.

Locket v. Ohio, 438 U.S. 586 (1978).

Meltsner, M. *Cruel and Unusual: The Supreme Court and Capital Punishment.* New York: Random House, 1973.

Moffitt, T. "Adolescence-Limited and Life-Course-Persistent Antisocial Behavior. A Developmental Taxonomy." *Psychological Review,* v.100 (1993).

Office of Juvenile Justice and Delinquency Prevention. *Serious and Violent Juvenile Offenders.* Bulletin. Washington, DC: U.S. Department of Justice, 1998.

Robinson, D. A., and O. H. Stephens. "Patterns of Mitigating Factors in Juvenile Death Penalty Cases." *Criminal Law Bulletin,* v.28/3 (1992).

Roper v. Simmons, 543 U.S. 551 (2005).

Sowell E. R., B. S. Peterson, P. M. Thompson, S. E. Welcome, A. L. Henkenius, and A. W. Toga. "Mapping Cortical Change Across the Human Life Span." *Nature Neuroscience,* v.6/3 (March 2003).

Sowell, E. R., P. M. Thompson, C. M. Leonard, S. E. Welcome, E. Kan, and A. W. Toga. "Longitudinal Mapping of Cortical Thickness and Brain Growth in Normal Children." *The Journal of Neuroscience,* v.24/38 (September 22, 2004).

Stanford v. Kentucky, 492 U.S. 361 (1989).

Steinberg, L. *Adolescence.* New York: McGraw-Hill, 2005.

Steinberg, L., and E. Cauffman. "Maturity of Judgment in Adolescence: Psychosocial Factors in Adolescent Decision-Making." *Law and Human Behavior,* v.20 (1996).

Streib, V. L. *Death Penalty for Juveniles.* Bloomington: Indiana University Press, 1987.

Streib, V. L. *The Juvenile Death Penalty Today: Death Sentences and Executions for Juvenile Crimes, January 1, 1973–June 30, 2000.* Ada, OH: Ohio Northern University Claude W. Pettit College of Law, 2000.

Thompson v. Oklahoma, 487 U.S. 815 (1988).

Trop v. Dulles, 356 U.S. 86 (1958).

Yurgelun-Todd, Deborah. "Inside the Teen Brain." (2002). PBS.org. http://www.pbs.org/wgbh/pages/frontline/shows/teenbrain/interviews/todd.html (Accessed September 2010).

7

Group Homes

Patricia E. Campie
National Center for Juvenile Justice

Shawn Marsh
National Council of Juvenile and Family Court Judges

G roup homes were created as an alternative to incarceration in the late 1960s as a response to research suggesting that the least restrictive and most therapeutic responses to delinquent behavior would be more successful when trying to impact the future behavior of young offenders, especially those with low-level offenses or short offending histories. Over time, these group home settings have been used to house more seriously delinquent youths with longer histories of deviance, as well as youths who come from abuse and neglect situations. Rather than mitigate the negative effects of incarceration on future reoffense, current research suggests that the intended pro-social supports in group home settings might be diluted by the higher concentration of negative peer influences in the group home setting and the relative lack of positive supports that might otherwise be available to the youths in their own community or family setting. The history of group homes in the United States has its beginnings in the 1960s; since that time, much research has been conducted on their effectiveness in reducing reoffense, and several positives and negatives of using these placements as a response to the problem of juvenile delinquency have arisen.

History of Group Homes for Delinquent Youths

Under the leadership of President Lyndon B. Johnson, the United States took its first serious look at the effectiveness of youth incarceration in 1967 through the work of the Commission on Law Enforcement and Criminal Administration. The commission found that incarceration did not result in positive outcomes for youths in terms of either lower recidivism or improvements in pro-social functioning or competency development. In fact, these institutionalized settings were also sometimes found inhumane, using more restrictive means than necessary, and applying these secure conditions to nonserious offenders, often at great expense. As a result, the commission recommended that community-based alternatives to incarceration be developed. Group homes became one of the options the juvenile justice system then turned to as a means to keep youths from secure confinement.

The earliest group homes designed specifically for juvenile justice populations were created around the theory that delinquent youths would benefit from being in a home-like environment where they could experience positive adult interactions and role models while learning pro-social skills with their peers in a group reinforcement setting. These Teaching-Family programs were evaluated using a rigorous study methodology in the mid-1980s, producing mixed results. Like many residential programs, recidivism rates were quite low while the youths were actively engaged in the group home setting. However, when compared to other nonresidential programming, reoffense rates were greater among group home participants during their stay than were reoffense rates among youths in nonresidential programs. One common limitation of these studies and similar early studies with programs of this type was the inability to randomly select youths to receive the group home intervention. So, it was not clear at the time whether these results were influenced by sample bias, where youths more at-risk for reoffense were sent to the group home setting, thus resulting in a higher likelihood that youths in those homes would reoffend, as compared to other youths who were placed in nonresidential settings.

Around this same time, the Adoption Assistance and Child Welfare Act was passed (1980). As part of that mandate, a new emphasis was placed on using the least restrictive means to provide youths with the child welfare services they needed. However, as the need for these services increased over time, more secure settings were used to provide these children with placement options that could provide these supports. Because of this, group home settings have become places where delinquent and dependent youths might be co-located, begging the question of how these settings are impacting new delinquent behavior among dependent youths, or reoffense behavior among delinquent youths.

Who Goes to Group Homes?

Most studies have continued to show that group home placements do not follow linear decision-making tracks, where one can predict which youths go to a group home versus an alternative placement, so it becomes difficult to tell how group homes are impacting particular types of youths. Looking retrospectively at populations most likely to be in a group home, data show that group homes are most often used to house older youths, more males than females, youths of color, and youths with more serious behavioral health problems and previous justice system involvement. Studies have also shown that many of the youths placed in group homes have a history of placement instability, where previous attempts to reunify the family or place the youths with kin care has not been successful. This placement shuffling has been associated with a wide range of negative outcomes for youths, from higher than average incidents of conduct disorder to greater prevalence of externalizing behaviors as compared to youths who do not have this placement instability history. Because of this, it can be difficult to discern whether the negative behaviors identified among youths in group home settings, as compared to youths in non-group home settings, is due to these placement instability impacts, or the placement in the group home setting itself. Added to this are the higher-than-average rates of recidivism that seem to attend youths who have spent time in group homes, as compared with their peers in alternative care settings.

The Contagion Effect

Research in the late 1990s explored the notion of whether the group home setting was itself a factor leading to greater delinquency and negative behaviors among youths. These studies suggested the presence of a contagion effect, which in essence allowed delinquent youths to "spread" their deviant ways to other youths in the group home setting simply by interacting with these youths, sharing stories, and teaching each other strategies for coping that often included delinquent behaviors. Further research in this vein argued that the isolation of the group home setting further reinforce deviant behavior because the setting often severed ties with the types of traditional community role models that youths would otherwise go to for guidance and support, as well as those peers or family members who provided pro-social bonding and positive impacts on these youths in their natural setting.

This can result in a dilution of positive supports and concentration of deviant supports within the group home setting. Also, because there is no individual risk/need method for deciding which youths go to which group home setting, youths are often mixed in terms of their offense history and severity, leading those with modest offending histories into a more vulnerable position when mixed with persistent or serious offenders in these settings. As such, the potentially positive effects of being in a structured, pro-social home setting, as originally envisioned by group home advocates in the 1960s, are often mitigated by the lack of proper assessments done to place these youths in the group home, or other settings most likely to address their criminogenic needs and give them the positive supports they need to keep them from reoffending.

Recent Trends

Over the past 10 years, most research has suggested that victims of child abuse and neglect are much more likely to engage in delinquent behavior as compared with youths who have no prior history of child abuse and neglect. Most of this research has focused almost entirely on a youth's risk for future delinquency. In a majority of these studies, dependent youths have had their delinquency futures compared with youths in the general population, rather than justice-involved youths. In addition, concerns over mixing dependent and delinquent youths in group home settings led to speculation that group homes might act as "deviancy schools," acting to turn dependent youths into delinquent youths as a result of the mixed-company group home setting.

Positive Peer Culture Program

A 2006 study conducted by J. P. Ryan and M. F. Testa explored the relationship between youths having a history of abuse and neglect and their future likelihood of offending as compared to delinquent youths with no prior history of abuse or neglect. The study was set in a group home environment where the Positive Peer Culture (PPC) program was implemented. The PPC program was designed to address the concern that mixing delinquent and dependent youths would create a deviant school setting. Harry Vorrath and

Larry K. Brendtro's book, *Positive Peer Culture* (1974), described the PPC framework, which called for a strength-based intervention that could be used within a full range of correctional, educational, treatment, and community settings for youths. The 2006 Ryan study included 286 youths who had been adjudicated delinquent. Just over 40 percent of youths in the sample had been arrested, but subsequent arrests were much more likely among those youths who had a prior history of physical abuse and neglect (50 vs. 37 percent). The study's conclusions pointed to more questions about the relationship between physical abuse and neglect and later delinquency, rather than simply assuming that these effects were produced from being in a group home environment with delinquent peers. The study was also able to show that the PPC program had little effect on reducing the recidivism of already delinquent youths, calling into question whether that program should be used in any group home setting, be it with dependent youths, delinquent youths, or a mix of both populations.

Since then, the research on the relationship between the use of group homes and the risk of future delinquency has continued to focus on dependent child populations that are mixed in the group home setting with delinquent youths. This research has found that children who have been physically abused or victimized are most vulnerable to developing delinquent behaviors after placement in group homes, rather than foster care homes. And, while about 40 percent of all arrests in the child welfare system are associated with a group home placement, only 26 percent of adolescents ever experience a group home placement.

Further, youths who enter the juvenile justice system from group home placements are more likely to be associated with a threat-related offense. This has led to speculation that these youths are either using verbal means more often to express their feelings when in group settings, or there may be a lower level of tolerance for these verbal exchanges in the group home setting. The research suggests that police are more likely to be called as a result of disruptions isolated to one youth, as these individual incidents might be seen as part of an escalation pattern that must be interrupted before the group becomes too unruly to control.

The research conducted on the pathways to delinquency for a dependent child placed in a group home setting has tried to control for factors that could explain a greater prevalence toward delinquency outside of group home setting effects (such as placement instability, age, gender, etc.). Despite this, there is a considerable gap in reliable data available at the case level in many jurisdictions, which makes it problematic to reliably identify the causal factors for predicting future offending among dependent children related to group home placement.

Pro: Benefits of Group Homes for Delinquent Youths

Home-Like Environment Helps Youths Transition

Structured, home-like settings supervised by positive adult role models who are trained to provide therapeutic or pro-social skill development activities can help youths transition back to their communities.

Research in the field of social cognition suggests that youths spending time with adult role models, observing and practicing new skills, is closely linked with the development of self-efficacy, which describes one's belief that they are capable of achieving a particular goal or series of goals based upon particular capabilities they judge themselves to possess. Although domain-specific, high self-efficacy is one of the strongest predictors of future behavior. In group homes, properly trained adults can successfully model pro-social attitudes and behaviors, problem-solving techniques, and peaceful conflict resolution skills for youths under their care. Further, adults who are able to successfully guide youths in practicing new positive behaviors and skills, and who reinforce these positive developments, can also help youths develop self-efficacy around important abilities linked with future success into adulthood. The types of abilities and skills that can be developed through this process could include teaching youths how to avoid negative peer influences and how to remain engaged in school. Evidence on the efficacy of peer group treatment is mixed. Success with this approach tends to vary as a function of the program model, appropriate staff training, and implementation fidelity, along with a youth's age, gender, and ethnicity. Still, this approach might provide the right opportunity for group home youths to make needed connections with positive adult role models and as a result impart to them a strong sense of program belonging. At least for some of these youths, group home conditions that can foster these connections can help youths experience improved outcomes as they transition to less restrictive settings.

Detention and correctional facilities are highly artificial settings with few characteristics that would suggest that they are good for encouraging or producing optimal human development. Although locked facilities are a necessary option when a youth presents substantial risk to self or others, these facilities typically offer only limited opportunities to learn and practice pro-social skills in a setting that mirrors life at home, school, or work in the community. A recent study released by the Bureau of Justice Assistance also suggests that abuse of youths in locked facilities, including sexual abuse, remains unacceptably high in many areas of the country. In contrast, group homes are often able to provide an environmental reality that is analogous to living in a traditional family home. For example, youths in a home-like setting have the opportunity to cook and share meals around a table, get fresh air and enjoy outdoor recreation, contribute to routine chores, and exercise increased levels of personal control. Efforts to "make life normal" are important for system-involved youths so that they engage in developmentally appropriate experiences as they would during the course of normal development as adolescents and young adults. This normalizing process can also increase the likelihood of youths completing a successful translation of skills between living situations as they move from the group home setting back into the community and on to adulthood.

Juvenile justice professionals have long recognized the importance of using graduated sanctions and incentives when working with system-involved youths. A robust continuum of sanctions for negative behavior and incentives (or rewards) for positive behavior that is meaningful, logical, and incremental is essential for encouraging behavior modification. Group homes provide one option on this continuum and allow more discrete "step up" or "step down" responses to behavior with youths in the system. For example, group homes historically have served an important transition and aftercare function for some youthful offenders leaving secure placement. Moving from a highly restrictive and structured setting such as a correctional setting back to the community can present substantial stressors and challenges for youths. Group homes, if operated by well-trained staff that provide intense supervision, and that involve natural family to the extent desirable and feasible, can serve in an important role for helping youths adjust to freedom and the risks (and rewards) it presents.

Less Restrictive Than Other Secure Placement Options

Group homes fall into the broad category of residential care, including halfway homes, campus-based homes, emergency shelters, and staff-secured settings. On the restrictive continuum, group homes fall between placement in the natural home on one end, and locked settings—such as detention, correctional facilities, or secure hospitals—on the other end. The seemingly universal belief that "children should be served in the least restrictive environment in which they can be safely treated," as articulated by Richard

Barth and colleagues in their 2007 study, suggests that group homes provide an important alternative when the youth cannot remain in his or her natural home, but when physically secure settings are unnecessarily restrictive. Group homes can be an important resource for communities that are looking for more cost-effective and community-based alternatives to traditional detention alternatives for delinquent youths. This is particularly true in light of the anticipated reauthorization of the Juvenile Justice and Delinquency Prevention Act (JJDPA) that would eliminate the valid court order exception, whereby a judicial officer can incarcerate a status offender for not following a court order for treatment, remaining in placement, or some other technical violation of a prior judicial order. This change in the JJDPA, coupled with intensive efforts across the nation to develop evidence-based alternatives to detention, could mean that group homes might offer a less restrictive placement option for juvenile justice systems moving away from incarcerating status offenders and other low-risk youths.

Less Expensive Than Other Secure Placement Options

Secure residential, detention, and correctional placements are expensive. Most physically secure placements operate 24 hours a day, seven days a week, 365 days each year—and thus must be staffed continuously. Further, extensive safety and security requirements in these settings often mandate a wide variety of expensive, and sometimes rapidly changing, security equipment requirements along with new staff training, protocols, and other measures that further increase the cost of operations, such as surveillance equipment and medical facilities onsite. Although the costs associated with secure placement vary substantially by jurisdiction, current estimates indicate that it costs an average of $43,000 per year in the United States to detain one youth offender. In contrast, the less-restrictive placement option of a structured and staff secure group home setting incurs substantially less in operating expenses, due to notable differences in costs associated with staffing levels and operating requirements.

Con: Drawbacks of Group Homes for Delinquent Youths

Mismatched System

Haphazard methods are used for determining which youths will be sent to which group home settings, often resulting in a mismatch between youth needs and risk and the services, staff training, and peer dynamics available within the group home.

In general, the field of psychological science has demonstrated how critical it is for interventions to be purposefully matched with the presenting problems, risks, assets, and trait characteristics of the clients served with these interventions. In the juvenile justice system, structured decision-making processes and needs assessments are used more frequently at probation and detention intake to identify the appropriate levels of services or placement based on the static and dynamic risks and needs of each youth, or client, who is served. By using a validated, culturally competent mental health and psychosocial assessment, justice practitioners can more accurately identify a youth's risk for future harm and delinquency, and then tailor the youth's rehabilitation plan to address the specific needs the child has for achieving full competency development. This assessment process should also be used to identify current strengths, or assets, that the youth might possess, or more broadly, are possessed by the family or community of the youth. With the more accurate identification of these assets, needs, and risks, service providers can develop or obtain evidence-based programs that are specifically designed to address these needs and risks.

Unfortunately, systemic pressures associated with a lack of resources, pressing scheduling demands, worry about detention counts, and long placement waitlists often put decision makers in the position to place youths simply where there is an open bed, rather than where the most good can be done. This results in youths being placed in group homes not suited to provide the ideal level, or type, of care required to produce the most optimal outcomes. These placement practices can also result in problematic mixtures of peer groups, such as delinquent youths living with dependent youths, or youths with victimization histories living with youths who have sexual offending histories.

Influence of Housemate Peers Versus Positive Support

The concentration of delinquent youths living together or delinquent youths living with youths who have been physically abused or neglected results in higher rates of initial or subsequent offending among both groups of youths (dependent and delinquent).

Deviancy training has emerged as a primary argument against housing low-risk youths with conduct-disordered youths, given evidence of iatrogenic effects. Iatrogenic effects are unintended negative consequences that are sometimes produced from participating in an intervention or prevention program. Deviancy training does not have overwhelming explanatory power in the current research to measure that theory's impact on predicting future offending behavior among nondelinquent youths mixed with deviant youths. There is also some evidence that an improved setting and comprehensive staff training, coupled with high-quality supervision practices, can offset the negative outcomes often associated with mixing low- and high-risk offenders. Nonetheless, social cognitive theory would again suggest that concentrating delinquent youths or delinquent and victimized youths together—without substantial safeguards and strong adult role models—is a potentially unproductive practice that can result in unintended consequences, such as increased delinquency among mixed-group, group home residents.

The relative isolation of group home settings separate youths from positive behavioral supports that they might otherwise have available to them in their natural family or community settings. Positive social supports are an essential component of encouraging resiliency and healthy human functioning across the lifespan. Resiliency is the ability to bounce back from adversity and adapt to new surroundings with relative ease, or at least with success. Placing youths outside of the natural home and in a group home setting can reduce social contact with parents, guardians, siblings, teachers, coaches, and other important familial contacts and persons of character. And even though there are verifiable differences between males and females in terms of the social supports they might prefer (i.e., practical versus emotional), increased distance from and hampered accessibility to existing supportive networks that youths are comfortable with can quickly erode this critical protective factor. The new social systems developed within the group home, while potentially beneficial in the short run, are not likely to replace the strong attachments youths have developed over many years, including family members.

Other More Cost-Effective Alternatives

The research evidence continues to suggest that intensive in-home treatment services can produce similar or better results than group homes, and at a fraction of the cost. Although not inexpensive, evidence-based treatments such as Functional Family Therapy (FFT) or well-coordinated wraparound services can provide an alternative to group home placement when the youth can remain in his or her home with adequate support and resources. This type of in-home solution also provides other benefits in terms of cost, including reducing the need to potentially separate siblings who have been adjudicated delinquent (an all-too-common event for many families), and bear the cost of two distinct group home settings within which youths are subsequently placed. In addition, by receiving services in the home, the entire family—and perhaps extended family and friends—can benefit from the therapeutic environment, where the approach is multisystemic, rather than focused on an individual youth's problem behavior. This multisystemic approach sees the family as a system that requires fine-tuning and support rather than focusing blame on any one person or any one isolated event, which is often the symptom of a problem rather than the root cause leading to many subsequent problems, and can come with additional costs down the road. Unfortunately, federal funding currently provides little impetus to place dependent youths back in the home environment, using scarce federal dollars instead to pay for foster care rather than in-home or wraparound services for children and families in need. A more flexible approach is needed for how these federal funds can be spent by local jurisdictions to encourage family unification, when appropriate, and the in-home, evidence-based services that are more cost effective than out-of-home placement alternatives.

Resistance From Local Community

Communities that can provide a strong, pro-social, resource-rich environment for misguided youths are unfortunately often the same places that resist the placement of youth group homes in their neighborhoods. Sometimes called the "not in my back yard" phenomenon, residents and business owners from these more affluent and livable communities report fears and concerns over their personal and property safety when faced with the prospect of having a youth group home in their midst. Citizens in these communities may call town hall meetings, engage local media, or stage a protest at local government offices to argue that a youth home will result in a range of negative outcomes such as reduced property values when congregate care is slated for their neighborhoods. Although there is little research on the subject, communities with a strong sense of cohesion and abundant resources seem to be most resistant to a group home in their area. Arguably, these locations might be the most desirable places to encourage pro-social development and opportunities for youths to connect with resources important to a successful future, such as good schools, viable employment, healthy recreation opportunities, and a peer network that will support other positive youth behaviors. Because of this tension, developing a plan for locating a group home setting can become driven mainly by the lowest common denominator of properties that are available where community receptiveness is at a premium, or at least where community resistance is minimal. Unfortunately, these locations may not be the places most optimal for encouraging the pro-social opportunities and environment that lead to healthy human development and access to important social capital (i.e., access to jobs, education, and healthcare).

Conclusion

Group homes have served as an alternative to incarceration in the juvenile justice system for well over 40 years. Originally envisioned to encourage pro-social development of low-risk youths or to support transition to the community from more restrictive settings, the emergence of group homes also reflected the advancements in social science that attempted to determine the most effective and healthy interventions for young people with problem behaviors. Few would argue that efforts to divert low-risk youthful offenders or adolescent-limited offenders from incarceration are aligned with the current fund of existing knowledge pertaining to adolescent development and trajectories of delinquency. Emerging evidence suggests that peer group interventions for problem behaviors—such as placement in a therapeutic group home—can result in unintended negative outcomes (e.g., the development or worsening of conduct disorder).

Although the literature on deviancy training is compelling, other lines of study caution that further research is necessary to fully understand the constellation of factors associated with outcomes of group interventions—such as setting effects, dosage, and post-intervention peer group contacts. Given the changing landscape of juvenile justice, including the likely elimination of the valid court order exception and increased emphasis on diversion, retaining a continuum of placement alternatives will be an important task for many jurisdictions.

Proponents of group homes urge further research to be focused on providing a better understanding of the complexities of peer group interventions and group home outcomes before removing this alternative completely from the toolbox of a modern juvenile justice system. However, any known shortcomings that can impact the quality of group home settings, such as having properly trained staff, providing an active programmatic schedule for youths, and ensuring access to family and pro-social community supports, should also be addressed. To the extent that group homes can provide this optimum environment for delinquent youths, they will be able to offer a more effective, short-term response to ensuring public safety and justice for victims, along with the long-term goals of providing youths with the competency development and rehabilitation opportunities they need to succeed in the future.

See Also: 2. Alternative Schools; 3. At-Risk Youth; 4. Boot Camps; 8. Juvenile Detention Facilities; 11. Juveniles in Adult Correctional Facilities; 13. Out-of-Home Placement; 20. Treatment and Rehabilitation.

Further Readings

Barth, R., J. Greeson, S. Guo, R. Green, S. Hurley, and J. Sisson. "Outcomes for Youth Receiving Intensive In-Home Therapy or Residential Care: A Comparison Using Propensity Scores." *American Journal of Orthopsychiatry,* v.77/4 (2007).

Braukmann, C. J., K. A. Kirigin, and M. M. Wolf. "Group Home Treatment Research: Social Learning and Social Control Perspectives." In *Understanding Crime: Current Theory and Research,* edited by T. Hirschi and M. Gottfredson. Beverly Hills, CA: Sage, 1980.

Child Welfare League of America. "Residential Group Care." http://www.cwla.org/programs/groupcare/groupcareaboutpage.htm (Accessed October 2010).

Dodge, K. A., and T. J. Dishion. "Deviant Peer Contagion in Interventions and Programs: An Ecological Framework for Understanding Influence Mechanisms." In *Deviant Peer Influences in Programs for Youth,* edited by K. Dodge, T. Dishion, and J. Landsford. New York: Guilford Press, 2006.

Jones, R. R., M. R. Weinrott, and J. R. Howard. *The National Evaluation of the Teaching Family Model.* Final report to NIMH Center for Studies in Crime and Delinquency, June 30, 1981.

Jonson-Reid, M. "Exploring the Relationship Between Child Welfare Intervention and Juvenile Corrections Involvement." *American Journal of Orthopsychiatry,* v.72 (2002).

Kirgin, K. A., C. J. Braukmann, J. D. Atwater, and M. M. Wolf. "An Evaluation of Teaching Family (Achievement Place) Group Homes for Juvenile Offenders." *Journal of Applied Behavior Analysis,* v.15/1 (1982).

Lilienfeld, S. O. "Psychological Treatments That Harm." *Perspectives on Psychological Science,* v.2/1 (2007).

O'Connell, J. P., Jr. *A Group Home Study: Washington State.* Olympia, WA: Law and Justice Planning Office, 1977.

Osgood, D. W., and L. Briddle. "Peer Effects in Juvenile Justice." In *Deviant Peer Influences in Programs for Youth: Problems and Solutions,* edited by K. Dodge, T. Dishion, and K. Landsford. New York: Guilford Press, 2006.

Piat, M. "Group Homes and the 'Not In My Back Yard' Phenomenon (NIMBY)—It Happened Close to Home: A Pilot Study." *Sante Mentale au Quebec,* v.29/1 (2004).

Rhule, D. M. "Take Care to Do No Harm: Harmful Interventions for Youth Problem Behavior." *Professional Psychology: Research and Practice,* v.36/6 (2005).

Ryan, J. P., J. M. Marshall, D. Herz, and P. M. Hernandez. "Juvenile Delinquency in Child Welfare: Investigating Group Home Effects." *Children and Youth Services Review,* v.30/9 (2008).

Ryan, J. P., and M. F. Testa. "Child Maltreatment and Juvenile Delinquency: Investigating the Role of Placement and Placement Instability." *Children and Youth Services Review,* v.27 (2005).

Vorrath, Harry H., and Larry K. Brendtro. *Positive Peer Culture.* Chicago: Aldine, 1974.

Weiss, B., A. Caron, S. Ball, J. Tapp, M. Johnson, and J. R. Weisz. "Iatrogenic Effects of Group Treatment for Antisocial Youth." *Journal of Consulting and Clinical Psychology,* v.73/6 (2005).

Widom, C. "The Role of Placement Experiences in Mediating the Criminal Consequences of Early Childhood Victimization." *American Journal of Orthopsychiatry,* v.61 (1991).

Zinn, A., J. DeCoursey, R. Goerge, and M. Courtney. *A Study of Placement Stability in Illinois.* Chicago: Chapin Hall Center for Children, 2006.

8

Juvenile Detention Facilities

Courtney A. Waid
North Dakota State University

W hen youths are arrested, the police officer making the arrest must decide whether to process the child formally or informally. Some children may be released to their parents/guardians if it can be determined that the child's return to court will be ensured; however, other children may be placed in secure detention facilities, which are similar to adult jails in physical structure and regime; or alternative detention settings, such as home detention or weekend reporting, when such alternatives are available and deemed appropriate. Each jurisdiction uses legal criteria to determine which youths should be detained in secure settings. These typically include (1) if the child is a threat to public safety, (2) if the child has inadequate supervision from a parent or guardian at home, and (3) if the child is considered a flight risk from the jurisdiction. If any of these conditions are assessed to be present, the child may be placed in secure detention.

However, secure detention is currently experiencing several problems, including overcrowding, physical plant deterioration, and a lack of programming (i.e., substance abuse reduction or educational) that detained youths may need. Furthermore, the majority of youths in secure detention are of minority status and in need of physical and mental health services. Given the concern over issues related to secure detention, many commentators have called for the increased implementation and use of alternatives to detention. The Juvenile Detention Alternatives Initiative (JDAI), sponsored by the Annie E. Casey Foundation, looked to reform detention for youths in three major metropolitan areas: Portland, Sacramento, and New York City. These first JDAI sites were considered a success, and the Casey Foundation developed basic recommendations for sites to follow when developing and implementing alternatives. Central to the development of adequate alternatives is the collaboration and buy-in of community members and juvenile justice stakeholders with able leadership, as well as detailed assessment throughout the program's development and implementation. While the detention of youths is a way to protect accused youths of harming themselves further and doing harm in the community, steps must be taken to ensure that youths have access to the best possible alternatives when and where appropriate.

Overview of Juvenile Detention: A Place and a Process

Often, the decision whether to process an accused youth either formally or informally is made with some input from juvenile court personnel, and various legal and extralegal factors will impact this decision as well. Although a large majority of juvenile cases are treated informally, the small percentage of cases treated in a formal manner will result in a petition to juvenile court, and hence an adjudication hearing in juvenile court. Because of the often lengthy delay between arrest to the date of adjudication hearings, a critical decision must be made, as juvenile justice system officials involved in the handling of formal cases must decide to either release the youth under arrest to the custody of a parent or capable guardian, or detain the youth, resulting in the placement of the child in the custody of the state.

Furthermore, juveniles who have been adjudicated and are awaiting placement/transfer to a residential commitment program may be held by the state as well. This process of placing the juvenile in custody after arrest and/or prior to transfer to a commitment facility is known as *detention*. Detention can take many forms, such as placement in a secure setting. Typically, a youth detention facility physically resembles a jail and/or prison for adults. At a glance from the outside, it is difficult to ascertain the differences between a detention center for youths and an adult jail. Constructed with cement and cinderblocks, cell doors are often made of steel bars, each equipped with locks. However, in the past decade, alternative methods of detention have been developed. This is especially important, considering the fact that the number of cases involving detention increased by just over a third in the 1990s. This increase included a larger proportion of females detained and a greater proportion of youths charged with offenses against a person. Furthermore, a concern over disproportionate minority confinement (DMC) has come to the forefront for juvenile justice, and this issue is especially important when considering decision making in the detention of youths.

Legal Criteria by State

Each state uses legal criteria to determine which children should be detained in a secure institutional setting, and are similar among states throughout the country. In the majority of jurisdictions, three key conditions are often utilized to determine if secure detention is necessary. First, and probably most importantly, the safety of the juvenile and the community must be considered. If the child is a threat to public safety (i.e., inflicting harm to neighborhood residents), or if he or she has a prior offense record (both violent and nonviolent), he or she is more likely to be detained in a secure detention facility. Second, if a child has inadequate supervision from his or her parents or guardian, or is of neglected or dependent status, he or she is more likely to be detained in a secure setting. Third, if the child is considered a flight risk from the jurisdiction and likely not to return to court for adjudication, disposition, and or program placement, he or she is likely to be placed in a secure setting. Some states have additional requirements. For example, Florida requires that a youth be detained in a secure setting if he or she has committed contempt of court by disrupting the court proceedings, disobeying court orders, and/or disrespecting authority on the court's premises. Generally, state statutes require that juveniles be released within 48 to 72 hours. During this time, a petition to juvenile court is typically filed, and some states have detention hearings. For this reason, bail is generally not utilized in the release of youths detained in detention facilities in the United States. For example, the state of Florida views youth as not having a right to bail; however, some states allow for it per the due-process revolution, which has sought to ensure the protection of constitutional rights for juveniles.

Reflecting on the criteria detailed above, the concept of detaining youths pending juvenile court hearings may seem very straightforward. However, the process of deciding to detain a child is quite ambiguous in the majority of jurisdictions throughout the United States. Because of the steadfast, almost routine reliance on secure detention in a local jail for alleged offenders over the age of 18, many citizens unaware of nuances between the adult and juvenile systems naturally conceptualize juvenile detention as a secure, institutional facility similar to an adult jail. In fact, some system personnel may not even be aware of these differences, and are often reluctant to examine potential and appropriate alternatives to secure detention for specific youths. Because of this, juvenile detention is multidimensional, as it entails more than just the physical structure. Granted, by strict definition, detention facilities serve to house those youths accused of delinquent acts. Detention can also be defined as a process involving the decisions that juvenile justice system officials make relating to the level of restriction that is needed to fulfill the detention goals of a particular youth's case. In considering detention as a process and not just a place, jurisdictions across the United States are beginning to make efforts to collect extensive information about potential alternatives to secure detention, and develop viable alternatives such as home detention, shelter care, and weekend reporting.

History of Juvenile Detention

The placement of youths in institutions for the purposes of detainment has a long history. Early detention facilities in America draw their roots from the refuge houses and training schools popular in urban locales in the 1800s. Refuge houses and training schools stressed extremely regimented scheduling of activities and corporal punishment for noncompliance. These facilities prevailed in the late 1800s and early 1900s. In the 1930s, during the peak of the Great Depression, many juveniles were sent to adult jails for detention. Many commentators and child advocates were concerned about the potential for harsh treatment of youths prior to court hearings, the denial of legal rights to youths, and the detainment of youths in facilities that were overcrowded and below standards for mental and physical well-being.

During this time, an inspector for the Federal Bureau of Prisons, Roy Casey, began examining these issues. He noted that the police and prosecuting attorneys were far too punitive with youths, and that the majority of children were detained with adults. Additional reports in the mid-20th century indicated that recordkeeping at adult facilities concerning youth matters was virtually nonexistent. Detention facilities specifically in operation for youths at this time lacked education and recreation programs, and social services were lacking. Recommendations for improving the detention process included stressing social services to meet the emotional needs of youths detained, revamping the court intake procedures to eliminate the potential for the misplacement of youths in detention (i.e., cases where secure placement was not necessary), and strengthening resources in the community to create a continuum of care for youths entering the system, thus eliminating the need for some youths to enter detention facilities.

However, as the 20th century progressed, more problems with secure detention arose. These problems included, but were not limited to, deplorable physical conditions such as poor heating, poor ventilation, and a lack of medical services (both for physical and mental needs) for the youths detained. During the 1960s, physical conditions of facilities improved due to a boom in construction, yet many of these facilities still resembled adult jails in appearance.

Profile of Detained Youths

The profile of youths placed in secure detention facilities across the United States does not reflect the sociodemographic characteristics of youths who comprise the general population. While males comprise a great proportion of the detention population, the rate of detention for females is increasing. When females are detained, they are more likely to be detained for status offenses than males. Minorities are disproportionately detained. This rate is not commensurate with the number of offenses that occur in communities across the nation. In the late 1980s, the problem of disproportionate numbers of minorities in confinement in juvenile justice systems throughout the United States was brought to the attention of the Office of Juvenile Justice and Delinquency Prevention (OJJDP) by the Coalition for Juvenile Justice. Initially, the DMC Initiative focused solely on confinement, not contact. In the 1988 Amendments to the Juvenile Justice and Delinquency Prevention (JJDP) Act of 1974, the U.S. Congress required that in order to qualify for federal funding, each state must take steps to address DMC. Specifically, under the Formula Grants Program, states were to assess how problematic DMC was, as well as develop efforts to reduce the proportion of minority youths detained or confined in secure juvenile detention facilities and other correctional settings if their representation exceeded the proportion of such groups in the general population. For purposes of this requirement, the OJJDP defined minority populations as African Americans, American Indians, Asians, Pacific Islanders, and Hispanics. Commentators who study DMC have noted that the decision to detain negatively affects children of minority status, as they are more likely to be placed in a secure facility than their white counterparts. Furthermore, minorities tend to be placed in secure detention facilities for longer periods of time than white children.

Children held in secure detention have a higher likelihood of mental/psychiatric disorders than youths in the general population. Compounding the mental health issues that a large proportion of youths face is the fact that many youths suffer from substance-abuse related problems that require therapeutic attention. Furthermore, some youths detained in secure settings find themselves in need of basic healthcare, as some children may not be receiving proper healthcare while living at home due to factors such as the child's parents' inability to pay for services. Other youths suffer from untreated sexually transmitted diseases such as chlamydia and gonorrhea upon admission to detention. The adverse conditions of confinement, such as overcrowding, could exacerbate these problems for youths experiencing them to any degree.

Alternatives to Secure Juvenile Detention

Secure detention, as it was conceptualized in the mid-20th century, prevailed in design and practice through the 1970s and 1980s. However, many status and minor offenders were being held in secure detention in the early 1970s. During this time, the federal government developed the Juvenile Justice and Delinquency Prevention Act of 1974, which encouraged the creation and implementation of alternatives to secure detention and residential confinement when and where possible and appropriate. Within the past decade, the continued overreliance on secure detention for youthful offenders has led to proactive reform initiatives in several jurisdictions across the country. The Juvenile Detention Alternatives Initiative (JDAI), sponsored by the Annie E. Casey Foundation, has the express goal of reforming detention practices for youths in several major metropolitan areas. The first JDAI sites included Portland, Sacramento, and New York. The reform efforts at these sites, which placed a heavy emphasis on the development, implementation, and evaluation of alternatives to secure detention, were monitored at various stages throughout the initiative, so that the keys to success could be shared with both urban and rural jurisdictions frustrated with current practices and wishing to make changes to current detention policy in their respective locales.

The JDAI initiatives in the cities of Portland, Sacramento, and New York were deemed a success because of the reduced reliance on the placement of youths in secure detention facilities. This was especially the case for youths who, considering the nature of their offenses and/or arrests, could better be served by detention in alternative settings. Thus, these findings offered some encouragement to parties interested in better serving youths through alternatives. Because of this, more alternatives to secure detention were developed in the three cities, each with the goal of providing services to youths that may match their needs, and their efficacy in various situations was documented. Most importantly, with the funding and recommendations provided by the Annie E. Casey Foundation, guiding principles to aid jurisdictions in the development and implementation of detention alternatives were documented. The recommendations from the Annie E. Casey Foundation include, but are not limited to: (1) the development of a juvenile justice committee of wide representation, which will facilitate the development of goals, oversee program implementation and delivery, anticipate potential obstacles and develop solutions to these obstacles, identify funding sources and secure available monetary grants, and sponsor external evaluation on a quarterly basis; (2) the development and use of appropriate screening instruments to aid appropriate program placement to best serve the needs of youths; and (3) the continued dissemination of information by juvenile justice personnel concerning the best alternative practices to secure detention.

These guidelines could prove to be critical in the reduced reliance on secure detention in U.S. jurisdictions, both urban and rural, as well as aid in the development and implementation of alternative detention programs such as foster care, home detention, and weekend reporting.

Planning for Change

Jurisdictions interested in following the recommendations of the Annie E. Casey Foundation must tightly coordinate and plan a vision for change. According to the Casey Foundation, meaningful and coordinated change can and will only occur when key policy-level actors—prosecutors, juvenile court judges, and juvenile probation officers—develop a collective vision and then implement the agreed upon plan of action based on the following seven principles:

1. Groups with the express intent to collaborate must be formed through dedication and may not be immediately successful, as ego, power, and ideology have to be negotiated between each of the system components represented.
2. Relevant stakeholders from a wide range of service agencies must be engaged and involved, as their knowledge must be relied upon when forming a continuum of care for youths.

3. The group must form a consensus regarding the need and direction of change, as goals must be articulated, tasks must be assigned, program deliverables outlined, and an evaluation plan put in place.
4. Effective collaboration requires negotiation among parties and willingness to compromise.
5. Strong and able leadership is required to broker and implement reform, perhaps in the form of coordinators hired specifically for leadership purposes.
6. Collaborations must include members or leaders with political and/ or policy clout to negotiate implementation.
7. Mandatory self-assessment must take place at many stages of the process, as well as a plan for outside process and outcome evaluations.

In general, institutions are resistant to change and reform, and juvenile detention is no exception. It is, however, only through meaningful collaboration that the failings of a system intent on relying on secure detention might be adequately addressed. Collaboration holds more promise for lasting juvenile detention reform than does the prospect of legislating change without the consensus of stakeholders, or of unilateral, self-serving change.

Pro: Benefits of Juvenile Detention Facilities

When a child commits a status offense or a delinquent act, the arresting police officer must make a critical decision: to detain or not to detain. If the child is a threat to himself or the public order of the community, it may be best for the youth in question to be detained in a secure facility so that officials may keep watch over him or her and protect the safety of the child as well as the community. Arrested children may be released to their parent(s) or a capable guardian; however, a youth may not have an individual who can provide adequate supervision and/or bring him to court for his initial appearance. In these cases, detention is necessary, as it will ensure the child will be present for his court date. Other children may be at risk of leaving the jurisdiction and not making their court appearance, and as with cases where the child lacks parental/guardian supervision, detaining him or her in a secure setting may be the only answer the juvenile justice system has to keep the child from fleeing from appearing before the judge at the initial appearance. While secure detention settings are often criticized for the problems they present, such as overcrowding and poor living conditions, they are not as "hard" as adult jail settings.

Even secure facilities can help juvenile justice system officials in the assessment and proper placement of children post-adjudication. Some secure facilities use risk assessment instruments to determine if children are in need of mental health, substance abuse, and educational services. The results of these assessments can be used by probation officers filling out presentence investigation reports (PSIs), which in turn are used by judges in determining the proper disposition for the child. If the child is in need of treatment at the disposition phase, these steps can be invaluable to system officials.

Con: Drawbacks of Juvenile Detention Facilities

Not all youths need secure detention, and many children would fare better in alternative settings such as foster care or weekend reporting. Alternatives to secure detention settings provide youths with needed services, more opportunities for medical and mental healthcare, and educational attainment and vocational training.

Proponents of alternative settings note that the secure detention of alleged delinquents should primarily be restricted to cases where youths are at risk of harming themselves and/or residents of their communities, as well as youths who are at risk of not returning to the juvenile court for both adjudication and disposition hearings. However, the juvenile justice process is very complex. In addition, the juvenile justice system has come to embrace a contemporary, adversarial nature since the due-process movement of the 1960s, lacks uniformity in determining the risks youthful offenders may present to both themselves and their communities, uses inadequate risk-assessment instruments at intake to determine the treatment needs of offenders, and juggles a myriad of extralegal factors (i.e., the socioeconomic status of a child and/or the availability of an intake officer to administer a risk assessment). All of these factors contribute to the fact that many juveniles posing little to no risk of harm to themselves or their communities and/or involvement in recurrent delinquent behavior are detained in secure facilities in many jurisdictions. This practice has resulted in the secure detention of youths accused of drug and minor property offenses, case backlogs in the juvenile courts, and overcrowding in institutional settings. All of this leads to rapid physical deterioration of the facility, which can result in unsafe conditions, which may be found at many secure detention facilities across the United States. In fact, these adverse, widespread conditions of confinement are considered by some commentators to be below the necessary standards for the protection of youths. Specifically, educational needs, healthcare services, suicide prevention, and psychiatric treatment (both individual and group approaches) are deficient in most secure detention facilities for youths in the United States.

Denial of Services

Whether the decision is conscious or not, many juvenile courts deny access to youths needing alternative services. Much of the time, it is because prosecutors, juvenile court judges, and juvenile probation officers are unaware of services available to youths in their jurisdiction. Furthermore, this denial of appropriate service is an administrative function, since few accessible alternatives to secure detention or funding for research and development are available in the majority of jurisdictions. Planning, implementing, and managing alternatives, as well as monitoring and tracking, require valuable staff time and the skills of qualified juvenile justice specialists and researchers. Nevertheless, if community stakeholders and system officials can agree to invest the resources available to them, alternatives to detention that are culturally relevant and available to youths can become alternatives for juvenile justice system officials to use on a routine basis when choosing programming for youths.

Because of this, the Annie E. Casey Foundation advocates jurisdictions develop a continuum of alternatives for youths in need of detention services. At the nonresidential end, home/community detention and day and/ or evening reporting are considered to be the best options for youths in need of services, with the latter requiring more intensive supervision from juvenile justice officials. These methods have shown that effective monitoring of youths can be achieved, and they have successfully reduced further involvement in the juvenile justice system in both urban and rural locations. Residential options include both shelter care and foster care. Shelter care is the most commonly used residential alternative for youths in their teens. This method of detention differs from a secure environment in that youths are typically housed for less than 30 days, and security is maintained through a low staff-to-youth ratio (typically 1:6). Probably most importantly, the physical environment is not reminiscent of the secure detention setting. In some jurisdictions, youths participating in shelter care attend public school. A less intensive program than shelter care is foster care, which is recommended for younger (i.e., pre-adolescent) children entering the system, specifically those posing a low risk of further delinquency involvement.

While alternatives to secure detention remove much of what is traditionally conceptualized as "hard" and routine about the detention process, juvenile justice system officials are encouraged by the Annie E. Casey Foundation to provide specific treatment services to youths who need individualized and intensive attention. However, there is the unintended consequence of youths remaining in programs for periods longer than necessary when treatment becomes a critical component to any alternative program.

See Also: 3. At-Risk Youth; 4. Boot Camps; 7. Group Homes; 13. Out-of-Home Placement; 15. Racial Disparities; 19. Serious and Violent Juvenile Offenders; 20. Treatment and Rehabilitation.

Further Readings

American Correctional Association. *Guidelines for the Development of Policies and Procedures: Juvenile Detention Facilities.* Laurel, MD: American Correctional Association, 1992.

American Correctional Association. *Standards for Juvenile Detention Facilities.* Laurel, MD: American Correctional Association, 1991.

Annie E. Casey Foundation. *Pathways to Juvenile Detention Reform.* Baltimore, MD: Annie E. Casey Foundation, Juvenile Detention Alternatives Initiative, 1999.

Bremner, Robert H., ed. *Children and Youth in America: A Documentary History.* Cambridge, MA: Harvard University Press, 1974.

Butts, Jeffrey A. *Offenders in Juvenile Court, 1994.* Washington, DC: Office of Juvenile Justice and Delinquency Prevention, 1996.

Casey, Roy. "Children in Jail." In *Delinquency and the Community in Wartime: Yearbook of the National Probation Association*, edited by M. Bell. New York: National Probation Association, 1943.

Cohen, Lawrence E., and James R. Kluegel. "The Detention Decision: A Study of the Impact of Social Characteristics and Legal Factors in Two Juvenile Metropolitan Juvenile Courts." *Social Forces,* v.58/1 (1979).

Dunlap, Earl L., and David W. Roush. "Juvenile Detention as Process and Place." *Juvenile and Family Court Journal,* v.46 (1995).

Frazier, Charles E., and Donna M. Bishop. "The Pretrial Detention of Juveniles and Its Impact on Case Dispositions." *Journal of Criminal Law and Criminology,* v.76/4 (1985).

Frazier, Charles E., and John C. Cochran. "Detention of Juveniles: Its Effects on Subsequent Juvenile Court Processing Decisions." *Youth and Society*, v.17/3 (1986).

Kobrin, Solomon, and Malcolm W. Klein. *National Evaluation of the Deinstitutionalization of Status Offender Programs—Executive Summary*. Los Angeles, CA: Social Science Research Institute, University of Southern California, 1982.

Krisberg, Barry, and Ira Schwartz. "Rethinking Juvenile Justice." *Crime and Delinquency*, v.29 (1983).

Lubow, Bart. "Successful Strategies for Reforming Juvenile Detention." *Federal Probation*, v.63 (1999).

National Conference on Prevention and Control of Juvenile Delinquency. *Report on Juvenile Detention*. Washington, DC: U.S. Government Printing Office, 1947.

Norman, Sherwood. "Detention Facilities for Children." *Proceedings of the National Conference of Social Work: 1946*. New York: Columbia University Press, 1947.

Norman, Sherwood. "Juvenile Detention." *NPPA Journal*, v.3 (1957).

Norman, Sherwood. *Standards and Guides for the Detention of Children and Youth*. New York: National Probation and Parole Association, 1958.

Office of Juvenile Justice and Delinquency Prevention. *Conditions of Confinement: Juvenile Detention and Corrections Facilities*. Washington, DC: Office of Juvenile Justice and Delinquency Prevention, 1994.

Pawlak, Edward J. "Differential Selection of Juveniles for Detention." *Journal of Research in Crime and Delinquency*, v.14/2 (1997).

President's Commission on Law Enforcement and the Administration of Justice. *Task Force Report: Corrections*. Washington, DC: U.S. Government Printing Office, 1967.

Roush, David W. *Desktop Guide to Good Juvenile Detention Practice*. East Lansing, MI: Center for Research and Professional Development, 1996.

Roush, David W. "Juvenile Detention: Issues for the 21st Century." In *Juvenile Justice Sourcebook: Past, Present, and Future*, edited by A. R. Roberts. New York: Oxford University Press, 2004.

Sanborn, Joseph B., and Anthony W. Salerno. *The Juvenile Justice System: Law and Process*. Los Angeles: Roxbury, 2005.

Sarri, Rosemary. *Under Lock and Key: Juveniles in Jails and Detention*. Ann Arbor, MI: National Association of Juvenile Corrections, 1974.

Schwartz, Ira. *(In)Justice for Juveniles: Rethinking the Best Interests of the Child*. Lexington, MA: Lexington Books, 1989.

Schwartz, Ira, Gideon Fishman, Radene R. Hatfield, and Barry Krisberg. "Juvenile Detention: The Hidden Costs Revisited." *Justice Quarterly*, v.4/2 (1987).

Steinhart, David. *Planning for Juvenile Detention Reforms: A Structured Approach*. Washington, DC: Department of Justice, 2000.

Wordes, Madeline, Timothy S. Bynum, and Charles J. Corley. "Locking Up Youth: The Impact of Race on Detention Decisions." *Journal of Research in Crime and Delinquency*, v.31 (1994).

9

Juvenile Gangs and Delinquency

Kristy N. Matsuda
University of Missouri, St. Louis

G angs have been the subject of much attention since the significant increase in gang-involved violence around the 1980s. The discussion around gangs is fraught with controversy and contradiction from the most basic level, such as how to define a gang, to the most complex, including what to do about them. The least debatable characteristic about gangs is that they are responsible for a disproportionate amount of delinquency. This fact makes gangs particularly interesting to the media, researchers, law enforcement, and policymakers. The depiction of gangs offered by these parties, however, do not always converge, as defining gangs is a problematic issue. Understanding gang composition and structure is a complex challenge as well, and there has been ongoing debate regarding the extent of gangs in America (and abroad), as well as the most appropriate and effective methods for addressing the problem. Many controversies surround gangs and the various methods of dealing with the gang problem in the United States, including law enforcement and intervention techniques.

The debate begins at the foundation of the gang problem. What is a gang? There is general agreement by law enforcement and researchers that some criminal outfits like the mafia or organized crime, prison gangs, outlaw motorcycle groups, and hate groups such as white supremacists should not be equated with criminal street gangs (e.g., the Bloods or Crips). Criminal street gangs are composed primarily of youths, whereas these other groups are adult criminal organizations and are therefore considered distinct.

Defining Juvenile Gangs

Aside from a broad focus on youth groups, the definition of a gang has been debated since the earliest qualitative work on street gangs. In short, interested parties have not been able to come to a consensus regarding what characteristics of gangs are universal enough to be shared among all gangs, but specific enough to distinguish gangs from any other youth group. This is particularly challenging when decades of research shows that most youths who engage in crime do so during adolescence, and usually in groups. So, what distinguishes a group of delinquent friends from a street gang?

Much of the preoccupation with gangs centers on the amount of crime that gangs commit. Gang members commit more crime than non-gang members, but researchers have been at odds with whether or not a commitment to crime should be included in the definition of a gang. It is circular logic to state that gangs commit more crime than non-gang youth groups, and to be classified as a gang, the group must commit crime. Without an acknowledgement of their criminal involvement, however, would a gang be distinguishable from any other youth group that shares a name, has colors or signs, or rituals and rules (e.g., fraternities, or sports teams)?

Media and pop culture depictions of gangs usually implicate race/ethnicity of members, clothing, territoriality, organizational structure, signs, colors, or monikers. There is no consensus regarding the appropriateness of including some or all of these gang descriptors. Some researchers have favored a broader definition of gangs to allow for applicability in a variety of contexts, such as defining gangs internationally. These definitions generally do not include culturally or regionally specific characteristics like race of members or group colors or dress. They may stress in a street-oriented way but do not require territoriality (i.e., gangs have their own defined area they defend). Others definitions require some semblance of structure or organization to be considered a gang. This may be problematic, because not all gangs are characterized by notable structure or organization. In short, researchers have proposed a number of gang definitions. Some are more popular than others, but none have a consensus.

Law enforcement definitions vary by jurisdiction. Many states do not legally define a gang, and those states that do have a definition do not often use the same definition. As legal consequences for gang membership have become more severe, courts have demanded an unambiguous definition of a gang to protect the constitutional rights of gang members. States that have attempted to use these strategies have been forced to adopt a concrete definition. One example that has withstood court challenge defines a gang as three or more people with the commission of crime as one of their "primary" activities, and that have a common name, or identifying sign or symbol.

Juvenile Gang Members and Their Lives

By the best research estimates, approximately 6–8 percent of the general population is gang-involved at any given time. However, the demographic characteristics of street gang members vary depending on the data source. Law enforcement portrayals of gangs suggest that gang members are predominantly male, adult, and minority organizations. Female gang members make up only about 10 percent of the national gang picture. White gang members are even rarer (nine percent), and only about one-third are juveniles.

Research on gang membership has offered a rather different picture of gang members. While empirical studies show that males are more likely to be gang-involved than females, the proportion of female gang members is far greater than is offered in law enforcement estimates. In addition, research shows that the peak of gang membership is in adolescence and not adulthood. The peak of gang joining is most often cited between 13–15 years of age and declines thereafter. Finally, studies have shown far more diversity in the race/ethnicity of gang members. Minorities are overrepresented in self-report studies and official data estimates, but the proportion of white gang members is far higher in research than law enforcement estimates.

Research on Gangs Across America

Research has offered a rich description of the lives of gang members and the dynamics of gang processes. Systematic research began with qualitative studies of gangs and gang members, such as Fredrick Thrasher's work in the late 1920s. Theories about gang formations were offered by Richard Cloward and Lloyd Ohlin, as well as Albert Cohen. Gang research has significantly benefited from decades of qualitative accounts of the lives of gang members and group processes. Researchers like Martin Sanchez Jankowski and William Whyte, for example, utilized a participant-observation technique. In other words, these researchers became involved in the everyday lives of gangs. Other in-depth accounts of gangs stem from authors' experiences with gangs via intervention programs (e.g., Malcolm Klein, James Short Jr., and Fred L. Strodtbeck).

Qualitative research on gangs has provided insight into the commonalities and differences in various types of gangs. James Diego Vigil and Joan Moore, for example, have highlighted the unique struggle of Chicano/a gangs for the past 30 years. Ko-Lin Chin and Sheldon Zhang have illuminated Chinese gangs in America, which are rarely studied. Although he did not specifically implicate African American gangs, Elijah Anderson's book *Code of the Street* is relevant to discussions regarding how attitudes and behavior may be affected by urban life. Scholars like Jody Miller and Meda Chesney-Lind have been central to the discussion of how girls' experiences in and around gangs are distinct from boys and non-gang girls.

The qualitative body of research is necessary, but generally only captures the experience of one or two gangs in one city (or in extraordinary cases, two or three cities) at a time. Qualitative studies have not utilized methods that allow for generalization of findings across gangs and/or research sites. This had led to an absence of any national picture of gangs.

Quantitative studies have been employed to understand the extent and characteristics of gang members across the United States (and abroad). National, quantitative studies are rare. One of the best-known is the National Youth Gang Survey, conducted by the National Gang Center, which polls a representative sample of law enforcement agencies about the gang problems in their jurisdictions. These data have been used to inform the prevalence of gangs and gang members, the areas in which they are common, and the demographic of gang members. In addition, researchers have also attempted to collect national data on gangs.

Cheryl Maxson and Malcolm Klein, for example, collected data from hundreds of law enforcement agencies in gang cities across the United States to understand the structure of gangs. Media depictions of gangs often include an emphasis on gangs as organized, long-standing, hierarchical groups with established syndicates that spread across the nation. Their study did confirm "traditional" gangs, which are most often captured by the media, as large, long-standing, hierarchical gangs with a wide range of gang member ages. However, they also concluded that this type of gang structure only characterized 11 percent of the gangs that were reported across the country. The most common structure of gangs were groups that had no formal organization (no subgroups), had less than 50 members, had been in existence for less than 10 years, had no pattern of territoriality, and had members around the same age. This gang structure accounted for 39 percent of the gangs reported. A large proportion of gangs were rather loosely structured groups of youths. Research has shown that these types of gangs are more fluid than traditional, highly structured gangs. It is not uncommon for these types of groups to dissipate on their own.

The media also commonly report that gangs specialize in a particular crime. In particular, media reports on gangs often stress gang involvement in the drug trade. The research on gang structures found that most of the gangs reported by law enforcement did not specialize in their offending. Only 17 percent of gangs were classified as specialty gangs. Research has shown that a majority of street gangs in the United States are not highly structured organizations, which makes the likelihood of successful criminal syndication unlikely. This is not to say that well-organized, criminal street gangs do not exist. They do, but they are the exception rather than the rule. Similarly, the notion of a transnational gang, a gang that sends members across the globe to start new syndicates, is also not the common gang structure.

Gang Locations

Gangs used to be mainly clustered around big cities, in particular Los Angeles and Chicago. But from the 1980s through the 2000s, every U.S. state has reported the presence of gangs. The growth of the gang problem in America is no longer confined to only highly populated cities. Gangs are consistently reported in mid-sized cities, suburban areas, and rural towns. A 1995 U.S. Department of Justice survey of urban, rural, and suburban law enforcement agencies estimates as many as 23,000 youth gangs exist in the country.

Gangs are also found all over the world, including Europe, Canada, and Latin America, though they may be more often referred to as *troublesome youth groups*. The extent of the global gang problem has not been established, as systematic data collection has not been attempted. The research that has been conducted on gangs in other countries has also shown that minority youths are more likely to join gangs. And comparative studies, between American versus European cities, for example, show similar prevalence of gang youths.

Gang Delinquency

Gang members commit a substantial amount of crime, which has been shown using both self-reported and official measures of crime. Research has consistently shown that gang members commit more delinquency than non-gang members. They also commit more violent crime than non-gang members. The word *more*, however, should be clarified. In one sample of youths, for example, approximately 30 percent of the youths reported gang involvement, but reported committing 68 percent of all violent crime and 86 percent of all serious offenses reported by the entire youth sample.

While gang members commit more violent crime than non-gang members, this is not to suggest that every gang is committing multiple violent crimes on an annual basis. Most jurisdictions with gangs report no more than one or two gang-related homicides a year. Larger cities report more homicides than smaller cities, but even most large cities report less than three gang homicides per year. Los Angeles and Chicago are two gang cities that are the exception to this rule. These two cities are the most heavily populated with street gangs and can report hundreds of gang homicides per year.

Researchers have been interested in why gang members are so delinquent. In particular, they have examined whether gang members are more delinquent and thereby seek out other people like them, or whether entrance into the gang increases delinquent behavior. Longitudinal research on gang offending shows that it is a little bit of both. Gang membership increases serious and violent offending in an individual who is an active member, but even after a member leaves the gang, their reported offending is still higher than non-gang members. Gang members are also more delinquent than delinquent youths who have non-gang delinquent friends. Research has also shown that non-gang youths who associate with gang friends are more likely to offend than non-gang youths who do not have gang friends. In sum, involvement or association with gangs significantly increases participation in delinquency.

Gangs and gang members may be responsible for a significant amount of crime, but most do not specialize in their type of offending. Gang members may shoplift, commit robbery, and participate in gang-on-gang violence. The exception may be juvenile tagging crews, who vandalize public spaces. These groups often engage solely in vandalism and are not usually included in studies of street gangs.

Not all gang members commit a lot of crime. There is variation in the extent of participation in illegal activities by gang members and gangs. Perhaps more importantly, even the most delinquent gangs and the most delinquent gang members are not offending all, or even most, of the time. While their involvement in crime often brings them the most notoriety, gang members spend most of their time in everyday activities, such as eating, sleeping, going to work or school, or hanging out.

Despite pop culture and/or media representation that gang membership is a permanent status, research shows that many gang members are only active for a short period of time, approximately one or two years. Gang members leave the gang life for a number of reasons, many related to the normal "aging-out" process that occurs with delinquent activity in general. Gang members become parents, get jobs, and experience or witness too many threats of violence against themselves or their loved ones. Interviews with current and ex-gang members suggest that members can leave the gangs without experiencing actual harm, suggesting the "blood in, blood out" notion made popular by movies may be exaggerated.

Responses to Gangs

There are many contradictions surrounding the understanding of gangs, as well as very little consensus regarding what to do about gangs. There are three primary methods of controlling gangs: suppression, intervention, and prevention. Suppression methods are efforts at reducing gang offending by increasing or changing the law enforcement emphasis on these groups. Intervention programs target youths who are already gang-involved and attempt to bring about or speed up the desistance process. Intervention programs have also been designed to target gang violence. Prevention techniques attempt to stop the gang from forming or reduce the incidence of gang member joining. These efforts have the broadest target population. Prevention efforts focus on the general population on youths who are at risk for joining gangs.

Police Suppression Techniques

Since the rise in gang activity almost three decades ago, the justice system has implemented numerous types of suppression techniques to combat the gang problem. In the 1980s and 1990s, law enforcement agencies all across the country increased the intensity of their policing of gangs. Police agencies began utilizing a range of techniques to suppress the gang problems in their jurisdictions, such as arresting gang members for minor offenses (e.g., wearing a gang sweater); following gangs members until they offended, and then arresting them; hot-spot policing; strip searches of suspected gang members; or dropping arrested gang members in rival gang territory. Many of these new tactics were found to be unconstitutional.

Suppression techniques today include more specialized policing, intelligence gathering, and prosecution. Police departments across the country began creating gang units, or specialized police units that were focused specifically on gangs and collecting gang intelligence. California implemented their CalGang database, a system designed to house information on identified gang members in the state. Individuals entered into the CalGang database can be subject to sentencing enhancements, civil gang injunctions, or any other prosecutorial tactic that is aimed specifically at street gang members.

With the increased attention to foreign threats, the enforcement of transnational street gangs like Mara Salvatrucha (MS-13) became a federal government priority. In 2005, the U.S. Immigration and Customs Enforcement (ICE), under the auspices of the Department of Homeland Security, took the lead on the intelligence gathering of transnational gangs. ICE conducts large-scale raids that end in the deportation and/or incarceration of foreign-born gang members. In addition to transnational street gangs, ICE has also been tasked with intelligence gathering and enforcement of prison gangs, hate groups, or other threat groups that span across state lines, thus falling within federal jurisdiction.

Prosecutorial and Legislative Suppression Techniques

Along with specialized police units, county prosecutors began increasing their focus on gang prosecutions. "Vertical" prosecution became a commonly exercised technique. The same prosecutor would be in charge of a gang case from beginning to end (instead of a number of prosecutors handling the case at each stage). This would increase familiarity with the case and create stronger ties between the district attorney and the investigating police unit. One example, Operation Hardcore, relied on vertical prosecution, and was designed to specifically handle the most serious gang cases, such as homicide or crimes involving gang leaders. Operation Hardcore also provided special training to prosecutors and avoided the use of plea bargaining. The program boasts a very high conviction rate, though the effect on gang crime has not been established.

Civil Gang Injunctions

Civil gang injunctions are a form of prosecutorial suppression. The strategy first gained ground in the early 1990s and has been increasingly used in jurisdictions with significant gang problems. Civil gang injunctions differ from other techniques in that they target a specific geographical area, such as a neighborhood, that has been inundated by a specific gang threat. A civil gang injunction seeks to prove that a gang is responsible for creating a public nuisance in the proposed area. If the prosecution can prove its case against the gang, the judge will order a permanent injunction against the gang. Any violation of the injunction will result in a fine or jail time.

To prove their case, prosecutors and police must be able to identify individuals and prove that they are specific gang members, show evidence of nuisance (i.e., declarations from community members), and be able to define the affected area. Thus, these cases require a great deal of data gathering. If the prosecutors are successful, however, the named gang is prohibited from engaging in a list of restricted activities. These activities can vary by the suit, but generally include congregating in certain locations, engaging in criminal activity, trespassing, public intimidation or harassment, or possessing items often associated with illegal activities.

Gang Interventions

Intervention strategies are targeted at current gang members to leave the gang or at gangs to reduce gang violence. There are numerous programs that have had this focus. Many researchers and practitioners agree that gangs cannot be controlled simply by law enforcement strategies. Intervention programs often link law enforcement agencies with other community groups in an attempt to reduce gang offending. One example of a suppression-intervention hybrid is the Boston Gun Project or Operation Ceasefire. Both programs intend to reduce gang violence (but not gangs). Meetings are held with gang members in the target areas, and both law enforcement and community members convey a desire to eliminate gang violence.

Community agencies also offer services to gang members. Law enforcement informs gang members that any nonviolent crime will be handled like any other crime, but any gang-involved violence will be subject to immediate and severe response from all players in the justice system. Though a rigorous evaluation of the programs has not been conducted, post-program rates of gang violence have been demonstrated in each site. One of the earliest types of gang intervention were programs that sent gang or "detached" workers into the community to interact with gangs in their environments and move them toward better relationships, work, education, or less gang cohesion.

More recently, interventions like CeaseFire in Chicago also rely on outreach staff or "violence interrupters" that work on the streets, building relationships with gang leaders and community members, and try to mediate the violence between gangs. The immediate program goal is to prevent the cycle of retaliatory violence that often characterizes gang crimes. An evaluation of the program shows that CeaseFire was associated with a decline in gang shootings, either homicide or reciprocal killings.

Gang Prevention

There are a number of gang prevention program models available. Many prevention models have been criticized for expecting reductions in gang joining and offending when they are designed to reduce juvenile delinquency or other problem behaviors such as truancy or bullying. The Gang Resistance Education and Training (G.R.E.A.T.) Program, which began in the early 1990s in the Phoenix area and quickly spread around the country, is a 13-lesson program taught to middle school students by local law enforcement officers. The original G.R.E.A.T. program was evaluated in the mid-1990s in a national, longitudinal study, which found no differences in the gang involvement and delinquency in G.R.E.A.T. versus non-G.R.E.A.T. participants. However, the evaluation results prompted a redesign of the program, and data is currently being collected to determine if the program has long-term effects.

Pro: Benefits of Gang Prevention Techniques

Law enforcement and gang expert practitioners were surveyed and asked to identify the type of gang strategy that was most often used, and the strategy they believed was the most effective. Results of the survey revealed that these experts agreed that suppression and enforcement techniques were the most often used, but were also seen as the least effective. There is wide support for the notion that only a balanced approach to gangs that incorporates suppression, intervention, and prevention will be effective in combating the gang problem in America.

Prosecutorial and Legislative Suppression Techniques

The increased intelligence gathering by police and prosecutors has had a number of effects in the new suppression techniques tailored toward gang members. The California Street Terrorism Enforcement and Prevention (STEP) Act was the first legislative attempt to define a gang, and made it illegal to engage in gang crime. Individuals that are determined to be a part of a gang can be required to register, and may be subject to gang enhancements and special prosecutorial handling (e.g., vertical prosecution and civil gang injunctions). Prior attempts to target gangs legislatively have been struck down by the courts for not providing a sufficiently explicit definition of a gang. The STEP Act, and other definitions like it, are specific and detailed enough to have withstood court challenge.

Federal law allows for the creation and maintenance of criminal databases, and some states have created gang-member databases. Again, a sufficiently narrow definition of a gang member—self-admitted, or demonstrates a number of gang-like qualities like dress, signs, associates—is created, and numerous state law enforcement agencies can share information about gang members and associates. This kind of intelligence gathering has been useful for gang prosecution and civil gang injunctions.

Gang Prevention

The G.R.E.A.T. middle-school program taught by local law enforcement officers is the only gang prevention program that has been evaluated by rigorous methodological standards and found to be promising or effective. When the program underwent a curriculum redesign that was fully implemented in 2002, a new evaluation of the program began in 2006 and continued through 2010. Short-term results from the evaluation of the revised G.R.E.A.T. program have shown that program participants report lower rates of gang membership and delinquency. Data is currently being collected to determine if the program has long-term effects.

Con: Drawbacks of Gang Prevention Techniques

While there is no shortage of motivation to combat the problem and numerous programs and policies have been designed, there have been very few success stories. The results of gang policies and programs may seem disheartening. The fact is that few programs that target gang prevention, intervention, or suppression have been found to be effective. This is large part because most programs and policies, especially suppression, have not been evaluated for effectiveness. Those that have been evaluated have not been tested with enough methodological rigor to make causal statements about program effect; that is, they cannot eliminate the possibility that a non-program related factor was the actual cause of the observed program effect.

Controversies Surrounding Suppression Techniques

In the 1980s, law enforcement instituted "gang crackdowns" in the form of massive sweeps of gang members like Los Angeles' Operation Hammer in the late 1980s. Over the course of a weekend, 1,000 police officers arrested over 1,000 people, and utilized mobile booking units to process suspected gang members quickly. This and other massive police sweeps were intended to increase gang member's perceptions of the consequences of their gang activity, but inevitably resulted in a majority of those detained being released without charges. Those arrested were usually charged with low-level offenses. Researchers like Malcolm Klein have argued that these kinds of tactics actually produced the opposite of the intended effect. Instead of deterring gang members, it more likely sent the message that the police did not have enough evidence to charge the individuals, so their criminal behavior would go unpunished.

Suppression techniques are the most common strategy for combating gangs in this country. First, to be able to successfully apply gang enhancements, registration, or civil gang injunctions, for example, an appropriate and sufficient definition of a *gang* and/or *gang member* must be established. The court has struck down laws that seek to affect gangs without establishing a sufficient definition. One problem with the increase in data gathering and record keeping is that there are more methods to get a gang member into the system than there are to get a gang member out of the system. Research has shown that active gang membership is only an average of one to two years, but the processes for being expunged from these gang databases and/or gang determinations are not well explicated. In the case of a gang injunction, siblings may be unable to travel in the same vehicle for as long as they reside in that neighborhood even if they leave the gang.

In addition, some researchers have urged that declaring an individual a "gang member" or a group a "gang" could unintentionally build group cohesion, thereby producing more gang-oriented individuals. Peripheral gang members may feel a bolstered sense of gang identity if they are told they are a dangerous gang member. Similarly, loosely bound deviant groups may take on a stronger gang identity if they perceive law enforcement view them as a credible threat. Individuals who are not gang members, but associate with gang members, may actually join the gang if they believe that law enforcement have already classified them as members and they are subject to gang penalties. Related gang members may be less likely to consider leaving the gang if they do not believe that they will ever be rid of the classification.

Civil Injunctions

Injunctions have been issued in a variety of locales. Most, however, take place in southern California, particularly Los Angeles. Few studies have examined the effectiveness of gang injunctions, and research results are mixed. Two studies show that gang injunctions increase crime in the area, and another showed a decrease. In addition, there is no research that examines if the effectiveness of gang injunctions is dependent on the type of gang, the area, or other potentially important characteristics. Civil gang injunctions have withstood constitutional challenges but are still controversial. If successful, a gang injunction can prohibit gang members from congregating in public together at any time. This includes family members that are named as members of the same gang.

Gang Interventions

Gang intervention programs that sent gang or "detached" workers into the community to interact with gangs in their environments have generally not been successful. Many of the first iterations of this technique actually resulted in an increase in delinquency and other negative outcomes in the treated group. Other versions of the same strategy showed small reductions in gang cohesion and small, short-term effects, but did not bring about any discernible, long-term change in gang behavior.

Conclusion

Decades of gang research and policy have made a few things clear. First, gang members are responsible for a great volume of delinquency, both violent and nonviolent. However, beliefs about who gang members are, what gangs look like, and the best way to handle the problem are continuously contested. Once gangs emerge, it is incredibly difficult to eliminate them. Some gangs, by virtue of their loose and informal group structure, may dissipate without intervention, but no strategies have been found to effectively force a gang out of existence. There have been no attempts to prevent gangs from forming or to improve the underlying reasons for their formation (e.g., marginalization in the community).

The numerous methods, policies, and programs to combat the problem of gangs have been largely unsuccessful. Most have not been evaluated for effectiveness, while those that do undergo evaluation have not been tested with adequately stringent methodological standards.

See Also: 5. Curfews; 17. School Violence; 19. Serious and Violent Juvenile Offenders.

Further Readings

Curry, G. David, and Scott H. Decker. *Confronting Gangs: Crime and Community*. New York: Oxford University Press, 2003.

Egley, Arlen, Jr., Cheryl L. Maxson, Jody Miller, and Malcolm W. Klein, eds. *The Modern Gang Reader*. Thousand Oaks, CA: Sage, 2006.

Esbensen, Finn-Aage. *Preliminary Short-Term Results From the Evaluation of the G.R.E.A.T. Program*. National Institute of Justice, 2008.

Howell, James C. *Youth Gang Programs and Strategies*. U.S. Department of Justice: Office of Juvenile Justice and Delinquency Prevention, 2000.

Huff, C. Ronald, ed. *Gangs in America III*. Thousand Oaks, CA: Sage, 2001.

Juvenile Justice Bulletin. "Gangs." (April 1998). http://www.ojjdp.gov/jj bulletin/9804/gangs.html (Accessed March 2011).

Klein, Malcolm. *The American Street Gangs: Its Nature, Prevalence, and Control*. New York: Oxford University Press, 1995.

Klein, Malcolm, and Cheryl L. Maxson. *Street Gangs: Patterns and Policies*. New York: Oxford University Press, 2006.

10

Juvenile Offenders in Adult Courts

Megan Kurlychek
University at Albany, State University of New York

T he historical precedent of providing differential treatment for juveniles who break the law dates as far back as the first written records of law found in the Code of the Hammurabi, 4,000 B.C.E. In general, the modified response to juvenile offending has consisted of some form of mitigation of punishment based on the presumption that youths are not fully culpable for their actions due to immaturity. In more modern times, this distinction has not only been drawn at the punishment stage, but an entirely separate system of justice, the juvenile court system, has evolved to process and respond to the delinquent behavior of youths.

However, the boundary between juvenility and adulthood is nebulous, and as such, many disagreements persist concerning which youths, and for which offenses, the more lenient juvenile justice system is appropriate. In this discussion, any youth under the age of 18 is considered a juvenile. Thus, the processing of such a youth in the adult criminal justice system is the topic at hand. To fully understand the implications of such processing, one must first hold a basic understanding of the distinctions between the adult and juvenile justice systems; then, which juveniles make it to adult court, and the differing opinions on the benefits and drawbacks of adult court for juveniles.

Differentiating Juvenile and Adult Justice

The practice of providing mitigated responses to the offending of juveniles is based on the premise that due to their youthful status, children are not capable of fully understanding the consequences of their actions. For example, 18th-century English common law prescribed a tripartite approach to the administration of justice. At the first level were children under the age of seven who were deemed incapable of having criminal intent, or what is referred to today as mens rea, and were therefore exempt from all prosecution and punishment. On the second tier were persons between seven and 14 years of age who were presumed to lack the mental capacity to form criminal intent; however, the prosecution could attempt to prove otherwise. The third tier was comprised of persons 14–21 years of age for which the above scenario was reversed. That is, they were presumed to have the mental capacities to be fully culpable for the crimes committed; however, the defense could argue otherwise.

While these early distinctions applied to different levels of prosecution and punishment in an adult system of justice, the 19th and 20th centuries witnessed the evolution of a totally separate system of justice for juveniles. This newly evolving juvenile justice system was not merely distinct from its adult counterpart in regards to the age of offenders brought before it, but in its very structure and purpose. The adult system maintains a focus on procedural justice and promotes the primary purposes of retribution for acts committed, as well as incapacitation to prevent future law-violating behavior. The juvenile justice system, however, emerged during the Progressive Era and was premised on the underlying notion that juveniles, being not yet fully developed, were still malleable to outside influences. Thus, the purpose of the juvenile justice system was to provide for children in danger of growing up to be criminals the necessary influences to turn them into productive adults instead. With a focus on rehabilitation and care, the juvenile justice system then emerged as a civil, not criminal court, and its structure did not provide for the focus on procedural protections and adversarial justice prescriptive of the adult system.

In addition to these key distinctions in purpose and process, other differences of note include that, for the most part, juvenile court proceedings and records have been maintained as confidential to protect the child from stigmatization. Moreover, a juvenile adjudication of delinquency has not held the same weight as an adult conviction in any subsequent adult court processing (e.g., considerations of prior record) and has not produced the same collateral civil consequences as an adult conviction, such as restrictions on educational loans, employment and housing opportunities, and the right to vote or hold office. Juvenile adjudications have also historically been open to expungement, meaning the youths can start over as an adult with a truly clean slate. Finally, the juvenile system, existing as a separate entity from the adult system, maintains separate facilities for the treatment and care of juveniles, meaning that youths processed in this system are not in contact with older, more experienced offenders.

However, since the evolution of this separate system of justice for juveniles, there have always been exceptions to the rule and ways to prosecute some youths as adults. While the juvenile justice systems of today differ significantly from the original model, most still maintain a focus on rehabilitation, thus making them a distinct entity from the adult criminal court. The decision to prosecute a youth as an adult therefore entails much more than symbolic gesture, but rather encompasses the fundamental differences in sentencing philosophies represented by the two systems. Criminologist Donna Bishops suggests that the transfer to adult court embodies a core status transformation from "redeemable youth" to "unsalvageable adult."

The current debate surrounding the prosecution of juveniles as adults encompasses arguments concerning the appropriateness of various mechanisms of transfer (the means by which the juvenile reaches adult court); the actual population of youths captured by such mechanisms; and ultimately, the adult court outcomes of these youths.

Mechanisms of Transfer

The oldest and most popular mechanism by which a juvenile can reach adult court is known as a judicial waiver. This practice dates as far back as the turn of the 20th century in the first juvenile court in the United States in Chicago. In his court, Judge Tuthill created a culture in which older juveniles with lengthy prior juvenile records (in other words, "experienced delinquents") were sent to the adult court for prosecution. His rationale for such transfer was that these older, experienced juveniles were beyond the rehabilitative reach of the juvenile court and could only serve to further corrupt more innocent and younger juveniles within the auspices of the juvenile courts. The practice of judicial transfer thus evolved at the local level, taking on the flavor and culture of individual courts, and differed greatly across jurisdictions and states. It wasn't until 1966 when the case of Morris Kent was decided by the U.S. Supreme Court that this mechanism became formalized and standards for transfer set. *In Kent v. United States*, the Court set forth criteria that must be met before a youth can be denied the protection of the juvenile court. These criteria include the right of the juvenile to be represented by a defense attorney at a formal waiver hearing and the requirement that the judge consider a host of individual and legal factors at the hearing, including: seriousness of the offense, whether the offense was against a person, the prosecutorial merit of the case, the sophistication and maturity of the juvenile, the prospects for adequate protection of the public, and the likelihood of reasonable rehabilitation of the juvenile. The Court also required a written transcript of the reasons for transfer to be provided. Although this particular case was based on interpretation of the juvenile code of Washington, D.C., and therefore applied only directly to this jurisdiction, other states quickly came into compliance with these prescribed practices to avoid questions of constitutionality.

A waiver hearing such as this is typically referred to as a *discretionary waiver hearing*. Similar to English common law, the youth is presumed to lack responsibility for his or her actions, and it is up to the prosecutor to convince the juvenile court judge otherwise. Over time, several variations on the theme of judicial waiver have also evolved, known as a presumptive waiver and a mandatory waiver. A presumptive waiver is most closely related to that which was assumed for juveniles 14–21 years of age in English common law. The presumption is that the youth is responsible for his or her actions, but the defense attorney has the opportunity to argue otherwise before the juvenile court judge. A mandatory waiver hearing further limits the discretion of the juvenile court judge in that the only issue at hand is whether or not the juvenile meets legislatively prescribed age, prior record, and current offense criteria for mandatory transfer.

Statutory or Legislative Exclusion

In addition to judicial waiver, another mechanism by which juveniles reach adult court is known as *statutory exclusion* or *legislative exclusion*. These laws give original jurisdiction over certain youths to the criminal courts, rather than to the juvenile courts. That is, these youths go directly to criminal court, and do not pass through the juvenile court on their journey. Statutory exclusion laws can be based upon age, offense, prior record, or any combination of the above. While not directly referred to as legislative exclusion, not all states maintain 17 as the maximum age of juvenile court jurisdiction. For example, North Carolina and New York maintain a maximum age of 15, meaning all 16- and 17-year-olds are denied the protections of the more rehabilitative juvenile justice system. Similarly, 11 states set the maximum age at 16, meaning all 17-year-olds are subject to adult penalties for all offenses.

Another method of reducing juvenile court jurisdiction places unfettered discretionary power in the hands of the prosecutor. Rather than providing original jurisdiction over certain offenses to either the juvenile court or the criminal court, 15 states have passed laws that provide both the juvenile court and the adult criminal court with what is termed *concurrent jurisdiction* over certain offenses, which means that both courts have original jurisdiction over the same offenses at the same time. The prosecutor is free to decide whether to process the case in juvenile court or in criminal court. Since the prosecutor decides whether or not the juvenile is tried in adult court, this type of transfer is often termed *prosecutorial waiver* or *direct file*.

Most states maintain more than one method of transfer, with 46 states maintaining judicial waiver, all 50 states and the District of Columbia maintaining statutory exclusion, and 15 states utilizing concurrent jurisdiction procedures.

Who Reaches Adult Court?

In regards to sheer number of juveniles reaching adult court, although there are no exact national figures available, statisticians from the National Center for Juvenile Justice estimate that most youths who reach adult court do so through statutory exclusion provisions. The most recent estimates suggest that between 200,000 and 300,000 youths under the age of 18 reach adult court each year through this mechanism alone. Regarding judicial waiver, estimates show that the popularity of this mechanism increased from the mid 1980s through the 1990s, with a more recent decline in numbers. For example, in 1985, 7,200 juveniles nationally reached adult court via judicial waiver. This number increased to 13,200 in 1994, but then declined to 6,300 in 2001.

This decline has been interpreted several ways; however, the most prominent assumption appears to be that juveniles who would have typically been waived to adult court are now being captured by the new and expanded transfer mechanisms, therefore decreasing the need for judicial waiver. Prosecutorial discretion is the least-common method for transferring juveniles, as it is available in only 15 states; however, in those states, it generally accounts for a large majority of transfers. For example, both prosecutorial discretion and judicial waiver are available in Florida, but in 2000, 95 percent of transfers were accomplished by prosecutorial discretion, and only five percent by waiver (hence supporting the previous interpretation of the decline in waiver usage). Moreover, in 2001, when there were 6,300 judicial waivers nationwide, Florida alone transferred over 2,000 juveniles to criminal court by prosecutorial discretion.

In addition to sheer numbers of juveniles reaching adult court, the question has also been raised as to whether the "right" youths are being transferred and whether one of these mechanisms of transfer is superior to the others in capturing the intended population of older, violent juveniles. While there is no conclusive evidence on this topic, early studies of judicial waiver found that those youths most likely to be waived were older youths with extensive prior records, regardless of the seriousness of the current offense. That is, the juvenile court judges, similar to Judge Tuthill, were transferring to adult court those juveniles who had exhausted the rehabilitative efforts of the juvenile system. However, data compiled by the National Center for Juvenile Justice show that while property offenses dominated the judicial waiver caseload in the 1980s, by 1993, offenses against persons were more prominent, indicating a shift in waiver decision making to perhaps focus more on the gravity of the current offense.

In addition, a greater portion of younger offenders with less substantial prior records also appear to be reaching adult court. Although no formal studies have been conducted to date, it is thought that these youths reach adult court primarily through statutory exclusion provisions, which often focus only on the seriousness of the current offense rather than the extralegal considerations present at a waiver hearing, such as amenability to treatment and culpability for offenses committed, which may have previously benefited such young, inexperienced delinquents.

Transfer Biases

Perhaps the most salient criticism of all transfer mechanisms is that they are either intentionally or unintentionally biased against certain types of offenders. First, it is well known that most juveniles transferred to adult court are male. Studies have found that over 95 percent of all transferees are male. While at first glance it might be assumed that this discrepancy could be explained away by frequency and seriousness of offending, a study of six states by the U.S. General Accounting Office found that within each offense category, males were still considerably more likely than females to be waived to adult court. For example, in California, a male charged with a violent offense was 42 times more likely to be waived to adult court than a female charged with a violent offense.

Research addressing racial bias in transfer decisions paints a slightly more abstract picture. On the surface, it is clear that minority youths are disproportionately represented in the number of youths transferred. Jeffrey Butts reported that while African American youths made up about 20 percent of the juvenile population in 1994 and 36 percent of juvenile court referrals, they represented more than half of all transfers. National data such as these may also significantly underestimate the actual numbers of minority youths transferred, as Hispanic youths are normally coded as "white," thereby masking their numbers in transfer decisions. A study by Elizabeth McNulty in Arizona found that while 29 percent of the juvenile population was Hispanic, 44 percent of the youths transferred to adult court in this state were Hispanic. However, many have argued that these racial disparities do not represent bias, but rather could possibly be accounted for by other legal determinants.

M. A. Bortner, Margory Zatz, and Darnell Hawkins provide an exhaustive review of the literature in this area and conclude that while race may not have direct effects on waiver decisions, it has been found to interact with offense type, particularly in relation to young, African American males charged with drug or weapons violations. These youths bear the unfortunate stigma of outwardly fitting the stereotype of the violent gangbanger so successfully portrayed by national media. In addition to drug crimes, some studies have also indicated that youths of color fare worse in waiver decisions when charged with a violent offense. For example, researchers Jeffrey Fagan, Martin Forst, and T. Scott Vivona found that in a four-city study spanning Boston, Detroit, Newark, and Phoenix, minority youths charged with homicide were more likely to receive a transfer than white youths charged with the same offense.

In addition, emerging research suggests that the increase in transfers, particularly those achieved through statutory exclusion provisions, only serves to perpetuate this pattern. While on the surface, these transfer mechanisms may seem race-neutral and focusing on offense severity, given the previously noted interaction effect between race and offense classifications, some scholars predict that these mechanisms reflect institutionalized racism. Preliminary studies of legislative exclusion have found that upward of 98 percent of youths captured by these provisions are minorities.

What Happens to These Transferred Youths?

The results of processing youths in the criminal courts are found in the adult correctional system, where on the average day in 2004, adult correctional facilities held about 9,500 youths under the age of 18. About 7,000 of these youths were held in adult jails nationwide, and the remaining 2,500 were held in state prisons.

A growing literature is developing that examines actual sentence and later life outcomes of these youths. Some of these studies compare juveniles transferred to adult court to similar juveniles retained in the juvenile system. Much of this work suggests that in adult court, the historical legacy of juvenile leniency remains. For example, research by M. A. Bortner reported that almost two-thirds of juvenile offenders sentenced in adult court received sentences to probation rather than a more severe adult penalty. Also, research by Simon Singer, and more recently by Aaron Kupchik, suggests that juvenile status is unrelated to early case processing, but serves as an important mitigating factor in the determination of punishment in adult court. This has led some to conclude that the prosecution of juveniles in adult court is more likely to symbolize toughness than to actually deliver it.

However, several more recent studies have found that significantly harsher punishments are meted out to juveniles in adult court when compared to juveniles in juvenile court, particularly for serious or violent offenses. For instance, a recent examination of Pennsylvania youths reported that after controlling for a broad range of factors, comparable juveniles were significantly more likely to be incarcerated in the adult criminal justice system, compared to youths maintained in the juvenile justice system. In addition, research by criminologists Megan Kurlychek and Brian Johnson has found that juveniles processed in the adult system receive even more severe penalties than similarly situated adult offenders. Specifically, studies by these researchers in both Pennsylvania and Maryland have found that juvenile defendants in adult courts are more likely than their young adult counterparts (aged 18–21) to receive sentences of incarceration and to be incarcerated for significantly longer periods, even after matching defendants on relevant legal and extralegal factors such as prior record, offense seriousness, mode of conviction, gender, and race.

While the verdict is still out on why these youths may be receiving harsher sentences, arguments presented include the fact that the mere transfer from the juvenile system may in some way stigmatize the offender in the eyes of the adult court, and/or that the juvenile, due to reduced decision-making capabilities, does not fully understand the adult criminal justice process and is not capable of making adequate decisions regarding his or her legal representation and defense. Regarding the later point, research has found that most juveniles under the age of 15 fall short of the standardized competence measures deemed appropriate for legal decision making. Even more importantly, these studies find that juveniles under this age do not comprehend the meaning of their right to remain silent, nor do they possess appropriate decision-making capabilities to understand the plea bargaining process.

In addition, much research has suggested that once incarcerated in adult prisons, the lifelong outcomes of these young offenders are dismal. In sum, these studies have found that juveniles in adult prisons are more likely to by physically and sexually assaulted by staff and other inmates; are more likely to suffer depression and other mood disorders; and perhaps most importantly, are more likely than youths processed in the juvenile justice system to later recidivate.

Pro: Arguments in Support of Juveniles in Adult Court

"Do adult crime, do adult time" was the battle cry of the 1990s, and perhaps one of the most persuasive political agendas of all time. The primary assumption behind this slogan is that if the crime is the same, the punishment should be the same, regardless of the age of the offender. If a homicide is committed, a person has lost his or her life. Surely, the punishment should be the same regardless of whether the perpetrator was a juvenile or adult. This focus on the offense and its consequences are hallmarks of the adult criminal justice system as compared to the more individual and rehabilitative focus of the juvenile system. Thus, from this perspective, the proper policy response is to transfer the juvenile to adult court, where he or she can be subject to the punishment proportional to the offense committed.

This argument was mainly promoted for crimes of violence in which there was direct physical injury to a victim. Transfer of such serious juveniles to the adult system also provided for more victim involvement in case processing as compared to the more secretive juvenile system, which had historically kept offenders' names and outcomes confidential. Thus, many victim advocacy groups support the transfer of serious and violent juveniles to adult courts.

The transfer of serious juvenile offenders to adult court also enhances the sentencing options, particularly in regard to potential time incarcerated.

For example, most states' juvenile justice systems can maintain jurisdiction over an adjudicated delinquent until his or her 21st birthday. That means for a 17-year-old offender, the maximum time of confinement is four years. Proponents of transfer insist that for older, serious offenders, these time limits do not sufficiently allow for either proper punishment of the offender, or protection of the victim and community from the offender.

Another advantage to transferring the most serious and violent juveniles to the adult system is that it allows the juvenile system to focus on the younger, more malleable offenders for which it was originally designed. Similar to the practices set forth by Judge Tuthill in the country's first juvenile court, the idea is twofold. First, older, experienced juvenile offenders are beyond the rehabilitative responses available within a juvenile court setting, and therefore are most necessarily a waste of scarce resources that could have been better directed at a younger, less delinquent youth. Second, if maintained in the juvenile system, these older, more serious youths would only serve to further corrupt the younger, more naïve youth. Thus, not only would the older offender not be reformed, but he/she may in fact also prevent the salvation of a more deserving child.

Types of Offender and Transfer Mechanisms

Among proponents of transfer, however, there are still divides over the exact type of offender who should be transferred and the most appropriate transfer mechanism. Regarding type of offender, the debate centers on whether youths should be transferred based on the seriousness of the current offense, or whether this decision should be determined by prior record, signifying a pattern of behavior and perhaps previous attempts of the juvenile system to reform the youngster; and age, with age serving as a proxy for both time left for the juvenile system to intervene and maturity/culpability for offenses committed. The arguments surrounding transfer mechanisms are even more divisive. Proponents of statutory exclusion promote it as the least-biased mechanism, as it reduces judicial and prosecutorial discretion and excludes entire classes of juveniles based on clear-cut age, offense, and prior record patterns rather than individual, and necessarily subjective, considerations of culpability and malleability. Proponents of judicial waiver maintain that the original *Kent* hearings are the best transfer mechanism, as they allow the juvenile court judge to fully examine the specifics of the case to ensure that only appropriate youths are being transferred. Those favoring prosecutorial waiver, though less numerous, adamantly affirm that the prosecutor is the correct authority to make this decision in the best interests of the state. That is, the prosecutor is the state's primary representative, and promotes the key purposes of justice, including protection of the public.

Con: Arguments Against Juveniles in Adult Court

Arguments against juveniles in adult court encompass an even greater variety of issues. First, even those that favor the transfer of some youths to adult court object to one or another of the transfer methods. For example, judicial waiver, the oldest and most popular means of transfer, is under fire for placing too much discretion in the hands of the judicial authority, which can lead to bias. While the *Kent* decision did set forth criteria for consideration at waiver hearings, there are no standard scientific assessments to determine such abstract concepts as "culpability" and "amenability to treatment," which leads to great disparity across jurisdictions and even between judges within the same jurisdiction. Criminologist Barry Feld argues that judges' application of such ambiguous criteria lead to arbitrary, capricious, and discriminatory transfer decisions. Research by the U.S. General Accounting Office has documented disparities in the use of waiver criteria across states, and research by criminologist Donna Hamparian has gone as far as to suggest that the judicial waiver is truly "justice by geography," meaning that one's status as juvenile or adult is more dependent upon where he or she resides than the offense committed.

The criticisms, however, do not end with judicial waiver; prominent scholar Frank Zimring lambasts statutory exclusion provisions for being grossly overbroad and leading to "subterranean discretion" in the hands of the prosecutor, who traditionally enjoys the authority to select which charges to file. In addition, the constitutionality of both statutory exclusion and prosecutorial waiver have been brought into question, as they circumvent the due-process protections provided through a formal waiver hearing as set forth in *Kent.* However, to date, the constitutionality challenges to these provisions have been unsuccessful. While opponents argue that the need for such a hearing is compelling based on the importance of the decision for the affected individual, the courts to date have determined that both legislative statute and prosecutorial charging are executive functions, and that by necessity, the constitutional separation of powers precludes the judicial branch from reviewing or controlling such executive functions.

Inherent in these various arguments regarding the modes of transfer is the second argument that somehow, the wrong youths might be reaching adult court and, more importantly, that these transfer decisions are racially biased. As demonstrated by the research, there is formidable evidence that existing transfer policies unduly impact minority male defendants. However, it remains unclear as to what extent this bias exists at the individual level (judicial decision making) or is intertwined with legislative classifications of offense categories and prescribed punishments.

Modern Advances in Adolescent Research

Moreover, some go as far as to argue that no youths below the age of 18 should ever reach adult court, thus making any method of transfer, or any youth, inappropriate. This particularly stringent argument is based not only upon the historical precedent of providing leniency to youths, but modern advances in medical and psychological research. According to research, there are several key differences between the adult and adolescent brain that specifically diminish the adolescent's culpability for actions committed. The most notable difference is the underdevelopment of the frontal lobe during adolescence. Since this portion of the brain controls reason, reflective thought, and impulse control, scientists posit that adolescents simply cannot understand and monitor their own behavior in the same way that adults can. Moreover, with this portion of the brain not yet developed, research shows adolescent thought to be more controlled by emotion and impulse, both of which can lead to deviant behavior. This finding of modern medicine in fact supports the original proposition of the Progressives, which was that these youths are indeed still malleable and can be reformed into law-abiding adults. In addition, it suggests that youths truly may not be culpable for their actions in the same way as an adult, thus making them less blameworthy and deserving of the benefit of treatment theoretically offered in the juvenile justice system.

Adult Court Outcomes for Youth

The final, and perhaps most compelling, argument surrounds the adult court outcomes of these youths. This particular argument encompasses three distinct components, including: the juveniles' competency to stand trial as an adult, biases in adult court sentencing outcomes of such youths, and life-long outcomes for youths held in adult prisons.

Regarding the first component, there is an expanding body of literature that suggests juveniles simply do not possess the mental abilities to fully understand the complicated procedures of the criminal justice system, and are thus at risk of forfeiting important rights and/or not being able to present a viable defense. A recent study by Thomas Grisso and colleagues specifically compared the abilities of adolescents and adults on a variety of legally relevant variables deemed "relevant for determinations of competence to stand trial." This study found several key distinctions that would disadvantage youths in adult court, including adolescents' tendency to underestimate risk, to not fully grasp the long-term consequences of their decisions, and to be more likely to confess or agree to a plea that represented compliance with authority. The authors further note that many youths, particularly those under the age of 16, performed at levels consistent with the definition of "incompetent to stand trial."

The research regarding adult court sentencing and later life outcomes further feeds the arguments against transfer of any youth to adult court. Specifically, this argument asserts that despite the aforementioned medical and social scientific research documenting differences in juvenile and adult decision making, impulsivity, and competency to stand trial, youths processed as adults actually receive more severe sentences than other adults, even when controlling for a variety of offense and offender-related characteristics.

Critics further argue that these youths then spend the most formative years of their development in adult prisons learning how to be better criminals, instead of how to be better citizens. Moreover, research shows that juveniles in adult prisons are more likely than adults to be victimized, both physically and sexually. Research also indicates that youths processed in the adult system are more likely than youths processed in the rehabilitative juvenile justice system to commit crimes in the future. Such findings have implications not only for these particular youths, but also for the overall crime rate in society and general safety and well-being of all citizens.

Conclusion

The arguments regarding the transfer of juveniles to adult court are necessarily complex, as they encompass both the difference between adolescents and adults and the inherent differences between the juvenile and adult justice systems. Transfer of at least some youths to adult court has been a hallmark of the American juvenile justice system since its inception. As such, it is likely to continue in some form long into the future. While the get-tough politics of the 1980s and 1990s sought to expand transfer mechanisms and the number of youths transferred, it appears the current trend is to take a second and closer look at transfer policies and perhaps limit the number and type of youths being transferred. Advances in developmental research and clinical assessment of competency will no doubt play a key role in the evolution of transfer policies in the years to come.

See Also: 1. Age of Responsibility; 3. At-Risk Youth; 8. Juvenile Detention Facilities; 11. Juveniles in Adult Correctional Facilities; 12. Legal Representation; 15. Racial Disparities; 18. Sentencing Options; 19. Serious and Violent Juvenile Offenders.

Further Readings

Bishop, Donna M., Charles E. Frazier, Lonn Lanza-Kaduce, and Henry George White. *Juvenile Transfers to Criminal Court Study: Phase I Final Report.* Washington, DC: Office of Juvenile Justice and Delinquency Prevention, Office of Justice Programs, 1998.

Boyce, Allison. "Choosing the Forum: Prosecutorial Discretion and *Walker v. State.*" *Arkansas Law Review,* v.46 (1994).

Butts, Jeffrey A. *Delinquency Cases Waived to Criminal Court 1985–1994: Fact Sheet #52.* Washington, DC: Office of Juvenile Justice and Delinquency Prevention, Office of Justice Programs, 1997.

Clarke, Elizabeth E. "A Case for Reinventing Juvenile Transfer: The Record of Transfer of Juvenile Offenders to Criminal Court in Cook County, Illinois." *Juvenile and Family Court Journal,* v.47 (1996).

Dawson, Robert O. "An Empirical Study of Kent Style Juvenile Transfers to Criminal Court." *St. Mary's Law Journal,* v.2 (1992).

Fagan, Jeffrey, and Franklin E. Zimring. *The Changing Borders of Juvenile Justice: Transfer of Adolescents to the Criminal Court.* Chicago: University of Chicago Press, 2000.

Feld, Barry C. "Abolish the Juvenile Court: Youthfulness, Criminal Responsibility and Sentencing Policy." *Journal of Criminal Law and Criminology,* v.88 (1997).

Fritsch, Eric, and Craig Hemmens. "Juvenile Waiver in the United States 1979–1995: A Comparison and Analysis of State Waiver Statutes." *Juvenile and Family Court Judges Journal,* v.46 (1995).

Greenwood, Peter. "Differences in Criminal Behavior and Court Responses Among Juvenile and Young Adult Defendants." In *Crime and Justice,* edited by Michael Tonry and Norval Morris. Chicago: University of Chicago Press, 1986.

Greenwood, Peter, Allan Abrahams, and Franklin E. Zimring. *Factors Affecting Sentence Severity for Young Adult Offenders.* Santa Monica: RAND, 1984.

Griffin, Patric, Patricia Torbet, and Linda Szymanski. *Trying Juveniles in Adult Court: An Analysis of State Transfer Provisions.* Washington, DC: Office of Juvenile Justice and Delinquency Prevention, Office of Justice Programs, U.S. Department of Justice, 1998.

Grisso, Thomas, and Robert Schwartz. *Youth on Trial: A Developmental Perspective on Juvenile Justice.* Chicago: University of Chicago Press.

Guttman, Catherine R. "Listen to the Children: The Decision to Transfer Juveniles to Adult Court." *Harvard Civil Rights-Civil Liberties Law Review,* v.30 (1995).

Hamparian, Donna, Linda Estep, Susan Muntean, Ramon Priestino, Robert Swisher, Paul Wallace, and Joseph White. *Youth in Adult Courts: Between Two Worlds.* Washington, DC: Office of Juvenile Justice and Delinquency Prevention, Office of Justice Programs, 1982.

Klein, Eric K. "Dennis the Menace or Billy the Kid: An Analysis of the Role of Transfer to Criminal Court in Juvenile Justice." *American Criminal Law Review,* v.35 (1998).

Kruh, Ivan, and Thomas Grisso. *Evaluation of Juveniles' Competence to Stand Trial.* New York: Oxford University Press, 2008.

Kupchik, Aaron. "The Correctional Experiences of Youth in Adult and Juvenile Prisons." *Justice Quarterly,* v.2/2 (2007).

Kupchik, Aaron. *Judging Juveniles: Prosecuting Adolescents in Adult and Juvenile Courts.* New York: New York University Press, 2006.

McCarthy, Frances Barry. "The Serious Offender and Juvenile Court Reform: The Case for Prosecutorial Waiver of Juvenile Court Jurisdiction." *St. Louis University Law Journal,* v.389 (1994).

Platt, Anthony M., and Bernard L. Diamond. "The Origins of the Right and Wrong Test of Criminal Responsibility and Its Subsequent Development in the United States: An Historical Survey." *California Law Review,* v.54 (1966).

Podkopacz, Marcy Rasmussen, and Barry C. Feld. "Judicial Waiver Policy and Practice: Persistence, Seriousness and Race." *Law and Inequality Journal,* v.14 (1995).

Poulos, Tammy Meredith, and Stan Orchowsky. "Serious Juvenile Offenders: Predicting the Probability of Transfer to Criminal Court." *Crime and Delinquency,* v.40 (1994).

Redding, R. "Juveniles Transferred to Criminal Court: Legal Reform Proposals Based on Social Science Research." *Utah Law Review,* v.3 (1997).

Sabo, Stacey. "Rights of Passage: An Analysis of Waiver of Juvenile Court Jurisdiction." *Fordham Law Review,* v.64 (1996).

Sanborn, Joseph B., Jr. "Policies Regarding the Prosecution of Juvenile Murderers: Which System and Who Should Decide?" *Law and Policy,* v.18 (1996).

Scott, Elizabeth S., and Thomas Grisso. "The Evolution of Adolescence: A Developmental Perspective on Juvenile Justice Reform." *Journal of Criminal Law and Criminology,* v.88 (1997).

Singer, Simon I. *Recriminalizing Delinquency: Violent Juvenile Crime and Juvenile Justice Reform.* New York: Cambridge University Press, 1996.

Snyder, Howard N., Melissa Sickmund, and Eileen Poe-Yamagata. *Juvenile Offenders and Victims: 2006 National Report.* Washington, DC: Office of Juvenile Justice and Delinquency Prevention, 2006.

Steinberg, Lawrence, and Elizabeth Cauffman. "Maturity of Judgment in Adolescence: Psychosocial Factors in Adolescent Decision-Making." *Law and Human Behavior,* v.20 1996.

Szymanski, Linda. *State Variation in Age Restrictions for Trying Juveniles in Criminal Court: NCJJ Snapshot.* Pittsburgh, PA: National Center for Juvenile Justice, 1997.

Torbet, Patricia, and Linda Szymanski. *State Legislative Responses to Violent Juvenile Crime.* Washington, DC: Office of Juvenile Justice and Delinquency Prevention, Office of Justice Programs, 1996.

Tuthill, Richard. *Report of the Cook County Juvenile Court.* Chicago: Cook County Juvenile Court, 1907.

United States General Accounting Office. *Juveniles Processed in Criminal Court and Case Dispositions.* Washington, DC: General Accounting Office, 1995.

Winner, Lawrence, Lonn Lanza-Kaduce, Donna M. Bishop, and Charles E. Grazier. "The Transfer of Juveniles to Criminal Court: Reexamining Recidivism Over the Long Term." *Crime and Delinquency,* v.43 1997.

Zimring, Franklin E. "The Treatment of Hard Cases in American Juvenile Justice: In Defense of Discretionary Waiver." *Notre Dame Journal of Law, Ethics and Public Policy,* v.5 (1991).

11

Juveniles in Adult Correctional Facilities

Margaret E. Leigey
College of New Jersey

Jessica P. Hodge
University of Missouri, Kansas City

Christina A. Saum
Rowan University

Juveniles in the United States are subject to incarceration in adult jails and prisons because they have been tried and sentenced in adult criminal court, or they are awaiting trial or sentencing. Over the past several decades, there has been an increase in the number of juveniles incarcerated in adult facilities, but the population remains small. Supporters of juvenile waiver (the process in which a juvenile's case is transferred to adult criminal court) and the incarceration of waived juveniles in adult institutions, maintain that the adult criminal justice system is better suited to handle serious juvenile offenders than the juvenile justice system. Alternatively, opponents of juvenile waiver and the co-incarceration of juveniles and adults argue that the adult system is not designed to handle these young offenders, and the issues associated with incarcerating adults and juveniles together outweigh any benefits.

Historically, juvenile detainees and those adjudicated delinquent were held in the same cells or holding areas as adults. Individuals were not separated based on the sex or age of the offender, provided that children were above the age of seven and could be held legally responsible for their actions. The practice of housing all offenders together was abandoned when a separate justice system for juvenile offenders emerged. The establishment of a separate system was intended to protect juvenile offenders from the negative influences of adult offenders, and to avoid the victimization that juveniles experienced when they were permitted to interact with adult offenders.

Methods for Transferring to the Adult System

There are several situations in which a minor, a person below the age of 18, can be tried in an adult court and receive a sentence of confinement in an adult facility. Juvenile justice systems in the United States define the maximum age of a juvenile differently. In most states, the juvenile court can hear cases involving individuals up to the age of 17; however, in about 15 states, the maximum age is 15 or 16. In other words, in a state with a maximum age of 16, a 17-year-old would have his or her case automatically heard in the adult criminal court, and could be sentenced to an adult jail or prison. Even children who qualify as juveniles due to their ages can have their cases heard in the adult courts. The process by which a juvenile's case is transferred to the adult system is also referred to as *waiver, remand, certification,* or *bind-over.*

There are three types of waivers that are utilized to transfer juvenile cases into the adult criminal court: a judicial waiver; a prosecutorial waiver, also known as *direct file*; or a legislative waiver, also referred to as *statutory exclusion.* With a judicial waiver and prosecutorial waiver, a juvenile court judge and prosecutor respectively determine whether the case should be heard in a juvenile or adult court. However, a legislative waiver occurs when legislation mandates that a juvenile's case, because of age and/or the nature of offense, be automatically heard in adult court. For example, if a juvenile commits a gang-related or violent offense, then his or her case would proceed directly through the adult system. In addition, several other scenarios allow for the possibility of juveniles to be treated as adults by the courts. First, as part of a blended sentence, a judge can impose a combination of juvenile and adult penalties; for example, when the offender reaches a certain age, he or she may be transferred to an adult facility to complete the remainder of the sentence. Second, under "once an adult, always an adult" legislation, juvenile offenders who have previously been adjudicated in the adult criminal court could be ineligible to have future cases heard in juvenile court. Third, legally emancipated juveniles would also have their criminal cases heard in the adult arena.

In the late 1980s and early 1990s, the rates of juvenile offending, and in particularly violent offending, increased in the United States. As a result, the juvenile justice system was criticized as ineffective in preventing juvenile crime. The different types of waiver mechanisms that were implemented and expanded upon during this time reflected the lack of confidence in the juvenile justice system and the more punitive attitude toward punishing offenders—juveniles or adults—in recent decades. While the rates of juvenile offending have declined since the mid-1990s, the "get tough" legislation remains in place in most jurisdictions.

The Supreme Court: How Harsh of a Sentence?

If their cases are transferred into the adult system, juveniles can receive the same types of criminal sanctions as adult offenders, including confinement in a jail or prison. Currently, the only sentence juveniles cannot receive in the adult court, as decided in the case of *Roper v. Simmons* (2005), is the death penalty. However, in the fall 2009 term, the U.S. Supreme Court heard oral arguments in the case of *Graham v. Florida* and a companion case, *Sullivan v. Florida,* to determine the constitutionality of life without the possibility of parole for juveniles convicted in adult criminal court of nonhomicide offenses. While both defendants have since reached the age of adulthood, they committed their offenses when they were below the age of 18. Sullivan was convicted of a sexual offense that occurred when he was 13 years of age, while Graham was convicted of an armed robbery that took place when he was 16 years of age. Under Florida law, they were tried in adult court and received sentences of life without parole. The specific question the Court was to answer was whether it was a violation of the Cruel and Unusual Punishment Clause of the Eighth Amendment for juvenile offenders convicted of crimes other than homicide to receive sentences of life without the possibility of parole. While juveniles convicted in adult court cannot receive death sentences, they are eligible to receive lengthy prison sentences, such as life with the possibility of parole.

The Supreme Court weighed in on the *Graham* case in May 2010 with their decision that juveniles who commit crimes in which no death occurred may not be sentenced to life in prison without the possibility of parole. In a 6–3 decision, five justices agreed that as a categorical matter, the Eighth Amendment's ban on cruel and unusual punishment forbids such sentences; The sixth vote, Chief Justice John G. Roberts Jr., noted that while the harshness of the defendant's sentence violated the Constitution, he endorsed only a case-by-case approach, saying that an offender's age could be considered in deciding life sentences.

The ruling was the first time the Court excluded an entire class of offenders from a particular punishment outside the context of the death penalty. As Justice Clarence Thomas wrote in dissent, "'Death is different' no longer."

A Glimpse at Daily Life

An offender's daily existence in a facility, whether juvenile or adult, is designed to be regimented. There is loss of freedom, privacy, and personal decision making. In addition, there are limited opportunities to see family or friends while offenders serve their sentences, or *dispositions* (the term used in the juvenile justice system). Confined juvenile and adult offenders must abide by the rules of the institution or else receive penalties such as loss of visitation or recreation privileges, and additional time added to the length of confinement. However, important differences exist between juvenile and adult facilities. Adult facilities are typically larger and more formidable in appearance than youth facilities. There is usually a larger inmate population in an adult jail or prison, and adult institutions are also more likely to have distant or hostile relationships between staff and inmates than in juvenile facilities. Conversely, staff members in juvenile halls are often referred to as counselors, reflecting the different orientations of juvenile and adult systems. Moreover, rather than the title of warden, the head administrator of a juvenile facility is referred to as a superintendent, and the juveniles are often called students. While the adult system emphasizes punishment, the juvenile justice system was founded on the principle that offending youths can be reformed or rehabilitated. Consequently, there are more opportunities for juveniles in the juvenile corrections system to participate in treatment programs, ranging from education to therapy, than what is available to them in adult facilities.

One provision of the Juvenile Justice Delinquency and Prevention Act (JJDPA) of 1974 mandates that juveniles whose cases are adjudicated in the juvenile justice system must be separated, in sight and sound, from adult offenders. For example, if a juvenile offender must be held in the same facility as an adult offender, he or she must be kept out of sight and earshot of the adult offender. This precaution is designed to prevent juvenile offenders from being victimized by adult offenders. However, this protective measure is not universally applied to juveniles whose cases are being handled in adult criminal court. Rather, in the United States, the federal and various state systems utilize a variety of institutional assignments for convicted juvenile offenders. Consistent with the JJDPA, some jurisdictions require that juveniles convicted in adult court serve their time in juvenile facilities. After reaching a specified age, for example 18 or 21, they could later be transferred to an adult jail or prison to serve the remainder of their sentences. Other jurisdictions choose to incarcerate juveniles in adult facilities. Some jurisdictions segregate the juvenile population in separate housing units; however, the possibility exists that juveniles could still interact with adult offenders in other locations, such as when receiving medical treatment.

Other jurisdictions make little distinction between juvenile and adult offenders and house juvenile offenders in the general population with adult offenders. Within this option, juveniles could have adult cellmates. They could also interact with adult offenders in other situations, including educational and vocational classes; counseling; recreational activities, such as sports; and at meal times.

A Profile of Juveniles in Adult Correctional Facilities

While there has been relatively little research conducted on juveniles who are serving time in adult facilities, especially females, one important exception was research conducted by Kevin Strom, a statistician at the Bureau of Justice Statistics. He analyzed data examining juveniles who were incarcerated in state prisons between 1985 and 1997.

Published in 2000, his report yielded several important findings about juveniles who were serving time in adult prisons. First, he noted that the population of juveniles who had been sentenced to serve time in adult state prisons had more than doubled within the time period of study. Despite the increase, however, the number of juveniles in adult prisons was about two percent in 1997, a small portion of the overall state prison population in the United States. More specifically, in 1997, there were 7,400 juveniles admitted to state prison and 9,100 juveniles in jails. Second, Strom found that the demography of the minor population was predominantly male, 16 or 17 years of age, and had educational deficiencies as they were below the appropriate level of education given their ages. A disproportionate number were also minority youths. Third, in a majority of cases, the most serious offense for which the juvenile was convicted was a violent offense (61 percent), followed by a property offense (21 percent), a drug offense (11 percent), and a public-order offense (five percent). In addition, Strom uncovered several trends in the prison sentences of juveniles. From 1985 to 1997, the likelihood of receiving a prison sentence increased. To put it another way, the likelihood of a juvenile defendant in this time period receiving a sentence of confinement, instead of a community-based sanction such as probation, increased. Strom also found that although the length of time served in the prison had increased, the length of the prison sentence had decreased over the time period. In other words, juveniles were sentenced to shorter prison terms, but they were serving longer portions of them.

Pro: Support for Juvenile Transfer to Adult Facilities

Advocates of juvenile transfer to adult court and juvenile incarceration in adult facilities rely on several arguments to support their position. They maintain that the juveniles whose cases are tried in adult court are serious offenders, and that the juvenile justice system is unable to properly handle their cases. They contend that the juvenile justice system is ineffective because of its perceived leniency, giving the perception that it coddles juvenile offenders; its greater emphasis on rehabilitation; and the limitations associated with the jurisdiction of the juvenile court, such as length of confinement. For example, many juvenile correction systems only have the power to confine juveniles until the age of 21. If a 17-year-old offender commits a robbery and his case is retained in the juvenile court, in most cases, the maximum time he can be confined is four years.

Supporters argue that juvenile offenders, regardless of their young ages, are a danger to society and cite the elements of specific cases, such as premeditation or brutality, to justify their stance. Due to the perceived insufficiencies of the juvenile system, advocates argue that the adult system is better suited to incapacitate juvenile offenders by imposing harsher sentences, including life sentences, than the juvenile justice system. Moreover, another argument for juvenile waiver and incarceration in jails or prisons is that juveniles who commit serious offenses should receive serious punishments. The adage "do an adult crime, do adult time" is a concise summary of this argument. According to this rationale, juveniles are capable of discerning right from wrong. They made the decision to offend and, as a result, need to be punished for their misbehavior. The punishments available in the adult system are considered more congruent with the harm the offense caused than the penalties available in the juvenile justice system.

A Deterrent Effect

Advocates maintain that juvenile offenders would be less inclined to commit future offenses if they received a more serious punishment. From this perspective, penalties in the juvenile justice system are not harsh enough to prevent either an offender from engaging in crime in the future or preventing other juveniles from offending. It is precisely because the adult system has more severe punishments available that it is believed the experience will have a longer-lasting effect. For example, after serving time in an adult jail or prison, the released offender will remember the negative aspects of punishment, including interaction with adult offenders and the monotony and limitations of prison life, and will decide not to offend in the future. In addition, advocates maintain that other juveniles would be less likely to commit an offense because of the possibility of having their cases tried in adult court and the threat of receiving adult penalties.

While the interaction between juveniles and adult inmates could be negative, and is considered to be one of the major issues associated with the incarceration of juvenile offenders in adult facilities, supporters point to the positive effects the interaction of the two groups could have on youths. For example, adult inmates could serve as mentors to the juvenile offenders, assist them as they adjust to confined life, and advise them to avoid the pitfalls they have encountered in their own lives.

To counter other issues associated with confining juveniles with adults, such as the increased risk of victimization and suicide with adult facilities, proponents argue that juveniles are responsible not only for the decision to offend, but for placing themselves in the situation in which victimization or mental health issues could occur. Advocates maintain that juveniles should have considered the consequences of offending and should be held accountable for their actions.

To support the arguments of juvenile waiver and incarceration in adult institutions, advocates cite two pieces of evidence: the higher rates of misconduct in prisons, and the higher recidivism, or reoffending, rates of juveniles released from adult institutions. First, juveniles in adult facilities are much more likely to be written up for failing to abide by institutional rules as compared to juveniles confined in juvenile facilities. Advocates use this finding to support the argument that waived juvenile offenders are a danger, that the public needs to be protected from them, and that the juvenile facilities are not equipped to handle this group of offenders.

Two methods have been used to examine the reoffending of juveniles waived into and subsequently released from the adult system. One method involves comparing the future criminality of a group of juveniles who were processed through the juvenile justice system to that of a group of juveniles who were transferred to adult court. To ensure a proper comparison, the two groups are generally matched on important indicators, including severity of the offense, prior record, and demographic characteristics such as age, gender, and race/ethnicity. The other method compares the reoffending rates of juveniles in two similar jurisdictions, one in which they were retained in the juvenile justice system, to a jurisdiction in which they were transferred to adult court.

Despite the method used or how recidivism is defined—for example, re-arrest, reconviction, or reincarceration—the increased recidivism rates of juveniles who have been incarcerated in adult facilities, as opposed to juveniles who committed similar offenses but were tried in the juvenile justice system, is well-documented. Advocates of the incarceration of juveniles in the adult system use this finding as strong evidence of the necessity of juvenile waiver and incarceration in adult facilities. Waived juvenile offenders were viewed as being less amenable to treatment or were identified as having the potential for being a future danger to society. For one or both of these reasons, they were transferred to the adult system in the first place. As such, their continued offending supports the decision to have them treated as adults. It also highlights the desire to distinguish between children who are thought to be capable of rehabilitation within the juvenile justice system, and to protect these children from juveniles who are viewed as being incapable of reform.

Con: Opposition to Juvenile Transfer to Adult Facilities

Opponents of juvenile waiver and the incarceration of juvenile offenders in adult facilities also rely on a variety of arguments for their position. The disproportionate representation of minority youth in adult facilities is a source of concern with regard to the fairness of the waiver process and to the sentencing decisions at adult levels. For instance, there have been allegations that prosecutors have reduced the charges against white juveniles, consequently making these juveniles ineligible for transfer, but not for minority juveniles who were accused of the same offenses or have similar criminal histories. While racial bias has been documented in case outcomes in the juvenile court, the existence of harsher sentences at the adult level is especially problematic to opponents.

A fundamental argument advanced by those who do not support juvenile waiver, and as a result, the incarceration of juvenile offenders in adult facilities, is that juveniles lack the capacity to fully appreciate the consequences of their actions or to make well-reasoned decisions. They cite adolescent brain research as evidence that the juvenile brain has not fully developed. As a result, they maintain that juveniles should not be treated as adults.

Well-Being and Victimization

The danger to the physical and mental well-being of juveniles if they are housed with adult offenders or in adult institutions is another cause of concern. Because of their smaller physical statures and inexperience with serving time in adult facilities, juvenile offenders are at an increased risk of victimization. They may be unable to defend themselves from adult men or women in physical confrontations or to ward off sexual assaults. Youths could also be more susceptible to manipulation by older offenders, such as being sexually exploited or engaging in rule violations in the prison, such as selling drugs. Research confirms that juveniles in adult facilities are more likely to be physically victimized, such as punched or pushed; sexually victimized, including forced or unwanted sexual contact; and economically victimized, including the theft or destruction of personal property, as compared to juveniles confined in juvenile facilities. The severity of the incidents is also greater in the adult system, as violent encounters are more likely to involve weapons. While the sexual victimization of juveniles occurs in prison, it is more likely to occur in jails. Opponents of juvenile waiver point out that those juvenile offenders who are subjected to sexual and other types of victimization in jails may not have been convicted yet. For instance, they could have been denied bail and are awaiting trial, and consequently, innocent juveniles may be subjected to victimization within adult jails.

The consequences of victimization while incarcerated are numerous, and include loss of status, loss of property, injury, and disease. Victimization could make juvenile offenders fearful, depressed, ashamed, or angry, all of which could increase the difficulty of serving a prison sentence or negatively impact the likelihood of being socially productive in the future. For instance, a juvenile offender who is physically assaulted in the institution may use violence in the future in order to prevent victimization. While protective custody units are designed for offenders who are unable to safely live in the general population, these offenders face restrictions in movement within the facility, which limits the opportunity to participate in educational and recreational programs. Another result of victimization is that juvenile offenders may feel compelled to join prison gangs as a means of obtaining protection. Gang affiliation has the potential to lead juvenile offenders farther away from a law-abiding future. Opponents also point out that victimization can occur not only from other inmates, but also from correctional staff, and cite specific cases of misconduct to bolster their position. The sexual exploitation and victimization of female juveniles by correctional staff is also of concern.

The risk of suicide is also higher for juveniles who are serving time in adult facilities as compared to the suicide rate in juvenile facilities. In fact, statistics demonstrate that the rate of suicide is also higher for juveniles confined in adult facilities than for adult inmates. As with sexual victimization, the risk of suicide is especially pronounced in jails. One explanation advanced by opponents to explain the greater likelihood of suicide is the additional stress, fear, and anxiety that juvenile offenders experience when imprisoned with adults.

Lack of Programs and Mismatch of Supervision

Due to the overcrowded nature of American prisons and jails, opponents are also concerned that juveniles have limited access to programs. If they are able to participate, opponents further contend that adult institutions, or the programming and services available in them, were not designed with juveniles in mind. While some jurisdictions have more programming and services designed to meet the needs of the juvenile offender population, others do not, and juvenile offenders have the same programming options as adults. Opponents reiterate that juveniles have different biological and psychological needs than adults and would consequently benefit from programming and services specifically designed for them. The limited relevant programming available to them is one explanation for the low participation and completion rates of juvenile offenders in adult facilities. In addition, juveniles may feel intimidated because of potential interactions with adult offenders. In sum, opponents maintain that juveniles should remain in institutions designed for them and with programming to meet their needs.

Those who do not support the incarceration of juveniles in adult institutions also object to the limited training that correctional staff members receive in interacting with young offenders. Correctional officers may have little experience in conflict resolution with juveniles, and consequently, may be unfamiliar with effective techniques. Previous research indicates that correctional officers report an unfavorable opinion of juveniles incarcerated in adult facilities and describe them as being difficult to supervise. The lack of training and the unfavorable attitudes toward juveniles are further reasons, according to opponents, to maintain the boundaries between the punishment of juvenile and adult offenders.

Recidivism Rates

While supporters of juvenile waiver and the incarceration of juvenile offenders in adult prisons use the increased recidivism rates of released offenders as evidence of the importance of strictly punishing juveniles, opponents interpret this finding as evidence of the inefficacy of transferring juveniles into the adult system and incarcerating juvenile offenders in adult institutions. They allege that punishment in the adult system causes a juvenile offender's behavior and judgment to worsen, not improve. For example, adult offenders could teach juvenile offenders new methods of engaging in crime or how to escape detection. They could also impart rationalizations for continued criminal involvement, sometimes referred to as *criminal thinking errors*. Furthermore, juveniles in adult facilities may act out because of the perception that their waivers and subsequent incarcerations in adult institutions were unfair or undeserved.

Labeling theory offers another perspective to consider when examining the increased recidivism of juveniles released from adult facilities. According to this theory, juveniles may be inclined to reoffend because of the negative consequences of waiver to the adult legal system and incarceration in adult facilities. The consequences of a felony conviction within the adult system are much more serious than in the juvenile justice system. As with adult offenders, juveniles who have been convicted of a felony in adult court are subject to the loss of the right to vote, serve in the military, own a firearm, sit on a jury, and hold public office.

In addition, a felony conviction disqualifies offenders from receiving some types of federal financial aid for education, and depending on the jurisdiction and offense, could also disqualify offenders from obtaining public housing or public assistance. As a felony conviction is a matter of public record, and its disclosure is legally mandated on future employment applications, released offenders could struggle with the ability to obtain legitimate employment. There are additional legal ramifications as well. A conviction in adult criminal court could permanently bar a juvenile from any future involvement in the juvenile justice system, and the conviction could be considered in habitual-offender statutes, such as three-strikes laws. As a result of these negative social and legal consequences, labeling theory would predict the offending rates for juveniles released from adult facilities to be higher than those of juveniles returning to society from juvenile facilities.

Length of Time Served

Finally, opponents argue that the length of time juvenile offenders serve in prison renders incarceration in the adult system unnecessary. One of the primary reasons for the waiver of a juvenile's case into the adult system is that the adult system has longer sentences available than in the juvenile system. While juveniles often are sentenced to longer periods than available in the juvenile justice system, the actual time an offender serves in prison is usually shorter than the original sentence. The average length of time juvenile offenders serve in jail or prison is of a short enough duration that juveniles could remain under the jurisdiction of the juvenile court. For example, a 16-year-old juvenile could receive a sentence of 10 years in the adult system. However, he could be released on parole after serving only three years, at the age of 19. Since many juvenile justice systems retain authority over confined offenders until the age of 21, the entire length of confinement could have been served in a juvenile institution.

In sum, opponents of juvenile waiver and the coincarceration of juvenile and adult offenders argue that the adult system is too dangerous and leads to increased offending. Moreover, because the juvenile justice system was designed with juveniles' unique treatment and rehabilitation needs in mind, this system remains the most appropriate setting to handle juvenile offenders.

See Also: 1. Age of Responsibility; 6. Death Penalty for Juvenile Offenders; 8. Juvenile Detention Facilities; 10. Juvenile Offenders in Adult Courts; 12. Legal Representation; 15. Racial Disparities; 18. Sentencing Options; 19. Serious and Violent Juvenile Offenders.

Further Readings

Allard, Patricia, and Malcolm Young. *Prosecuting Juveniles in Adult Court: Perspectives for Policymakers and Practitioners*. Washington, DC: The Sentencing Project, 2002.

Austin, James, Kelly Dedel Johnson, and Marie Gregoriou. *Juveniles in Adult Prisons and Jails: A National Assessment*. Washington, DC: U.S. Department of Justice, Bureau of Justice Assistance, 2000.

Bishop, Donna, and Charles Frazier. "Consequences of Transfer." In *The Changing Borders of Juvenile Justice: Transfer of Adolescents to the Criminal Court*, edited by Jeffrey Fagan and Franklin E. Zimring. Chicago: University of Chicago Press, 2000.

Centers for Disease Control and Prevention. *Effects on Violence of Laws and Policies Facilitating the Transfer of Youth From the Juvenile to the Adult Justice System*. Atlanta, GA: CDC, 2007.

Fanning, Thomas R., Donald C. Jaskulske, and Tammy L. Zimmel. "Institutional Adjustment for Youthful Offenders in Adult Facilities." In *Journal of Correctional Best Practices: Juveniles in Adult Correctional Systems*, edited by Barry Glick and Edward E. Rhine. Lanham, MD: American Correctional Association, 2001.

Fritsch, Eric J., Tory J. Caeti, and Craig Hemmens. "Spare the Needle but Not the Punishment: The Incarceration of Waived Youth in Texas Prisons." *Crime and Delinquency*, v.42/4 (1996).

Gaarder, Emily, and Joanne Belknap. "Little Women: Girls in Adult Prison." *Women and Criminal Justice*, v.15/2 (2004).

General Accounting Office. *Juvenile Justice: Juveniles Processed in Criminal Courts and Case Dispositions*. Washington, DC: General Accounting Office, 1995.

Glick, Barry, and William Sturgeon. *No Time to Play: Youthful Offenders in Adult Correctional Systems*. Lanham, MD: American Correctional Association, 1998.

Glick, Barry, and William Sturgeon. *Recess Is Over: A Handbook for Managing Youthful Offenders in Adult Systems*. Lanham, MD: American Correctional Association, 2001.

Griffin, Patrick, Patricia Torbet, and Linda Szymanski. *Trying Juveniles as Adults in Criminal Court: An Analysis of State Transfer Provisions*. Washington, DC: Office of Juvenile Justice and Delinquency Prevention, 1998.

Hartney, Christopher. *Youth Under Age 18 in the Adult Criminal Justice System*. Oakland, CA: National Council on Crime and Delinquency, 2006.

Hartney, Christopher, and Fabiana Silva. *And Justice for Some*. Oakland, CA: National Council on Crime and Delinquency, 2007.

Human Rights Watch and Amnesty International. *The Rest of Their Lives: Life Without Parole for Child Offenders in the United States*. New York: Human Rights Watch, 2005.

Kuanliang, Attapol, Jon R. Sorensen, and Mark D. Cunningham. "Juvenile Inmates in an Adult Prison System: Rates of Disciplinary Misconduct and Violence." *Criminal Justice and Behavior*, v.35/9 (2008).

Kupchik, Aaron. *Judging Juveniles: Prosecuting Adolescents in Adult and Juvenile Courts*. New York: New York University Press, 2006.

Lane, Jodi, Lonn Lanza-Kaduce, Charles E. Frazier, and Donna M. Bishop. "Adult Versus Juvenile Sanctions: Voices of Incarcerated Youth." *Crime and Delinquency*, v.48/3 (2002).

Lanza-Kaduce, Lonn, Donna M. Bishop, Charles E. Frazier, and Lawrence Winner. "Changes in Juvenile Waiver and Transfer Provisions: Projecting the Impact in Florida." *Law and Policy*, v.18/1–2 (1996).

Leigey, Margaret E., Jessica P. Hodge, and Christine A. Saum. "Kids in the Big House: Juveniles Incarcerated in Adult Facilities." In *Juvenile Corrections*, edited by Rick Ruddell and Matthew O. Thomas. Richmond, KY: Newgate Press, 2009.

Liptak, Adam. "Justices Limit Life Sentences for Juveniles." *New York Times* (May 17, 2010) (Accessed October 2010).

McShane, Marilyn D., and Frank P. Williams III. "The Prison Adjustment of Juvenile Offenders." *Crime and Delinquency*, v.35/2 (1989).

Memory, John M. "Juvenile Suicides in Secure Detention Facilities: Correction of Published Rates." *Death Studies*, v.13 (1989).

Mlyniec, Wallace J. "The Hidden Evil of Children Living in Jail." *Children's Legal Rights Journal*, v.21/1 (2001).

Myers, David L. "The Recidivism of Violent Youths in Juvenile and Adult Courts: A Consideration of Selection Bias." *Youth Violence and Juvenile Justice*, v.1/1 (2003).

Orenstein, Bruce W., and Robert B. Levinson. "Juveniles Waived Into Adult Institutions." *Corrections Today*, v.58/4 (1996).

Podkopacz, Marcy R., and Barry C. Feld. "The End of the Line: An Empirical Study of the Judicial Waiver." *Journal of Criminal Law and Criminology*, v.86 (1996).

Redding, Richard E. "Juvenile Offenders in Criminal Court and Adult Prison: Legal, Psychological, and Behavioral Outcomes." *Juvenile and Family Court Journal*, v.50/1 (1999).

Reddington, Francis P., and Allen D. Sapp. "Juveniles in Adult Prisons: Problems and Prospects." *Journal of Crime and Justice,* v.20/2 (1997).

Steiner, Benjamin, and Emily Wright. "Assessing the Relative Effects of State Direct File Waiver Laws on Violent Juvenile Crime: Deterrence or Irrelevance?" *The Journal of Criminal Law and Criminology,* v.96/4 (2006).

Strom, Kevin J. *Profile of State Prisoners Under Age 18, 1985–97.* Washington, DC: U.S. Department of Justice, Bureau of Justice Statistics, 2000.

Winner, Lawrence, Lonn Lanza-Kaduce, Donna M. Bishop, and Charles E. Frazier. "The Transfer of Juveniles to Criminal Court: Reexamining Recidivism Over the Long Term." *Crime and Delinquency,* v.43/4 (1997).

Wolfson, Jill. *Childhood on Trial: The Failure of Trying and Sentencing Youth in Adult Criminal Court.* Washington, DC: Coalition for Juvenile Justice, 2005.

Woolard, Jennifer L., Candice Odgers, Lonn Lanza-Kaduce, and Hayley Daglis. "Juveniles Within Adult Correctional Settings: Legal Pathways and Developmental Considerations." *International Journal of Forensic Mental Health* v.14/1 (2005).

12

Legal Representation

Patricia E. Campie
Linda Szymanski
National Center for Juvenile Justice

The juvenile justice system does not have a long history requiring the provision of legal counsel, as compared to the requirements long in place for adult defendants in the criminal justice system. Spurred mostly by the Supreme Court's near-unanimous (8–1) opinion in the seminal case of *In re Gault* in 1967, juvenile courts around the United States began the slow process of ensuring that juveniles were properly represented by legal counsel when facing charges of criminal conduct in the juvenile court. Throughout the 1970s, legal representation advocacy groups for youths emerged across the country, and by the end of that decade, the American Bar Association (ABA) had released the first comprehensive guide and standards for the representation of juvenile defendants, among other due process protections afforded by the *Gault* decision. More than 40 years after *Gault*, many states and local jurisdictions still do not have adequate legal representation practices in place, most notably for indigent juvenile defendants. And, while gains have been made to ensure adequate representation among youths who have the means to afford representation, state and local laws as well as individual judicial practice in the courtroom do not always result in the full and meaningful legal protections envisioned by the *Gault* opinion or the ABA standards created in 1979. The American history of legal representation for juveniles, germinating from the *Gault* decision of the 1960s, has traversed four decades to culminate in some notable recent trends. Attitudes and opinions have emerged on both sides of the issue of how to apply the full measure of due process protections regarding the right to counsel to juveniles.

History of Legal Representation for Juveniles

The due process revolution of the 1960s, largely associated with the U.S. Supreme Court under the leadership of Chief Justice Earl Warren, included a series of cases regarding youth defendants in juvenile court and culminated in the landmark *In re Gault* decision. The *Gault* decision was the first of its kind, in that the Court recognized that juveniles appearing on criminal charges in juvenile court should be afforded the same right to legal representation as that afforded to adult criminal defendants. The Court in *Gault* recognized that "[t]he probation officer cannot act as counsel for the child. His role ... is as arresting officer and witness against the child. Nor can the judge represent the child." Further, with many of these youths facing potential terms of incarceration if adjudicated delinquent, the Court reasoned that defense counsel was especially important for helping youths "to cope with problems of law, to make skilled inquiry into the facts, to insist upon regularity of the proceedings, and to ascertain whether [the client] has a defense and to prepare and submit it."

The 1970s was a groundbreaking decade for legal advocacy groups for youths across the country. By the end of that decade, the American Bar Association (ABA) had released the first comprehensive guide and standards for the representation of juvenile defendants, as well as other due process protections afforded by the *Gault* decision. These standards formed the basis for developing state legislation, influencing local practice, and generating ongoing monitoring of the provision of legal representation for youths. In the federal arena, juvenile justice was also starting to emerge as an independent area of national concern at this time, and with this came the Juvenile Justice Delinquency and Prevention Act (JJDPA), which established the federal Office of Juvenile Justice and Delinquency Prevention (OJJDP). Among other consequences, the JJDPA created the National Advisory Committee for Juvenile Justice and Delinquency Prevention, a body tasked with creating national juvenile justice practice standards and policy guidelines. These standards, published in 1980, called for legal representation for all youths in delinquency matters, beginning at the first point of contact in the juvenile justice system.

The 1990s: Assessing Due Process for Juveniles

In 1993, the Due Process Advocacy Project was funded by OJJDP to help states and local jurisdictions develop the capacity needed to fully implement the legal counsel protections envisioned in the *Gault* decision, the ABA guidelines, and the standards from the National Advisory Committee. This work culminated in the first comprehensive assessment of how well each of the 50 state-level and District of Columbia jurisdictions was performing in the provision of counsel to all youths appearing in juvenile court on a criminal charge. This 1995 report, *A Call for Justice: An Assessment of Access to Counsel and Quality of Representation in Delinquency Proceedings*, found that while some youths were receiving enthusiastic, well-informed, and effective counsel during court proceedings, all too often the majority of youths either had no counsel or had received legal representation that was little more than a token act and not of a quality that would be deemed consistent with the intent of *Gault*.

Often referred to as *kiddie court,* data generated from the project showed that some attorneys did not always take these juvenile court proceedings seriously, even expressing disdain and dismay when they were assigned to the juvenile court, where the cases weren't viewed to be as important as those in adult criminal court. At this time, it was common practice for attorneys to be informally and formally rewarded by their employers for litigation efforts in adult criminal court settings, but practicing in juvenile court was not seen as service that would result in promotions or other employment accolades. Added to this view regarding the unimportance of youth proceedings in juvenile court was the finding that public defenders had very high turnover rates (every 24–36 months) and handled inordinately high caseloads (up to 500 per year). Most alarming, almost half of the cases reviewed for this project also found that youths had no lawyer present at all during proceedings, having waived their right to counsel due to suggestions by the defense bar and other court personnel that the case wasn't really important enough to require the presence of counsel. Finally, this report also found that almost one-third (32 percent) of public defenders were not able to take cases on appeal from the juvenile court, and of the remainder who could, only 23 percent had ever done so. Appointed lawyers were in no better shape, with only one out of five (20 percent) able to take a case on appeal actually doing so in the year prior to the project's assessment.

Where effective defense counsel practices were found, the following system features were identified as keys to their success: (1) attorneys had smaller caseloads; (2) attorneys had early case involvement; (3) attorneys had the ability to represent the client in other matters (i.e., special education); (4) attorneys had multifaceted training, which was ongoing; (5) resources were readily available to attorneys; (6) attorneys had access to additional community and court-related supports and resources; (7) there was an effective process for supervision of attorneys; and (8) a professional culture valued practice in the juvenile court.

The report offered specific recommendations for states and local jurisdictions to improve the practice of defenders in juvenile court. Specifically, states and local jurisdictions were advised to:

- Provide adequate funding and staffing resources to support the work of juvenile defenders;
- Provide assurance that comprehensive, juvenile court-specific training is provided to defenders with responsibilities for representing youths in juvenile court;
- Ensure that reasonable caseloads are maintained for defense attorneys so that each youth can receive the quality representation required for their case;
- Ensure they are encouraging attorneys to specialize in juvenile law practices and make sure they are eligible for promotions and recognition on an equal footing with attorneys representing adult clients in criminal court;
- Ensure they are adopting minimum standards for legal representation in juvenile court; and
- Ensure they are collecting data that will routinely be used to monitor caseloads, assessing adequacy of training, addressing discrepancies in salaries, and other factors impacting the provision and quality of counsel for juveniles.

The report also included a detailed list of implementation strategies that states, defender offices, courts, and even law schools could use to help support the pursuit of these broader recommendations.

In response to the findings of this report, legal advocacy groups mobilized to develop more comprehensive training for public defenders, and to provide states with regular assessments of how well their state was measuring up to the new ABA standards. These standards were restated in 2009 by the National Juvenile Defender Center in terms of five core duties:

1. Duty to Represent the Client's Expressed Interests (ABA Model Rules of Professional Conduct (Model Rules): Preamble; 1.14(a) Client with Diminished Capacity; 1.2(a) Scope of Representation and Allocation of Authority between Client and Lawyer)
2. Duty of Confidentiality and Privilege (Model Rules: 1.6 Confidentiality of Information)
3. Duties of Competence and Diligence (Model Rules: 1.1 Competence, 1.3 Diligence)
4. Duty to Advise and Counsel (Model Rules: 2.1 Advisor)
5. Duty of Communication (Model Rules: 1.4 Communications)

In 2005, a state-by-state comparison was completed detailing how each of the 51 jurisdictions in the country have organized their defense counsel systems for ensuring juveniles the right to counsel, especially around the issue of juvenile indigent defense, or public defense systems. This state-by-state comparative analysis found that 22 states and the District of Columbia have state or jurisdiction-wide systems that provide juveniles with state-funded representation through the adjudication phase. In two of these jurisdictions, Florida and Tennessee, juvenile defense counsel are elected officials. The remaining 29 jurisdictions use a system that is funded primarily through county-level or judicial circuit budgets, although some of these jurisdictions use a blended funding scheme where the provision of some services is funded through state dollars. In terms of oversight, 15 states currently provide centralized control over the public defender services available to juveniles in those states. Fifteen other states perform in a partially centralized oversight role with regard to these services, which typically include things like hiring, compensation, practice standards, and training. The remaining 21 jurisdictions have no supervisory body providing oversight of juvenile defense bar staffing or practices. In Tennessee and Florida, professional associations provide this supervisory oversight role for the elected officials who occupy public defender positions in each state. The National Juvenile Defender Center provides an online tool that profiles each state's structure and process for providing legal counsel to juveniles. This tool provides the most up-to-date information on the current state of legal representation for juveniles.

The Case of Roper v. Simmons

In their 2007 *Rutgers Law Review* article, Donna M. Bishop and Hillary B. Farber used the U.S. Supreme Court case of *Roper v. Simmons* (2005), the case that invalidated the death penalty for crimes committed by juveniles under the age of 18, to make some interesting points about a juvenile's right to counsel and the waiver of that right.

In *Roper*, the U.S. Supreme Court found three characteristics of juveniles that distinguish them from adults: (1) a lack of maturity and an underdeveloped sense of responsibility; (2) a greater vulnerability or susceptibility to negative influences and outside pressures, including peer pressure; and (3) more transitory personality traits. Using the *Roper* decision as background, Bishop and Farber "discuss research on adolescent decision making, then consider its implications for juveniles' capacities to understand and then invoke or waive constitutional rights," such as the right to counsel. Bishop and Farber look at the evidence from psychology and neuroscience in three key areas: cognitive development, neuropsychological research, and psychosocial factors affecting adolescent judgment.

The authors then go on to identify four psychosocial factors affecting adolescent judgment: susceptibility to external influence, orientation toward risk, limited temporal orientation, and limited capacity for self-regulation.

Currently, state and federal courts are divided on how far they want to stretch the *Roper* decision to cover other facets of juvenile law. Some courts have strictly limited their findings about the adolescent brain development of juveniles only to death penalty cases, while others seem to be more interested in applying the *Roper* findings overall to a juvenile's right to counsel and his or her waiver of that right.

Current Issues in Legal Representation for Juveniles

Ineffective Assistance of Counsel

If a juvenile asserts the claim of ineffective assistance of counsel regarding a delinquency petition on appeal, the juvenile bears a two-pronged burden to support this claim. To succeed in this appellate argument, he or she must show that counsel's representation fell below an objective standard of reasonableness under prevailing professional norms for demonstrating effective assistance of counsel. Then, the juvenile must show a reasonable probability that, but for counsel's errors, the results of the proceeding would have been different.

For example, in the 2009 case of *People v. Edward S.*, the California Court of Appeals applied this two-pronged test to its reasoning and held that the juvenile had been denied effective assistance of counsel by the public defender, and that the public defender's deficiencies prejudiced the juvenile by distorting the outcome that prevailed from those proceedings. Specifically, the California Court of Appeals found that (1) the public defender's failure to investigate potentially exculpatory evidence was deficient; (2) the public defender's failure to seek an adequate continuance to permit him to fully investigate and competently defend the juvenile was deficient; and (3) that the public defender's failure to move for a substitution of counsel knowing he was unable to devote the time and resources necessary to properly defend the juvenile was deficient. The California Court of Appeals concluded that in this case, the juvenile showed that, as a result of the public defender's deficient performance, the jurisdictional proceedings were fundamentally unfair and unreliable, and that there was a reasonable probability that, absent the errors, the fact finder would have had a reasonable doubt respecting guilt. In this case, the judgment was reversed and remanded to the juvenile court with directions to conduct a new jurisdictional hearing.

Another example of the appellate court finding ineffective assistance of counsel was in an unpublished 2009 Washington Court of Appeals case (*State v. D.S.*). In that case, the Washington appellate court found that the juvenile's defense counsel's failure to object, when the court twice continued a restitution hearing beyond the 180-day limit without good cause, denied the juvenile offender the effective assistance of counsel. The first continuance order arbitrarily set the hearing for one day beyond the 180-day limit, and the second continuance was in order to allow the state to remedy an insufficiency in its evidence. The appellate court reasoned that had counsel properly objected to the second order, the court would have denied restitution.

Right to Conflict-Free Counsel

Some state appellate courts have taken the juvenile's right to counsel even further, and have upheld a juvenile's right to conflict-free counsel. For example, in 2007, in *A.P. v. State*, the Florida District Court of Appeal held that a juvenile's waiver of the right to conflict-free counsel was not knowing and voluntary in a delinquency proceeding. Although the juvenile was advised about the nature of the conflict, namely that the public defender had previously represented the victim in an unrelated case, there was no indication in the record that the juvenile understood how this conflict could affect her defense, nor was she informed of her right to obtain conflict-free counsel.

In 2009, the state appellate court in New Jersey ruled that attorneys must be present when juveniles are read Miranda rights for any alleged crimes involving them and other family members. The court stated that lawyers should be the responsible for explaining the Miranda rights, rather than the juvenile's parents. The court argued that parents may have a conflict of interest when both the victims and the accused are family members. The case involved a 14-year-old girl who was accused of sexually assaulting her nephew, a four-year-old boy, in 2007.

Right to Consult With Counsel Without Parents

Does a juvenile client have the right to consult with and confide in his attorney without his parents present? This question was recently faced by the Washington Supreme Court in *State v. A.N.J.* (2010). In this case, the juvenile (accused of first-degree child molestation) was always accompanied by his parents when he met with his public defender. Citing Washington State Bar Association (WSBA), American Bar Association (ABA), and local defense bar standards in his appeal, the juvenile criticized his public defender for not meeting with him privately and creating a confidential attorney/client relationship with him. On the juvenile's behalf, a local law professor condemned the constant presence of the juvenile's parents. A juvenile, he argued, may be more candid with his lawyer and more willing to express his own views if his parents are not present. Among many other things, that candor cannot be accomplished when the meeting is held jointly with the parents. There is a substantial risk that the juvenile will defer to the parents under such circumstances when advice on the decision to plead guilty or to go to trial is provided. Thus, the law professor suggested, by failing to establish a confidential relationship with the accused juvenile, the public defender undermined the attorney/client relationship, undermined the client's autonomy, and potentially waived the attorney/client privilege in the process. In this case, the Washington Supreme Court found that a juvenile client should be given the opportunity to consult with and confide in his attorney without his parents present. However, the state's high court went on to hold that the failure to provide that opportunity to a juvenile defendant is a factor that may be considered by a court when considering whether a plea was knowingly, voluntarily, and intelligently made, but was not dispositive in this case.

Trial Court Abusing Discretion

How "real" must the juvenile's representation be? The Maryland Court of Special Appeals answered this question in *In re Shawn P.* in 2007, holding that the trial court abused its discretion by denying the request of juvenile's counsel for a continuance, or in the alternative, by refusing to afford counsel the opportunity to confer with the juvenile. In that case, a public defender happened to be in the courtroom at the same time as an underrepresented juvenile. The trial court appointed the public defender to represent the juvenile "on the spot" and denied the public defender's request for a continuance of the case. The trial court also refused to afford counsel an opportunity to confer with the juvenile. The trial court refused the public defender's requests to postpone the case after counsel implored the court to avoid violating the provisions of the statute and rule governing waiver of counsel in delinquency proceedings. The public defender was afforded absolutely no time to familiarize himself with the facts of the case, and the juvenile was forced to proceed without any opportunity for consultation regarding his options or the implications of a delinquency adjudication, a fact that was obviously known by the trial court. The Maryland appellate court found that the trial court had abused its discretion, and vacated and remanded the case.

Supervising Good Juvenile Defense Bar Practices

Do juvenile defense attorneys have a special property interest in their specialty practice of family court, and what happens when a court decides to evaluate the quality of legal services rendered by lawyers who handle juvenile delinquency cases? It might seem like a good idea, until all the attorneys who were rated as underperformers and are no longer recommended to handle delinquency cases file a federal lawsuit, as happened in the District of Columbia courts in *Roth v. King* (2006).

In the 2002 Appropriations Act for the District of Columbia, a joint congressional committee issued a statement strongly urging the D.C. Superior Court to evaluate the quality of the legal services rendered by lawyers appointed under the Criminal Justice Act to handle juvenile delinquency cases. The D.C. court was urged to take immediate and affirmative steps to ensure that lawyers who lacked the requisite training, experience, and skill were not appointed to delinquency cases. Responding to that directive, the chief judge of the Superior Court of the District of Columbia appointed an ad-hoc committee to recommend panels of qualified attorneys to represent indigent parties in Family Court. From among the 351 applications received, the committee ultimately recommended 75 attorneys for a juvenile delinquency panel, 77 attorneys for a guardian ad-litem panel, 181 attorneys for the Counsel for Child Abuse and Neglect (CCAN) panel, and 34 special education advocates. On March 26, 2003, after reviewing the committee's report, the chief judge issued an administrative order that established the Family Court Attorney Panels in accordance with the committee's recommendations.

Prior to the establishment of the Family Court Attorney Panels, the Superior Court did not designate attorneys for such panels. Rather, the Court simply appointed counsel from lists of volunteers that had been maintained by the CCAN Office or the D.C. Public Defender Service (PDS). Any lawyer who desired to be on the volunteer lists was included, without any inquiry into the lawyer's qualifications. Lawyers whose names appeared on these lists were not guaranteed any appointments, however. Inclusion merely indicated to Superior Court judges that a lawyer was interested in receiving appointments. This regime was changed with the issuance of the administrative order, which provided that, in most cases, judges in Family Court must appoint attorneys from the appropriate panel list to represent indigent parties. Attorneys not on the panels could continue to represent their clients, but they would not be eligible to receive compensation under the Criminal Justice Act or the CCAN statute. On May 21, 2003, the non-panel attorneys, who claimed to represent a class of attorneys who allegedly suffered harm as a result of the administrative order, filed suit in District Court against the judges of the Superior Court who participated in developing and implementing the panel system. These attorneys alleged they had a "property interest" in their "specialty practice" in Family Court, and that the administrative order violated their Fifth Amendment rights by "taking" their property without due process.

The U.S. Court of Appeals, D.C. Circuit held that the non-panel attorneys had no "property interest" in their "specialty practice" in the Family Court, and that the administrative order resulted in no unlawful "takings." The federal appellate court further explained that: there was no statute, regulation, or court rule that guaranteed any member of the bar compensated Family Division appointments before the administrative order was promulgated. The judges of the Superior Court always had discretion to decide which attorneys would be appointed to handle Family Division cases, and to decide the basis upon which such appointments would be made. Prior to the adoption of the administrative order, no law or rule ensured appointment for attorneys who met particular criteria, and no law or rule restricted the discretion of a presiding judge to terminate a lawyer's appointment for cause. The Superior Court simply appointed counsel from lists of volunteers that had been maintained by the CCAN Office and PDS. Any lawyer who desired to be on a volunteer list was included, without any inquiry into the lawyer's qualifications. However, inclusion on a list merely indicated to Superior Court judges that a lawyer was interested in receiving appointments; it did not guarantee appointment. In short, before the issuance of the administrative order, no member of the bar could claim entitlement to appointments in the Family Division.

Therefore, the attorneys' desires for compensated appointments amounted to nothing more than "expectations," not "entitlements." There never has been a statute or rule, or even a practice, securing attorneys' right to compensated Family Court appointments. Furthermore, a lawyer's inability to make a living as a family court practitioner without such appointments does not create an entitlement.

Pro: Benefits of Legal Representation for Juveniles

Legal representation provides youths with the constitutional protections needed to help ensure a fair outcome, especially when that outcome could involve a term of incarceration. Recent U.S. Supreme Court decisions illustrate just how high these stakes can be for juveniles. For example, in the 2005 case of *Roper v. Simmons*, the death penalty was invalidated for juveniles who had committed their capital crimes under the age of 18. Before then, such juveniles could be executed. Then in 2010, in the case of *Graham v. Florida*, the Supreme Court held that under the U.S. Constitution, it was considered cruel and unusual to permit a juvenile offender to be sentenced to life imprisonment without the possibility of parole for a nonhomicide crime that they committed when they were under 18. As these cases show, legal representation is a necessity for a juvenile facing this bleak future.

Legal representation elevates the field of juvenile justice to a level commensurate with the public policy expectation that public resources in the juvenile court are used effectively and efficiently to prevent future delinquency and improve public safety. Locally, nationally, and internationally, the argument is made that juveniles are not yet fully formed adults, are immature, and do not always make the wisest decisions. Once again, legal counsel is necessary to ensure that these same bad decisions aren't repeated and do not perpetuate the cycle of delinquency.

Legal representation supports the concept of using the juvenile court as a system of support for young people by providing legal advocates who can help youths and their families navigate the legal process as well as the other systems (schools, child welfare, physical/mental health) that are invariably impacted when a youth becomes involved in justice. Many jurisdictions provide or require special training for juvenile legal advocates because of the unique nature of their role in the system. Such advocates walk the fine line between being a social worker and advocating for a young client's rights.

Con: Drawbacks of Legal Representation for Juveniles

While full constitutional protections for youths in criminal delinquency proceedings is desirable, the traditional public defender approach used in adult criminal court is not sufficient to provide the additional supports many of these youths may need (educational advocacy, family support, mental health services, etc.). Representing juveniles requires "lawyering plus." In addition to all the necessary traditional legal skills, a juvenile public defender needs to understand adolescent development and behavior. Such an attorney also needs a good working knowledge of the kinds of community resources available to support a troubled juvenile during this difficult time. Given life's realities, all of this extra effort (outside the scope of traditional attorney work) is subject to many constraints, such as time, money, interest, and capability. The average attorney with a general practice may not be able to devote this extra effort to a particular type of case, particularly if juvenile work does not represent the bulk of his or her caseload.

Lack of Oversight

Juvenile justice practices vary by local jurisdiction, and the resources needed for effective responses to juvenile crime also vary considerably from place to place; yet effective oversight for supervising good defense bar practice, through training and standards adoption, is better placed at the state level of authority. This very real dilemma often forces a juvenile defender to ignore or avoid innovative training because his or her local jurisdiction cannot afford or refuses to adopt such practices. This mindset can also encourage corruption if there is no one accountable to challenge it. Unfortunately, entrenched attitudes are always at risk of being leveraged for personal gain. For example, two juvenile judges in Pennsylvania were recently getting kickbacks from certain detention centers for every juvenile they sent there. Few, if any, of these juveniles were represented by counsel. "Business as usual" kept this unfortunate practice in operation for a number of years and created quite a judicial scandal when uncovered.

The Dilemmas of Counsel

The use of defense counsel in juvenile proceedings could be seen as a step toward criminalizing delinquent behavior along the lines of the "adult crime, adult time" public policy stance of the late 1990s, where youths are treated as adults even though adolescent development research clearly indicates that youth decision-making and subsequent delinquent behaviors require a much different response than what is needed to prevent or reduce adult reoffending. This argument is often made in favor of abolishing the juvenile court altogether. Representing a juvenile can present an attorney with a set of dilemmas. What if the attorney believes his or her client is guilty, but in need of treatment? Is the attorney's job to get the young delinquent off "scot-free" from the bad behavior, without receiving any treatment? Or should the attorney work to get treatment for the juvenile as a disposition option? Does the attorney in this kind of case represent the best interests of the child or the best interest of his or her client? And, finally, what role do the juvenile's wishes play in deciding courtroom strategy? The questions become very tricky and lead some to argue that juvenile courts are no longer useful—that juvenile offenders should have all the rights and punishments of adults. These commentators argue that if juveniles had all the rights of adult defendants in criminal court, the immaturity of adolescent decision making would not matter. The issue is very complex and moves very far away from the traditional paternalistic role of the juvenile court.

Conclusion

Although there are still considerable gaps in both providing access to counsel and ensuring quality of legal representation, especially among youths who are already marginalized due to location, race/ethnicity (including language), or socioeconomic factors, the current state of legal representation for youth has seen considerable improvement since the *Gault* decision four decades ago. More than a dozen states have created commissions to study their juvenile justice systems, and many states are currently considering the adoption of a statewide oversight authority to supervise the provision of legal services for juvenile defendants. While state fiscal realities are still grim, there has been increased funding for defender organizations as well as more specialized training for lawyers working with youths. States continue to explore and adopt better performance standards for lawyers, and are actively working to prohibit the waiver of counsel, which has been used in too many cases as an informal way of reducing the need to provide legal services to juveniles. An egregious example of the misuse of this waiver right recently surfaced in the Luzerne County, Pennsylvania, scandal, where nearly all justice-involved youths were routinely being adjudicated delinquent and sent to secure placement without the benefit of counsel during juvenile court proceedings.

States have also been active with their legislative reforms impacting juvenile right to counsel, such as the Georgia Indigent Defense Act of 2003, the Louisiana Juvenile Justice Reform Act of 2003, and the Mississippi Juvenile Delinquency Prevention Act of 2006. The OJJDP-funded *Call to Action* report from 1995 recommended changes in the way law students are educated with regard to juvenile law matters. Since then, modest advances have started to take hold in this realm, with new juvenile justice clinical education courses created at the University of Maine and University of Richmond in Virginia, while a Juvenile Justice Center has been created at Barry Law School in Florida.

Since the ABA released the first comprehensive guide and standards for the representation of juvenile defendants in the 1970s, more than 40 years after *Gault*, many states and local jurisdictions still do not have adequate legal representation practices in place, most notably for indigent juvenile defendants. And, while gains have been made to ensure adequate representation among youths who do not have the means to afford representation, state and local laws as well as individual judicial practice in the courtroom do not always result in the full and meaningful legal protections envisioned by the *Gault* opinion or the ABA standards created in 1979.

See Also: 10. Juvenile Offenders in Adult Courts; 14. Parental Responsibility Laws; 18. Sentencing Options.

Further Readings

American Bar Association. *A Call to Justice: An Assessment of Access to Counsel and Quality of Representation in Delinquency Proceedings.* Chicago: American Bar Association, 1995

Bishop, Donna M., and Hillary B. Farber. "Joining the Legal Significance of Adolescent Developmental Capacities With the Legal Rights Provided by *In re Gault.*" *Rutgers Law Review,* v.60/1 (2008).

Blitzman, Judge Jay D. "*Gault's* Promise." *Barry Law Review,* v.9 (2007).

Foxhoven, Jerry R. "Effective Assistance of Counsel: Quality Representation for Juveniles Is Still Illusory." *Barry Law Review,* v.9 (2007).

In re Gault, 387 U.S. 1 (1967).

Krake, Kellie M. "*In Re Gault*: Do Its Promises Still Protect Juveniles?" *Wisconsin Lawyer,* v.80/11 (November 2007).

Levick, Marsha, and Neha Desai. "Still Waiting: The Elusive Quest to Ensure Juveniles a Constitutional Right to Counsel at All Stages of the Juvenile Court Process." *Rutgers Law Review,* v.60/1 (2008).

L.H. v. Schwarzenegger, 519 F.Supp.2d 1072 (E.D. Cal. 2007).

Mantel, Barbara. "Public Defenders: Do Indigent Defendants Get Adequate Legal Representation?" *CQ Researcher,* v.18/15 (April 18, 2008).

Markman, Joanna S. "*In Re Gault*: A Retrospective in 2007: Is It Working? Can It Work?" *Barry Law Review,* v.9 (2007).

Mlyniec, Wallace J. "*In re Gault* at 40: The Right to Counsel in Juvenile Court—a Promise Unfulfilled." *Criminal Law Bulliten,* v.44/3 (May–June 2008).

National Juvenile Defender's Center. http://www.njdc.info/state_data.php (Accessed September 2010).

People v. Edward S., 92 Cal.Rptr.3d 725 (2009).

Pennsylvania Supreme Court. *In re J.V.R. and H.T.* (2008).

Rutgers Law Review Symposium 2007. "The Promise of *In re Gault*: Promoting and Protecting the Right to Counsel in Juvenile Court." *Rutgers Law Review,* v.60/1 (2008).

Santiago, Katherine. "N.J. Court Says Juveniles' Miranda Rights Must Be Read by Lawyer in Family-Related Crime." *The Star-Ledger/New Jersey Real Times* (August 12, 2009).

Solomon, Gary. "I Got the Post-*McKeiver* Blues." *Rutgers Law Review,* v.60/1 (2008).

13

Out-of-Home Placement

Jamie J. Fader
University at Albany, State University of New York

O ut-of-home placements are residential programs for youths who are adjudicated delinquent (found guilty) by the juvenile court. They may include foster care, group homes, independent living programs, ranches, boot camps, treatment camps, farms, or institutional programs such as training schools or residential treatment centers. Out-of-home placements are typically contrasted with community-based services for delinquent youths. They are designed to remove youthful offenders from the criminogenic influences of delinquent peers, impoverished neighborhoods, or lack of parental supervision. Residential placements are also used when youths have needs that cannot be met in the community, such as severe mental health or substance abuse problems, or when there is abuse or neglect at home.

Finally, they are a common dispositional option for delinquent youths who have committed serious offenses or who have lengthy criminal histories. The use of residential placements is controversial because they occupy the boundary between punishment and treatment, two seemingly contradictory goals that are simultaneously held by the juvenile justice system. Those who are concerned about crime control generally support the use of such placements, whereas those who view juvenile offenders as vulnerable youths often argue that they are overused. Out-of-home placements made national attention in early 2009 when two judges in Luzerne County, Pennsylvania, were accused of accepting $2.6 million in kickbacks in exchange for sending delinquent youths to two private correctional facilities. Many were denied the right to counsel and placed outside of their homes despite only having committed low-level offenses.

Residential programs vary widely, particularly those for delinquent youths. Within facilities, youths may receive any (or many) of the following interventions: behavior modification, token economies (accumulating points to receive privileges), cognitive-behavioral treatment, military discipline, group and/or individual counseling, family counseling, mentoring, substance abuse education and/or treatment (including 12-step programs), vocational training, life skills training, work readiness and job placement, and college preparation. These facilities are also required by law to provide educational programming for school-age youths, although this also varies widely in terms of quality and accreditation. Facilities differ in their commitment to a therapeutic treatment program. Many resemble adult prisons, with nominal rehabilitative programming and little contact with the outside world, while others use evidence-based practices to design programs that employ techniques shown in research to be effective in curbing future juvenile offending.

In 2005, the courts committed 140,100 youthful offenders to out-of-home placements. This was a 30 percent increase in commitments since 1985, although a peak of 163,000 commitments occurred in 1997. As a percentage of post-adjudication decisions, 22 percent of youthful offenders were court-ordered to out-of-home placements, down from 32 percent in 1985. Violent offenders were the most likely (25 percent) to be committed to these programs, and drug offenders (19 percent) the least likely. Although the Juvenile Justice and Delinquency Prevention Act of 1974 mandated the deinstitutionalization of all status offenders, approximately five percent of young people in facilities were there for status offenses. Males were more likely (24 percent) than females (17 percent) to be sent to out-of-home placements. Black youths were slightly more likely (26 percent) than their white counterparts (21 percent) to go to residential programs.

Many states have enacted legislation that requires juvenile judges to use residential placements sparingly, only when the youth's needs or public safety concerns prevent the use of programs in the community. For this reason, and because out-of-home placements are so costly compared to their community-based counterparts, these programs typically house the most serious cases in the juvenile justice system.

History of Out-of-Home Placements
Early Beginnings

Although many trace the origins of the American juvenile justice system to the establishment of the Juvenile Court in Cook County, Illinois in 1899, reformers first established out-of-home placements for wayward youths 75 years earlier. The first House of Refuge was instituted in New York City in 1825, soon followed by homes in Boston (1826) and Philadelphia (1828). By 1868, there were more than 20 similar institutions across the United States, with 40,000–50,000 young residents. These early reformatories were based on their British predecessors, but differed in two key respects. First, they housed children for vagrancy as well as petty crimes, attempting to prevent crime among poor youths before they encountered the "slippery slope" of criminality. Second, they used indeterminate sentencing to encourage compliance of their residents. These institutions were privately run—most often by religious organizations—but received increasing amounts of funding from the state as they became more firmly established.

These early reformatories were based on a congregate model containing dormitory sleeping areas, a large cafeteria, and workshops. Architecturally, they resembled the factories, prisons, workhouses, and hospitals of the time. Conceptually, they represented new definitions of both childhood and punishment, culminating in a commitment to removing young people from adult prisons and offering rehabilitation in lieu of punishment. The education provided inside these institutions, and at reformatories opened in the latter half of the 19th century, emphasized the acquisition of skills for agricultural and industrial work for boys, and preparation for domestic servant positions for girls. Boys learned chair caning, shoe repair, and brass-nail making, while girls were trained to do laundry, cooking, and cleaning. In addition to preparing youths for future employment, this work was an important source of revenue. Youths spent an average of two to five years inside these reformatories, typically followed by an apprenticeship.

The Child-Saving Era of Progressive Reformers

Toward the end of the 19th century, this congregate model largely fell out of favor among reformers. Institutions had become quickly overcrowded and, as a result, began to serve as way stations for young people who would be "placed out" on farms or out west as apprentices or indentured servants.

With "sentimental pastoralism" as a guiding philosophy, Progressives strove to remove children from densely populated urban areas that they viewed as the breeding grounds for poverty and vice to rural settings characterized by fresh air and abundant space. The cottage, or family, plan moved troubled youths into smaller, decentralized, cottage-style reformatories run by house parents: upstanding, Christian married couples who were instructed to treat residents lovingly and as members of their own family. During this period, Charles Loring Brace, founder of the Children's Aid Society, also instituted his "orphan train" program, transporting more than 200,000 children out west to be adopted by pioneer families.

The character of out-of-home placements—their architecture, setting, size, and strategies for addressing delinquency—has historically been guided by evolving standards of how policymakers and the public define social constructs such as "children," "crime," and "punishment." Before the advent of the 19th century, children did not constitute a distinct social category; with the family as the basic unit of economic production, they worked alongside their parents and childhood was not viewed as a distinct developmental phase. However, by the time the first Houses of Refuge were built, reformers began to attribute special significance to children as a result of new conceptions of their innate innocence and malleability. Given their particular amenability to intervention, children were targeted in the hopes that moral guidance and hard work could reshape them into productive and law-abiding citizens.

Reformers during this child-saving era constructed the problem of delinquency out of their concerns about poverty and immigration. The New York House of Refuge, for instance, was established by the Society for the Prevention of Pauperism. Paupers were not just viewed as poor, but poor because they engaged in crime and vice. Reformers worried that, if left unchecked, poor immigrants would spread their immorality to others. Therefore, the activities of lower-class immigrant children—their failure to attend school, their begging or wandering the streets, and their search for amusement at arcades—became defined as delinquency. Because treatment in reformatories was offered "in the child's best interests" and was not designed to be punitive, legal rights were not extended to children or their families. When reformers of the 1960s became disillusioned with the rehabilitative model and acknowledged that many reformatories appeared to have conditions similar to adult confinement (such as overcrowding and violence), many due process rights, such as the right to counsel, were extended to juveniles.

The Get-Tough Movement to Modern Placement

In contrast to the child-saving movement, the get-tough movement of the 1990s defined children as adult-like individuals whose violence was unprecedented and defied all logic. Rising youth crime rates during the early 1990s (at the height of the crack trade) spurred a moral panic among the public, who demanded that young people who "do adult crime do adult time." Juvenile justice policymakers, convinced that nothing worked to rehabilitate youthful offenders, turned to harsher punishments, including increased use of out-of-home placements (particularly ones that looked most like prisons) and expanded legal definitions of which children qualified for punishment in adult courts, jails, and prisons. Classical conceptions of crime as freely chosen (instead of being the product of poor environments) led to deterrence- and incapacitation-based approaches to addressing delinquency. During this time, boot camps and wilderness programs proliferated, based upon the assumptions that delinquent youths needed better discipline and more structure in their daily routines.

Modern out-of-home placements are built both in the congregate and cottage models, with the family-style programs often reserved for dependent youths and nonserious delinquent youths with substantial problems in their own homes and families. These settings offer residents greater freedom to move about the campus between cottages, school, and recreational activities than their more structured congregate counterparts, which may have fences, locks, or even bars. Out-of-home placements are still overwhelmingly located in rural areas as a result of philosophical and practical concerns. Many still endeavor to remove delinquent youths from the criminogenic influences of cities, although rural settings are also perceived as more palatable to the law-abiding public, who frequently express concern when such facilities move into their neighborhoods.

Recently, many states have built smaller facilities set closer to residents' homes. The Missouri Model of juvenile justice, which has garnered substantial attention because of its impressive rates of success with serious youthful offenders, is based on an open-dorm model with no more than 48 residents at each facility. Residential facilities in Missouri aim to "treat kids like kids," allowing them to wear their own clothing and staffing counselors who aim to develop positive relationships with young people. The California Division of Juvenile Justice (formerly known as the California Youth Authority) has recently closed its largest facility in response to legislation requiring juveniles to be committed to county facilities wherever possible. With eight of 13 state-based facilities now closed, the number of youthful offenders in jail-like settings has declined from 10,000 to approximately 1,700. The Office of Juvenile Justice and Delinquency Prevention (OJJDP) Comprehensive Strategy for Serious, Violent, and Chronic Juvenile Offenders offers states a model of graduated sanctions, encouraging development of a range of community-based residential placements as well as placement alternatives. As a result, states all over the country are shutting down large facilities and diverting children and funds to smaller, more localized residential placements.

Pro: Benefits of Out-of-Home Placement

Because the juvenile justice system still retains a commitment to the philosophy of parens patriae, or the state acting as parent, judges and other decision makers often view out-of-home placements as a necessary means of removing delinquent youths from harmful home and family situations. Since there is such a great degree of crossover between dependent and delinquent youths, maltreated children are often viewed as predelinquent. Victims of abuse or neglect are 25 percent more likely than their counterparts to engage in delinquency (and later adult offending), and a substantial proportion of delinquent youths have histories of child welfare system involvement. Moreover, young people growing up in families characterized by abuse or neglect are more likely to run away from home, a status offense that can lead to arrest and later placement. Juvenile justice decision makers often deem out-of-home placements as the preferred option for youths whose parent(s) are incarcerated, battling drug or alcohol addiction, actively involved in offending themselves, or otherwise determined to be the cause of their children's delinquency. Delinquent youths with troubled home environments may be viewed by judges as less blameworthy for their offenses, and court-committed to the same or similar placements used for dependency (i.e., child abuse/neglect) cases. These placements are more likely to fit the cottage model and to incorporate the involvement of "house parents" who take on parental roles and responsibilities for their young charges.

Supporters of out-of-home placements argue that they frequently offer treatment for youths that is limited or unavailable in community-based programs. Delinquent or dependent youths with substance abuse or mental health problems (or both, termed *co-occurring disorders*) often require treatment that is more intensive than that which can be provided on an outpatient basis. Residential Treatment Facilities (RTFs), highly structured therapeutic facilities for youths suffering from addiction or mental illness, are much smaller in number (and far more expensive) than other types of out-of-home placements. Youths often have to travel out of state to attend these programs. These facilities are also often the only programs that will accept sex offenders, fire starters, or developmentally delayed children.

Because residential placements are so highly routined, they are often the preferred disposition when the juvenile court determines that a young person lacks structure or discipline in the home. Regardless of the programmatic regime, most facilities are organized around a predictable daily and weekly schedule in which expectations for behavior are clearly stated at the outset. Young people wake up at the same time each day, maintain hygiene, eat a nutritious breakfast, and go to school or work. Many delinquent youths, particularly those whose parents or guardians are absent or battling addictions, were never required to be home at a specified hour or to attend school regularly. Perhaps because of the importance of structure and routine, some research has found that placement in a training school, combined with military service, leads to desistance (or termination) of offending. Youths may develop positive relationships with pro-social adults while at these facilities. Staff members often serve as role models, encouraging delinquent youths to develop realistic and achievable aspirations for the future that can be achieved through legal means.

Perhaps the most commonly used rationale for committing delinquent youths to out-of-home placements is public safety. One of the most robust and consistent findings in the criminological literature is the roughly eight percent of offenders who commit over 50 percent of offenses and consume a disproportionate share of policing, court, and corrections budgets. This small but apparently intractable group of serious, violent, or chronic offenders poses a threat to the community and need to be incapacitated, or kept off the streets, to avoid further harm to others. Public safety was the rallying cry for increased use of residential facilities during the "get tough" movement of the 1990s, although recent trends suggest that out-of-home placements—at least the ones that look most like adult prisons—will increasingly be reserved for the most serious, violent, or chronic juvenile offenders.

Con: Drawbacks of Out-of-Home Placement

Despite the benevolent intentions of the child savers who were responsible for building the network of reformatories, reports of overcrowding, abuse, and other adverse conditions of confinement are recorded as far back as a century ago. One survey of both detention facilities and training schools found that overcrowding is still pervasive today; nearly half (47 percent) of facilities are over capacity. Moreover, overcrowded facilities are more likely to have the highest incidence of resident-on-resident and resident-on-staff injuries. The U.S. Department of Justice has initiated legal action against facilities in 11 states where supervision was deemed substandard or abusive. Between 2004 and 2007, 13,000 claims of abuse were made by residents of custodial facilities, including beatings, sexual abuse, and the use of aggressive restraint techniques. At least five young people died while being forcibly restrained during this reporting period. The U.S. Justice Department found 2,821 sexual abuse allegations made by staff inside these institutions in one year alone.

Psychological and Developmental Problems

Opponents of out-of-home placements argue that confinement in these facilities may aggravate mental health problems if they are not treated properly. In one random, 30-day study period, approximately 1.6 percent of residents committed 1,487 acts of suicidal behavior while confined in institutions. Suicidal behavior inside facilities is more common where there is no screening, where there are higher rates of staff turnover, and where residents are isolated in single rooms. Although it is difficult to establish causal order because young people with mental health problems are more likely to be institutionalized than their counterparts, there is some evidence that the onset of major depression can occur after being confined.

Developmental psychologists have recently exposed the harmful effects of youth confinement on the developmental processes leading adolescents into healthy adult roles. They point out that the successful transition to adulthood requires young people to develop a sense of social competence and mastery over their worlds, autonomy from parents and others, and self-direction. These building blocks of maturity are compromised when young people are sent to residential placements and cut off from the support of positive role models and community institutions such as schools, resulting in what some have termed *arrested development*. Moreover, most programmatic regimes inside these institutions emphasize total control over the youths (specifying all activities from how youths' beds are made to how they are expected to comport themselves as they move around campus), inhibiting the development of autonomy and self-direction. Months and even years spent inside juvenile correctional facilities can put youths "off time" in reaching important turning points such as high school graduation or establishing stable employment histories. Although it is difficult to establish causality because residents of out-of-home placements are already more likely to be behind in school, only 12 percent of formerly incarcerated youths have a high school diploma or GED by the time they reach young adulthood, compared to 74 percent of nondelinquents. Less than a third is either in school or employed a year after leaving facilities.

Disruption of Relationships

Opponents of out-of-home placements contend that the physical distance between out-of-home placements and the communities from which young offenders are typically drawn can disrupt meaningful relationships with family members and other pro-social adults and peers, weakening social bonds that are necessary to prevent further offending. For example, a disproportionate number (25 percent in California) of young men in juvenile facilities are fathers, traditionally considered a risk factor for later offending. However, new research on parenthood and crime suggests that establishing strong bonds with children may be a "turning point" leading young fathers out of criminal careers as they take on the adult responsibilities associated with fatherhood. Several features of residential facilities make the establishment and maintenance of father-child bonds more difficult. First, these institutions are located an average of 58 miles from residents' homes. The distance to facilities and their location in rural, hard-to-reach areas make visitation more difficult, especially for poor families who do not have a car or money for gas, or who are required to work on visiting days. Second, visitation policies that restrict the number of potential visitors can discourage visits from children with different mothers. Finally, family members can be denied entry on visiting days for a number of reasons, including failure to comply with the dress code or a lack of proper identification. One study found that family members who had made the long trip out to the facility were turned away after being informed that the resident they were visiting (or his dorm) had been put on "lockdown" (denied all privileges) for misbehavior.

Culture Shock

The cultural distance between residential facilities and youths' homes and communities can also inhibit the process of transferring new social skills and behaviors to settings that are wholly different from the one in which they are learned. Ethnographic research conducted in inner-city neighborhoods has documented a unique set of behavioral expectations (the "code of the street") that regulates interactions between residents and allows them to safely navigate otherwise dangerous terrain. When young people from these neighborhoods arrive at out-of-home placement facilities, they are often required to suspend street behavior and comport themselves as middle-class citizens as part of their commitment to conformity. Prolonged eye contact, slang, strutting, and clothing made by urban companies are all discouraged because of their potential to lead to fighting and their association with street culture and crime. Young people are often required to inform staff about any misbehavior by their dorm-mates, which is typically considered "snitching" by inner-city residents. Meanwhile, new ways of thinking and behaving are taught and practiced. However, once young people return to the urban milieus in which the code of the street prevails, it is especially difficult to translate skills that were learned and rehearsed inside the walls of an institution.

Out-of-Home Versus Community-Based Interventions

Opponents of residential placements for juvenile offenders point out that confinement in these facilities for the purpose of enhancing public safety can backfire, increasing both the likelihood and frequency of later offending. Several mechanisms may be responsible for the exacerbating effect of juvenile incarceration. First, the time spent inside residential facilities can delay important transitions to adulthood, putting youths "off time" in their acquisition of adult skills. These young people may not "age out" of delinquency as do their counterparts who begin to take on adult roles and statuses in their early to mid-20s. Second, juvenile justice processing, especially confinement in out-of-home placements, may more firmly adhere delinquent labels to youths. Once young people begin to view themselves as delinquent, opportunities for engaging in law-abiding activities are perceived as inconsistent with that role. Finally, peer contagion (the grouping of delinquent youths with one another) increases the likelihood of reoffending when young people come together to share delinquent norms or even teach each other new techniques for offending and avoiding detection. Systematic analyses of program evaluations find that interventions bringing delinquent youths together are 30 percent less effective than those that deliver services in individual or family contexts.

New research, particularly powerful experiments using random assignment to treatment and control groups, concludes that the most effective treatments for delinquency are community- or family-based interventions. Multisystemic Therapy (MST), for example, has been identified as a model program by the Center for the Study and Prevention of Violence's Blueprints program after demonstrating its effectiveness in many rigorous studies across multiple locations. MST approaches antisocial behavior as embedded in a network of intersecting systems, including individual, family, and extrafamilial (peer, school, or neighborhood) factors. Young people in these programs receive strategic family therapy, structural family therapy, behavioral parent training, and cognitive behavior therapies. Evaluations of the MST program have found 25–70 percent reductions in long-term arrest rates, 47–64 percent reductions in out-of-home placements, significant improvements in family functioning, and decreased mental health problems for serious juvenile offenders. Similarly, Functional Family Therapy (FFT), another family-based, Blueprints-endorsed program, brings together trained probation officers, mental health technicians, and degreed mental health professionals to enhance protective factors and reduce risk of future offending. Services are delivered in homes, schools, clinics, juvenile court, community-based programs, and at the time of reentry from residential placement. FFT has been shown to effectively treat adolescents with conduct disorder, oppositional defiant disorder, disruptive behavior disorder, and who exhibit drug or alcohol abuse and other delinquency and violence. Many of the interventions identified as models by the Blueprints program are far less expensive than institutional placements, which cost an average of $241 per youth per day (ranging between $24 in Wyoming and $726 in Connecticut). MST earned $13.36 in public safety benefits for every dollar invested in the program, while FFT earned $10.69 for each dollar spent. Given that two-thirds of youths are committed to out-of-home placements for nonviolent offenses, states could save large sums by diverting youths to these less expensive and more effective interventions.

Outdated Theories and Programs

Critics of out-of-home placements argue that, where any sort of programmatic theory exists inside juvenile treatment, it is often outdated and/or has received no empirical support. The widespread use of criminal thinking errors—which posits that offenders have unique thinking patterns that are responsible for their lawbreaking—is one example. Often, the "therapeutic" component is really punitive (as in the case of boot camps), based on the theory that harsh discipline will bring about personal reform. Few of these programs have undergone evaluation, relying instead on reactive monitoring by state and local funding agencies (after an incident has occurred). These efforts tend to emphasize outputs and compliance with minimum standards for service provision, such as staff-to-client ratios, instead of outcomes, such as recidivism. Accountability, then, rarely means that facilities must demonstrate that they actually reduce young people's risk of reoffending after release. In Philadelphia, where a groundbreaking system of outcomes-tracking existed for 10 years, the failure rate varied widely across juvenile facilities, but averaged 40 percent.

Disproportionate Numbers of Minorities

Finally, opponents of out-of-home placements point to a growing body of research that exposes their disproportionate use for racial and ethnic minorities and their role in exacerbating social inequality for young people of color. Although the body of literature on disproportionate minority confinement is mixed, the majority of studies find that race plays an independent role at many decision points in the justice process. In 2006, African American males were 4.4 times and African American females 2.8 times more likely than white youths to be committed to out-of-home placements. American Indian and Alaskan Native males were 2.9 times and females 4.7 times more likely than their white counterparts to be confined in such facilities after being adjudicated for delinquency. These differences remain when controlling for offense type: black youths were 5.1 times more likely to be committed to residential placements for drug offenses than white youths. Some have argued persuasively that, when considering the unintended negative consequences of placement outlined above, youth incarceration plays a key role in what has been termed *cumulative disadvantage*, interacting with other forms of discrimination and systematic disadvantage to reduce life chances for African American and other poor youths of color.

Conclusion

In sum, concerns about the financial costs associated with out-of-home placements and the potentially detrimental effects of confinement in such facilities will likely discourage their widespread use in the future. Although the public has been largely unaware of the operation of these facilities, recent publicity around the "kids for cash" judicial scandal in Pennsylvania and high-profile cases of resident injuries and deaths inside juvenile institutions have generated additional scrutiny. There is already evidence of their declining popularity since the height of get-tough policies in the 1990s and the closing of large institutions in states such as California and New York. Experimental research on the effectiveness of alternatives to out-of-home placements has identified several programs such as Functional Family Therapy (FFT) and Multisystemic Therapy (MST) that allow young people to remain in their communities and strengthen social bonds with significant others while significantly reducing their risk of future offending. Combined with the success of the Missouri Model, which employs small, cottage-type facilities close to youths' homes, this evidence has prompted policymakers in many jurisdictions to divert young people to community-based programs. Nevertheless, out-of-home placements have a long history in the United States and are unlikely to disappear any time soon. Because the juvenile justice system must balance youths' best interests with public safety concerns, out-of-home placements will continue to play an important role for youths whose homes are judged to be unsafe, whose needs cannot be met in the community, or who present a danger to others.

See Also: 2. Alternative Schools; 3. At-Risk Youth; 4. Boot Camps; 7. Group Homes; 8. Juvenile Detention Facilities; 11. Juveniles in Adult Correctional Facilities; 14. Parental Responsibility Laws; 15. Racial Disparities; 16. Scared Straight Programs; 17. School Violence; 18. Sentencing Options; 19. Serious and Violent Juvenile Offenders; 20. Treatment and Rehabilitation.

Further Readings

Alexander, Jim, and D. S. Elliott, eds. *Functional Family Therapy: Blueprints for Violence Prevention, Book Three*. Boulder, CO: Center for the Study and Prevention of Violence, Institute of Behavioral Science, University of Colorado, 1998.

Anderson, Elijah. *Code of the Street: Decency, Violence, and the Moral Life of the Inner City*. New York: W.W. Norton, 1999.

Bernard, Thomas J. *The Cycle of Juvenile Justice*. New York: Oxford University Press, 1992.

Bishop, Donna M., and Charles E. Frazier. "Race Effects in Juvenile Justice Decision-Making: Findings of a Statewide Analysis." *Journal of Criminal Law and Criminology*, v.86/2 (1996).

Chung, He Len, Michelle Little, and Laurence Steinberg. "The Transition to Adulthood for Adolescents in the Juvenile Justice System: A Developmental Perspective." In *On Your Own Without a Net: The Transition to Adulthood for Vulnerable Populations,* edited by D. Wayne Osgood, E. Michael Forster, Constance Flanagan, and Gretchen R. Ruth. Chicago: University of Chicago Press, 2005.

Fader, Jamie J. "You Can Take Me Outta the 'Hood, but You Can't Take the 'Hood Outta Me: Youth Incarceration and Reentry." In *Against the Wall: Poor, Young, Black, and Male,* edited by Elijah Anderson. Philadelphia, PA: University of Pennsylvania Press, 2008.

Fader, Jamie J., et al. "Factors Involved in Decisions on Commitment to Delinquency Programs for First-Time Juvenile Offenders." *Justice Quarterly,* v.18/2 (2001).

Gatti, Uberto, Richard E. Tremblay, and Frank Vitaro. "Iatrogenic Effect of Juvenile Justice." *Journal of Child Psychology and Psychiatry,* v.50 (2009).

Gorsuch, K. R., et al. "Missouri Department of Youth Services: An Experience in Delinquency Reform." In *Missouri and Hawaii: Leaders in Youth Correction Policy,* edited by the Center for the Study of Youth Policy. Ann Arbor, MI: Center for the Study of Youth Policy, 1992.

Henggeler, Scott W., et al. *Blueprints for Violence Prevention, Book Six: Multisystemic Therapy.* Boulder, CO: Center for the Study and Prevention of Violence, 1998.

Howell, John C., ed. *Guide for Implementing the Comprehensive Strategy for Serious, Violent, and Chronic Juvenile Offenders.* Washington, DC: U.S. Department of Justice, Office of Justice Programs, Office of Juvenile Justice and Delinquency Prevention, 1995.

Inderbitzin, Michelle. "Inside a Maximum-Security Juvenile Training School: Institutional Attempts to Redefine the American Dream and 'Normalize' Incarcerated Youth." *Punishment and Society,* v.9 (2007).

Justice Policy Institute. "The Costs of Confinement: Why Good Juvenile Justice Policies Make Good Fiscal Sense." *Justice Policy Institute* (May 2009).

Kelly, Barbara Tatem, Terence P. Thornberry, and Carolyn A. Smith. "In the Wake of Child Maltreatment." (August 1997). *Juvenile Justice Bulletin.* U.S. Department of Justice. http://www.ncjrs.gov/pdffiles 1/165257.pdf (Accessed September 2010).

Leiber, Michael J. "Disproportionate Minority Confinement (DMC) of Youth: An Analysis of State and Federal Efforts to Address the Issue." *Crime and Delinquency,* v.48/1 (2002).

Lipsey, Mark W., David B. Wilson, and Lynn Cothern. "Effective Intervention for Juvenile Offenders." *Juvenile Justice Bulletin* (April 2000). U.S. Department of Justice. http://www.ncjrs.org/pdffiles1/ojjdp /181201.pdf (Accessed September 2010).

Miller, Jerome G. *Last One Over the Wall: The Massachusetts Experiment in Closing Reform Schools.* Columbus, OH: Ohio State University Press, 1998.

Nurse, Anne M. "The Structure of the Juvenile Prison." *Youth and Society*, v.32/3 (2001).

Parent, Dale G. "Summary of Conditions of Juvenile Confinement Study." *Prison Journal*, v.73/2 (1993).

Platt, Anthony M. *The Child Savers: The Invention of Delinquency.* Chicago: University of Chicago Press, 1977.

Pope, Carl. E., R. Lovell, and H. M. Hsia. "Disproportionate Minority Confinement: A Review of the Research Literature From 1989 Through 2001." *Juvenile Justice Bulletin* (2002).

Program Development and Evaluation System. Crime and Justice Research Center. http://www.temple.edu/prodes (Accessed September 2010).

Puzzanchera, Charles, and Melissa Sickmund. *Juvenile Court Statistics 2005.* Pittsburgh, PA: National Center for Juvenile Justice, 2008.

Sampson, Robert J., and John H. Laub. *Crime in the Making: Pathways and Turning Points Through Life.* Cambridge, MA: Harvard University Press, 1993.

Sampson, Robert J., and John H. Laub. "A Life-Course Theory of Cumulative Disadvantage and the Stability of Delinquency." In *Developmental Theories of Crime and Delinquency,* edited by Terrence P. Thornberry. New Brunswick, NJ: Transaction Publishers, 1997.

Schneider, Eric C. *In the Web of Class: Delinquents and Reformers in Boston, 1810s–1930s.* New York: New York University Press, 1992.

Sickmund, Melissa, T. J. Sladky, and Wei Kang. "Census of Juveniles in Residential Placement Databook." (2005). http://www.ojjdp.ncjrs.org /ojstatbb/cjrp (Accessed September 2010).

White, Helene R., et al. "Effects of Institutional Confinement for Delinquency on Levels of Depression and Anxiety Among Male Adolescents." *Youth Violence and Juvenile Justice*, v.8/4 (October 2010).

14

Parental Responsibility Laws

Gilbert Geis
University of California, Irvine

L aws that hold parents legally responsible civilly or criminally for outlawed behavior of their children have a checkered history in the administration of justice. There are advocates who believe that such statutes are the only practical way to put parents on notice that they must guide their children into acceptable paths or suffer legal consequences for their failure to do so. Others insist that the laws are both undesirable and ineffective. Their arguments focus on matters of family privacy and discrimination against the underclass. They also maintain that the parental responsibility laws are oversimplified attempts to deal with a notably complex social problem.

Three major considerations have fueled the drive to enact parental responsibility laws. The first is the inability of persons injured or deprived by an act of an underage person to obtain compensation from the youth who has harmed them. A minor is much less likely than his or her parents to afford payment for damages he or she has inflicted, such as a broken window from a baseball game or a pedestrian's broken arm from a careless act of bicycling. These laws, imposing civil liability on parents, are long-standing and commonplace.

A second concern involves protecting youths from acts by adults that contribute to, or are likely to contribute to, a minor's delinquent behavior. These statutes typically ensnare persons others than parents, such as liquor store owners who sell alcoholic beverages to underage customers. But they also can be employed against parents in regard to matters such as failure to see that their child attends school with some regularity or obeys curfew regulations. These laws have rarely been enforced after an early period of unrealistic expectations.

Some generations later, parental responsibility laws were reconfigured with renewed anticipation that they would have a significant impact on wayward young people. The major consideration prompting this third form of parental responsibility laws is the belief by the public and authorities that better measures had to be put in place in an attempt to curtail what was seen as out-of-control juvenile gang behavior: drive-by shootings, gang-against-gang warfare, narcotic use and sales, intimidation of the innocent, scrawled graffiti, and other disruptions of calm and safe existence, particularly in depressed urban areas.

Contributing to Delinquency

The idea of punishing parents for the misdeeds of their children has deep roots in American soil. A 1645 Massachusetts colony law, citing biblical precedent, declared that a court could sentence to death (none in fact did) a child whose parents found him or her unrepentant and incapable of control, unwilling, in the words of the law, "to obey the voice of his Father … or Mother, being his natural parents." The same law provided that the parents of a child found guilty of stealing could be held liable to repay the victim for the loss.

Approaches such as this were reflected in "contributing to delinquency laws." Their passage was first advocated by groups such as the Society for the Prevention of Cruelty to Children, founded in New York in 1875, that advocated a statute providing for "the prosecution of parents or others who ill-used and brutally treated the young and defenseless." The parental responsibility movement gained momentum in 1899 with the Illinois legislature's authorization of the country's first juvenile court, an American innovation that soon spread worldwide. The expressed aim of the juvenile court was to restore wayward youths to law-abiding ways by providing the kind of enlightened treatment that should have been afforded by their parents.

In 1903, Colorado's legislature included a pioneering provision in its state juvenile code that called for the punishment of adults "contributing to delinquency." In short order, as the Colorado Supreme Court noted in the 1909 case of *Gibson v. People*, the contributing statute had been "cordially welcomed" by the bar, the pulpit, and the press as a much-needed, forward-looking move. Contributing laws would be enacted in short order in all states except Maine and Georgia.

In contrast to the benevolent philosophy and compassionate ideals that led to the formation of juvenile courts, the new laws became entwined with statutes that called for the full force of the criminal law to descend on irresponsible parents of juvenile delinquents. If children no longer could be held personally responsible for their behavior, responsibility would have to be placed on other persons, rather than being located in inanimate and complex social forces. To view ineffective parents as products of the same processes that sent their offspring astray would not be an acceptable principle in a society that strongly believed in individual choice and in parents' guilt for the misdeeds of their offspring.

The contributing laws made it a misdemeanor (only rarely would it be classified as a felony) to aid, encourage, or cause any child under a specified age to become or to remain dependent, neglected, or delinquent. The law in Alabama was typical. It spelled out actions that were outlawed if they were deemed to contribute to delinquency—specifying words, acts, threats, commands, or persuasions—and noted that it was now against the law to induce or endeavor to induce a child to perform any act or to follow any course of conduct that would cause or manifestly tend to cause the child to become or remain delinquent. In Pennsylvania, such a provision was found to be adequate grounds to convict a person who purchased stolen goods brought to him by two minor boys. Similarly, parents who have knowingly accepted items stolen by their children have been prosecuted under contributing to delinquency laws.

Examples of Applied Delinquency Laws

The 1958 case of *State v. Gans* illustrates the application of a contributing statute. The adoptive parents of an 11-year-old girl had taken her from Ohio to West Virginia where, having misrepresented her age, she was married. On their return to Ohio, the parents were charged with contributing to the delinquency of their daughter under a statutory provision that outlawed actions causing or intending to cause delinquency. The court ruled that the

delinquency need not be forthcoming; the statute, it decreed, sought to fore-
stall this undesirable outcome. The judge noted that, after all, "a disease is
much easier to prevent than to cure," an arguable proposition. The likely
delinquent act, the *Gans* decision declared, was truancy; marriage was seen
as encouraging school absences, a matter made more unfortunate because
the 11-year-old had been a good student. And even if her school attendance
remained satisfactory, the judge observed, "the more successful her marriage would be the more it could tend to cause her to act so as to adversely
affect the morals of her classmates."

The contributing statute proved a convenient vehicle for action against
persons involved in behaviors that shocked or unnerved the community.
Thus, a father in New York was convicted of contributing to the delinquency of a minor when he left a loaded gun in an accessible buffet drawer,
and his three-year-old found the weapon and injured another child with it.
When parents in the state of Washington withdrew their son from school
to teach him at home, the court found the home tutoring inadequate, declared the child a delinquent, and prosecuted the parents for contributing to that condition. In Illinois, parents who instructed their child not to
pledge allegiance to the flag because it was against their religious principles
were sentenced to one-year jail terms, but in this case, the appellate court
reversed the verdict on the ground that it stretched the statute beyond its
tolerance level.

Hostile community attitudes toward nonconforming parents were not
without limits. In a widely publicized New York case, the conviction of
an allegedly heavy-drinking, promiscuous, neglectful mother, sentenced to
jail for contributing to her 14-year-old son's delinquency, aroused an out-
burst of sympathetic reactions, and the appellate division, apparently sympathetic to her situation, reversed her conviction on the technical ground
that the prosecution had introduced inadmissible hearsay evidence. Similarly, the courts exonerated a woman, who had accepted gifts and apparently been sexually involved with man who was a father, from the charge
of contributing to the delinquency of his children. In California, a man
who lived with a woman without the benefit of marriage was said not to
have contributed to her children's delinquency because it had not been
demonstrated that his behavior had directly brought about their delinquent behavior.

But recourse to the contributing statutes in such situations indicates their
flexibility and the potential for abuse. The legal counsel for the National
Council on Crime and Delinquency pinpointed what he deemed the illogic

of contributing laws. In New York, he noted, parents could be held criminally liable if their child was a habitual school truant, but if the same child murdered someone, the parents could not be held liable.

Empirical Inquires

Herbert Lou, a leading authority on the history of juvenile courts, summed up the situation in 1927 by pointing out that although adult contributing laws had been in force for many years, they had not been generally enforced (with the exception of a few places), and had not produced the anticipated results. This claimed failure to curb delinquency, in addition to instances of abuse of the law, and the appearance of other statutes that outlawed specified adult wrongdoing, led to the general disuse of contributing laws after the first quarter of the 20th century.

A couple of decades later, Paul Alexander, a judge in Toledo, Ohio, studied the impact of prosecutions for contributing to delinquency. He reviewed 1,027 cases between 1937 and 1946, of which about one-half involved parents. Three-quarters of the parents pleaded guilty or were convicted, and of these, one-quarter received jail sentences. On the basis of his research, Alexander concluded that there was no evidence whatsoever that punishing parents had any impact on curbing juvenile delinquency.

More recently, a 1996 study by the federal Department of Heath and Human Services (HHS) examined the results in 16 states that had enacted civil parental liability laws and compared the rates of juvenile crime in these states with the rates in the remainder of the country. The study found that the juvenile delinquency rate in the 16 states was higher than the national average. While the results suggest that the laws had not been effective, they are not conclusive. The laws may have come into being because the particular states that created them were beset with a higher level of delinquency than that elsewhere. The new laws could have had a mild impact and still left delinquency rates exceeding the national average.

Parental Responsibility Reestablished

A Michigan case that received widespread publicity reflected the revival of the doctrine of parental responsibility. The site was St. Clair Shores, Michigan, a middle-class suburban city about 13 miles northeast of Detroit. A six-person jury in 1965 took 15 minutes of deliberation to convict Susan Provenzino, a bookkeeper, and Anthony Provenzino, a restaurant chef, the

parents of 16-year-old Alex, of improper supervision of their child in violation of a two-year-old ordinance that placed a responsibility on parents to
"exercise reasonable control over their children." The Provenzino's attorney submitted evidence that the parents were fearful of their son, that he
had refused their insistence that he undertake a counseling regimen, that
he had attacked his father with a golf club, and that, all told, he was "out
of control." The youth was a drug seller and abuser and had committed
seven burglaries, including the theft of $3,500 from the church the family
attended. The prosecutor told the jury that the parents should have searched
the boy's room when he was away to locate evidence of his wrongdoing.
When the police made such a search, they found a stolen gun and knife and
a marijuana plant.

The prosecutor apparently scored points with the jury when he had the
parents grant that they were not aware of their child's recent school grades.
A commentator on the case believed that the jury's view of the father as
"unmanly" and "weak" had contributed to the guilty verdict. The prosecutor asked for a civil fine of $27,000, but the judge fined each parent $100
and imposed a $2,000 levy for court costs in addition to a $13,000 yearly
sum to cover Alex's care in a detention facility. The fine ultimately was
remitted by the county court on the ground that it had not been proven,
as the ordinance required, that the parents had not sought counseling for
their son.

Up Close and Personal

The focus on the responsibility of parents and guardians picked up speed
toward the end of the 20th century, as gang violence became a prominent
issue in American domestic life and policies. One example of this aggressive
approach appeared in a 1985 Wisconsin law that made both parents and
grandparents financially and criminally responsible, with a possible two-
year jail term and/or a fine up to $10,000, if their unmarried minor children
bore children. Some 14 adults were prosecuted before the law was allowed
to expire on the grounds that it had not proved effective. More to the point
was an enactment in the state of Washington that allowed the imposition of
a fine of up to $5,000 against the parents of a minor who defaced a public
building.

An ordinance enacted in 1989 in Dermott, Arkansas, a city with about
4,700 inhabitants, represented a particularly harsh expression of retribution directed against parents of offending children. The Dermott City

Council, in the wake of a gang street fight the night before and a crime increase during the summer school recess, decreed a possible sentence of two days in the open-air stockade for parents whose children under the age of 18 violated the city's 11 P.M. to 5:30 A.M. curfew. Further penalties could include publication of a parent's picture in the local newspaper over the caption "Irresponsible Parent." If parents maintained that they were unable to control their children, they had to sign a statement to this effect, and the youngster would be referred to the juvenile court. The parents then had to pay $100 for each child referred or perform 20 hours of community service.

The most prominent parental responsibility drive took place in California in 1988, when the state legislature added to the contributing law the sentence that "a parent or guardian to any person under the age of 18 years shall have the duty to exercise reasonable care, supervision, protection, and control" over their minor or child. Convictions could result in a fine no greater than $2,500 and a one-year jail term.

Louisiana's parental responsibility law, passed in 1995, took the unusual step of spelling out precisely the behaviors it outlawed. A parent could be held criminally responsible for "improper supervision" if he or she allowed a child to associate with a person known by the parent to be a member of a street gang, a convicted felon, a drug user or dealer, or a possessor of an illegal weapon. Similar penalties could be levied if the parents permitted their child to enter a place known by them to house what could be considered sexually indecent activities or prostitution, underage drinking, gambling, narcotics, or illegal weapons.

Another prominent example was the 1997 law in Silverton, Oregon, said to be the first of the new wave of parental responsibility local ordinances. In Silverton, a town of 6,170 persons, parents could be charged with the misdemeanor of "failing to supervise a minor" when a youngster under the age of 18 violated any provision of the Silverton Municipal Code. Seven parents were arrested in the first two and a half months of the existence of the responsibility provision. The case of 48-year-old Roberta Olsen was typical; her 11-year-old son gave her the slip when she tried to pick him up after school. Meanwhile, he went to a local drug store and shoplifted some items. The court dismissed the case, but not before the Silverton approach had commanded national attention and duplication in numerous other Oregon jurisdictions. The Silverton mayor reported a 45 percent reduction in juvenile crime in his city and a reduced level of truancy since the enactment of the ordinance.

Street Terrorism Enforcement and Prevention Act

The Street Terrorism Enforcement and Prevention Act (STEP) carried the legislative justification that "the State of California is in a state of crisis which has been caused by violent street gangs whose members threaten, terrorize, and commit a multitude of crimes against the peaceful citizens of their neighborhood." The legislative statement took note of the fact that there were 600 criminal street gangs in California, and that during 1987, there were 328 gang-related murders in Los Angeles, an increase of more than 80 percent over the number during the previous year. The STEP Act also established criminal penalties for gang participation and sentence enhancements for gang-related conduct, and defined certain buildings in which gang activities took place as public nuisances, subject to law enforcement actions.

The STEP measure mandated a parental diversion program that allowed the probation department, under specified circumstances, to send parents or guardians to an education, treatment, or rehabilitation program prior to a court trial. Satisfactory completion of the program would result in dismissal of criminal charges.

There was irony in the first case tried under the new law when Gloria Williams was charged after her 12-year-old son was suspected of having participated in a gang rape. When investigators came to the Williams's home, they found photo albums with pictures of Ms. Williams posing with gang members, spray-painted graffiti adorning the walls of their living quarters, and other gang-related contents. When it became known that Ms. Williams had participated in a parenting course two months earlier, the prosecutor dropped the case, saying that it would violate the spirit of the law since the accused mother had already undergone parental education.

Are the New Laws Constitutional?

The opinion of Justice Stanley Mosk in *Williams v. Garcetti* (1993), writing for a unanimous, seven-person California Supreme Court bench, addressed one of the more prominent objections to the parental responsibility condition that had been added to the 1909 contributing statute. The issue before the Court was whether the amendment was so vague and overbroad as to offend constitutional guarantees that demanded that there be enough specificity in a provision so that reasonable people would know what they could and could not do legally.

The state's Supreme Court upheld the law against a challenge by the American Civil Liberties Union and Gary Williams, a law professor filing the case as a concerned taxpayer. To avoid a verdict declaring a statute unconstitutionally vague, two criteria had to be met: The law had to be definite enough to provide a standard of conduct for those whose activities are proscribed, and a standard for police enforcement and ascertainment of guilt.

Before the case reached the Supreme Court, a trial court had ruled that the law was in accord with constitutional guarantees, but an appellate court had decided otherwise, ruling the law unconstitutionally vague but offering no judgment on the issue of overreach.

Justice Mosk, an eminent legal scholar, wrote the Court's opinion. He thought that the objection on the ground of vagueness was inadequate because the new provision was merely making clearer what had been long-established parental obligations under the existing contributing statute. It was the standard of "reasonableness" that carried the argument for the Court's decision, although it was granted that "there is no formula for the determination of reasonableness." The ruling also had a curious sentence. It declared that "a parent can be convicted [criminally] only for gross or extreme departures from the objectively reasonable standard of care." It is the use of the term *objectively* that is puzzling, since the opinion had earlier granted that reasonableness is essentially an ambiguous standard. Mosk also suffused his ruling with dicta, suggesting that unless its enforcers were scrupulous (he wrote that he saw no reason why they would not be), the law could be employed in an abusive manner, especially in marginal cases where arguable subjective judgments might be employed.

There are myriad arguments both favoring and opposing parental responsibility laws. The key question for those favoring the laws is: Who can be blamed? On the other side are those who see the problem as: What can be blamed? For proponents of parental responsibility laws, the target is readily determinable; for the opponents, the remedy is much more uncertain and far from easily implemented.

Pro: Arguments Supporting Parental Responsibility Laws

Frustration with youthful aberrancy is the major underlying condition and emotion leading to parental responsibility laws. One person arguing forcefully for attributing children's behavior to their parents noted the poet Ralph Waldo Emerson's comment, "men are what their mothers made them," and Abraham Lincoln's observation, "All that I am or hope to be, I owe to my angel mother." For those favoring the responsibility laws, bad kids are the products of bad parenting.

Advocates typically support their position by maintaining that parental responsibility measures are necessary to make inattentive parents monitor the behavior of their offspring more carefully. It is argued that the courts as well as family and youth service agencies have undervalued or ignored the role that parents play in their children's misbehavior, and what can and should be done about it. They often maintain that it is not their desire to be punitive (except in the very worst cases), but rather to make parents aware of the harmful consequences that can ensue from what is regarded as their failure to supervise their children satisfactorily. The law is deemed to provide a learning experience, not only to those being dealt with, but also to other parents who become aware of the punishment that might be inflicted on them if they do not adequately perform as parents.

The laws also are seen by proponents as having a symbolic impact, demonstrating that authorities are concerned about and trying to contain juvenile delinquency. A 1996 *New York Times*/CBS poll found that 72 percent of the population believed that parents should be held responsible for crimes committed by their children. Politicians are compelled to respond to such results; those who fail to do so might well have to seek other employment.

Some who favor the laws believe that they are not stringent enough. One of their major suggestions is the imposition of strict liability so that parents are automatically assumed to have failed to provide effective supervision of an errant offspring. Otherwise, to find parents culpable, it often becomes necessary to demonstrate their intentional encouragement of the undesirable behavior.

Con: Arguments Opposing Parental Responsibility Laws

Opponents of parental responsibility laws insist, among other things, that they represent but another instance of discrimination against members of minority groups who undoubtedly are the violators most targeted. Underclass parents often are overwhelmed by poverty and live in neighborhoods saturated with illegal activity. Single parents holding down jobs, it is argued, should not be penalized for consequences, that for all practical purposes, are beyond their control. How can a parent, for instance, reasonably keep a child from violating curfew laws if the child is determined to do so? In addition, opponents argue that poor parenting is hardly the sole cause, if a cause at all, of juvenile delinquency, and that the children of even model parents can go astray for reasons that have nothing to do with what their parents have or have not done.

Opponents also claim that parental responsibility regulations further disrupt what often already are dysfunctional family situations, and provide a weapon that children may use to harass beleaguered parents. Youngsters can threaten their parents with law enforcement retaliation if they are not allowed to have their way.

Those who find the parental responsibility laws irresponsible also note that a likely reaction of abusive parents concerned about the laws would be to inflict further physical punishment on a wayward child in the hope that it would keep him or her on a law-abiding path. If the penalty is a monetary fine, it would only further impoverish a family already severely pressed economically. A sentence to jail could deprive the children of whatever parenting they might have been receiving and encourage further depredations.

Opponents of the parental liability laws also note that parents seeking to protect themselves against the possibility of being held responsible for their children's unacceptable behavior might emancipate the youngsters, a legal tactic that absolves them from responsibility for any aspect of the child's situation. Emancipation of a minor involves a petition for an order, usually from family court, citing reasons why parents no longer are to be legally responsible for their child. Often, the child has to be living separately and to be self-supporting.

Objections also focus on the fact that convictions can be obtained without proving that the adult's behavior was the cause of the minor's wrongdoing. Critics taking this position maintain that parental responsibility laws ought only to incriminate parents who aid and abet their child's illegal acts, such as purchasing a weapon for an adolescent's use or knowingly allowing narcotics to be stored in their house by gang members. They also cite appellate court opinions that have ruled that strict liability laws imposing parental responsibility are unconstitutional. In New Hampshire, for instance, a father was convicted when his sons were apprehended for driving a snowmobile on a public thoroughfare at a higher than permissible speed. The appellate court ruled that a penalty had been imposed on the father only because of his status as a parent, and that this was a violation of his constitutional rights.

Others insist that the privacy of family affairs dictates that the government ought not to intrude with so far-reaching an invasive process into family activities and arrangements.

Conclusion

There is the underlying question of whether the parental responsibility laws accomplish the purpose they seek to achieve. The 1968 Seebohm Report in Great Britain, which sparked the first generic social services departments, recognized that services needed to reflect the fact that children live in families and communities, and noted that it is "both wasteful and irresponsible to set experiments in motion and to fail to record and analyze what happens." The government commission report added that it makes no sense in terms of administrative efficiency, and that however little intended, the failure to evaluate what is done indicates a careless attitude toward human welfare. This observation applies to the lack of solid information about the consequences of parental responsibility laws.

In the aftermath of widespread publicity over the Silverton ordinance, many small Oregon cities and towns enacted similar ordinances. A survey of the state's police chiefs and district attorneys found that the ordinances were rarely enforced at the time.

Criminologists who specialize in the study of juvenile delinquency tend to be scornful of parental responsibility laws. Barry Krisberg, president of the National Council on Crime and Delinquency, called the enactments "country club criminology," made to appease and please suburban residents. If so, is this because the laws were not meant to be enforced strenuously, because they are unenforceable, because prosecutors do not find them useful, or for other reasons? The judgments to date have relied almost exclusively on anecdotal evidence. The failure to empirically determine the consequences of the existence and the usage of parental responsibility laws is particularly unfortunate. At the same time, accurate experimental evidence will not resolve the judgmental issue. If the laws only prevent a few acts of serious subsequent delinquency, they may not be worthwhile endeavors from a cost-benefit basis.

See Also: 3. At-Risk Youth; 5. Curfews; 7. Group Homes; 13. Out-of-Home Placement; 15. Racial Disparities.

Further Readings

Alexander, Paul W. "What's This About Punishing Parents?" *Federal Probation*, v.12 (March 1948).

Brank, Eva M., Stephanie C. Kucera, and Stephanie A. Hays. "Parental Responsibility: Organization and Policy Implications." *Journal of Law and Family Studies,* v.7 (2005).

Chapin, Linda A. "Out of Control: The Uses and Abuses of Parental Liability Laws to Control Juvenile Delinquency in the United States." *Santa Clara Law Review,* v.37 (1997).

Cosgrain, Michelle L. "Parental Responsibility Laws: Cure for Crime or Exercise in Futility?" *Wayne Law Review,* v.37 (1990).

Davidson, Howard. "No Consequences: Re-Examining Parental Responsibility Laws." *Stanford Law and Policy Review,* v.7 (1995).

Demitris, Jason Emilios. "Parental Responsibility Statutes—and the Programs That Must Accompany Them." *Stetson Law Review,* v.27 (1997).

DiFazio, James Herbie. "Parental Responsibility for Juvenile Crime." *Oregon Law Review,* v.80 (2001).

Geis, Gilbert. "Contributing to Delinquency." *Saint Louis University Law Journal,* v.8 (1963).

Geis, Gilbert, and Arnold Binder. "Sins of Their Children: Parental Responsibility for Juvenile Delinquency." *Notre Dame Journal of Law, Ethics and Public Policy,* v.5 (1991).

Gibson v. People, 99 Pac. 33 (Colorado 1909).

Gladstone, Irving A. "The Legal Responsibility of Parents for Juvenile Delinquency in New York State: A Developmental Review. *Brooklyn Law Review,* v.21 (1955).

Greenwood, Christine T. "Holding Parents Criminally Responsible for the Delinquent Acts of Their Children: Reasoned Responses or 'Knee-Jerk Reactions'?" *Journal of Contemporary Law,* v.23 (1997).

Harris, Leslie Jean. "An Empirical Study of Parental Responsibility Law: Sending Messages, but What Kind and to Whom?" *Utah Law Review,* v.5 (2006).

Ihrie, A. Dale III. "Parental Delinquency: Should Parents Be Criminally Liable for Failing to Supervise Their Children?" *University of Detroit Mercy Law Review,* v.74 (1996).

Laskin, Elena R. "How Parental Liability Statutes Criminalize and Stigmatize Minority Mothers." *American Criminal Law Review,* v.37 (2000).

Lou, Herbert H. *Juvenile Courts in the United States.* Chapel Hill, NC: University of North Carolina Press, 1927.

Nicholas, Deborah A. "Parental Liability for Youth Violence: The Contrast Between Moral Responsibility and Legal Obligations." *Rutgers Law Review,* v.53 (2000).

Scarola, Tami. "Creating Problems Rather Than Solving Them: Why Criminal Parental Responsibility Laws Do Not Fit Within Our Understanding of Justice." *Fordham Law Review,* v.66 (1997).

Schmidt, Paul W. "Dangerous Children and the Regulated Family: The Shifting Focus of Parental Responsibility Laws." *New York University Law Review,* v.73 (1995).

Seebohm Report. *Report of the Committee on Local Authority and Allied Personal Social Services.* London: HMSO, 1968.

Soden, Glenn W. "Contributing to Delinquency: An Exercise in Judicial Speculation." *Akron Law Review,* v.9 (1976).

State v. Gans, 151 N.E.2d 709 (Ohio 1958); cert. denied, 359 U.S. 945 (1959).

Thurman, Tammy. "Parental Responsibility Laws: Are They the Answer to Juvenile Delinquency?" *Journal of Law and Family Studies,* v.5 (2003).

Tyler, Jerry E., and Thomas W. Sagady. "Parental Responsibility Law: Rationale, Theory, and Effectiveness." *Social Science Journal,* v.37 (2000).

Williams v. Garcette, 853 P.2d 507 (Calif. 1993).

Zelman, Courtney L. "Parental Responsibility Acts: Medicine for Ailing Families and Hope for the Future." *Capital Law Review,* v.27 (1998).

15

Racial Disparities

Tommy J. Curry
Texas A&M University

In the last several decades, racial disparities in the juvenile justice system have received renewed attention in academia. Following the amendments to the Juvenile Justice and Delinquency Prevention Act of 1992, the last several decades have seen the activity of various governmental and nongovernmental agencies dedicated to investigating the causes of black and Hispanic over-representation in the juvenile justice system. Alongside the work of national and local agencies, the scholarly interest in racial disparity in the juvenile justice system shown by academics has produced noteworthy contributions to identifying the presence of this particular racial disparity, however, this research has not provided social scientists and activists with an identifiable cause. According to Timothy Bray, Lisa Sample, and Kimberly Kempf-Leonard in *Justice by Geography,* "though there is an accepted wide consensus that differential treatment exists ... despite increasing sophistication and rigor of empirical research, we have not adequately explained the reasons for it." Like many other areas of social inquiry, the discovery of race and ethnic disparity and racial bias in social systems lead to seemingly endless apologetics of the systems accused of inequality rather than culpability for the identifiable patterns of discrimination or racist acts, especially when dealing with issues associated with crime.

Take, for example, one of the most recent reports funded by the Office of Juvenile Justice and Delinquency Prevention's Program of Research for

209

the Causes and Correlates of Delinquency. Even when David Huizinga, Terence Thornberry, Kelly Knight, and Peter Lovegrove identified racial bias and implicated this bias in the harsher sentencing and treatment of minorities, there seemed to be a complex nexus of variables that "expectantly" concludes that despite the presence of observations needed to substantiate the argument that racial bias exists in the juvenile justice system, one cannot conclude that the culmination of these observations and events point to racial bias, because there could be other alternative causes. But many scholars like Barry Krisberg have begun criticizing the enduring practice of "abstracted empiricism," whereby social scientists continue to treat race as "just another 'variable' rather than try [to]understand race as a profoundly important part of one's social and psychic existence from birth through death." These scholars insist that using statistical controls to parcel out, and in some sense determine, what alternative factors could explain the relationships found between race and the effect of juvenile justice on minorities is "sociologically naive." In the foreword to *Our Children, Their Children*, Barry Krisberg argues the problems with this approach:

> [these investigators think] if other factors appear to explain the observed empirical relationships, then race is not the real etiologic factor. But this position is sociologically naïve ... race is expressed in other social, economic, cultural and psychological factors .... [It] affects where one lives and how much education one receives. [It] influences life expectancy and access to health care. Race and social class, and race and geography are intertwined. So when analyses show that "other variables" reduce the variance explained by race, they are simply identifying the intervening variables through which race affects life outcomes. That the researchers find any residual race effect at all suggests ... that they have not measured all the pertinent intervening factors, or that they have inexactly measured another factor that I would call racism.

Racism, or the practice through which social, cultural, and economic conditions are used to enforce theories of racial inferiority, is the "ghost in the machine." For the last three decades, the research by criminologists and social scientists has continued to document the presence of disparity as either occurring in or based on differential offending—which suggests that differences in sentencing and conviction are based in the incidence, seriousness, and reoccurrence of delinquent activity by minorities, or differential treatment. This in turn suggests that the overrepresentation of minorities in the juvenile justice system is due to some structural or social inequity. Unfortunately, as Alex Piquero notes in a 2008 article titled "Disproportionate Minority Contact," a determinative analysis between these two approaches is not only difficult, but may in fact be impossible. Despite the means we have to describe this phenomenon, the reality, says Donna M. Bishop in her much-cited 2005 article "Racial and Ethnic Differences in Juvenile Justice Processing," is that "nationally, youths of color—especially African Americans and Hispanics—are arrested in numbers greatly disproportionate to their representation in the general population. They are overrepresented among young people held in secure detention, petitioned to juvenile court, and adjudicated delinquent." For those who are adjudicated delinquent, they are exiled to the deep end of the system, confined in large public state institutions rather than private treatment facilities focused on rehabilitation. Those deemed unfit for the juvenile justice system are usually African American.

While there are myriad ways to interpret this unfortunate racial reality, several major debates about racial disparity in the juvenile justice system, its relationship to racism, and critical literature surrounding alternative accounts of disproportionate minority confinement have come to the fore, particularly those given by "otherness" studies and abolitionists.

Policy and Paradigm

The Juvenile Justice and Delinquency Prevention Act of 1974 (JJDP) has undergone a series of amendments to address the persistent overrepresentation of minorities in the juvenile justice system. In 1988, for example, Congress mandated that states take concrete steps to address the presence of disproportionate minority confinement in their states. According to this earlier provision, under the Formula Grants Program, each state must address efforts to reduce the proportion of minority youths detained or confined in secure detention facilities, secure correctional facilities, jails, and lock-ups if their numbers exceed the proportion of such groups in the general population. In 1992, a subsequent amendment to the JJDP made redress of disproportionate minority confinement (DMC) a core requirement for states participating in the Formula Grants Program. According to the 1992 amendments, Congress conditioned full funding of states participating in the Formula Grants Program on their compliance with and monitoring of DMC. Failure to comply with the guidelines of the 1992 amendment could result in up to 20 percent of the funding being withheld.

In 2002, the federal government recognized the continued importance of DMC monitoring throughout the country and made further amendments to the JJDP that expanded its concerns beyond confinement toward contact. In short, the additional amendments required that states participating in the Formula Grants Program address juvenile delinquency prevention efforts and system improvements designed to reduce, without establishing or requiring numerical standards or quotas, the disproportionate number of juvenile members of minority groups who come into contact with the juvenile justice system. Remarking on the paradigmatic shift from early articulations of the DMC that concentrated primarily on "disproportionate minority confinement" to "disproportionate minority contact," Carl E. Pope and Michael Leiber note that there is now a federal commitment toward examinations of the overrepresentation of minority populations "at all decision points in the juvenile justice continuum." This expanded focus pushes states, local agencies, and social investigators to consider the facts that reach their culmination in confinement, not confinement as an end to itself.

Report of Accountability

In an effort to increase the accountability of the 2002 amendment, the 2002 revision mandates that states report their progress in a three-year report, which encompasses five areas: (1) identification (the determination of the extent to which DMC exists), (2) assessment (to assess the reasons for DMC); (3) intervention (to develop and implement intervention strategies to address these identified reasons for DMC); (4) evaluation (to evaluate the effectiveness of the chosen intervention strategies); and finally, (5) monitoring (to note the change in DMC trends and adjust intervention strategies as needed). According to the Office of Juvenile Justice and Delinquency Prevention, minority populations are not simply isolated to black and Latino youth incarceration rates in comparison to whites, as is usually reflected in the academic literature. For the purposes of the JJDP, minority populations include American Indian, Alaska native, Asians, blacks or African Americans, Hispanics or Latinos, and native Hawaiians and other Pacific Islanders.

Recent social investigations have shown that minority youth representation is present in every state and exists at every level of the juvenile justice system and decision point, including arrest, secure corrections, secure detention, and transfers to adult court. While there is variation in overrepresentation depending on state and locale, on average, note Carl E. Pope and Michael Leiber, "the greatest overrepresentation seems to be at secure detention and secure corrections, followed by transfer to adult court." This multifaceted expression of overrepresentation in the juvenile justice system, from contact to disposition, is the terrain the new amendment to the JJDP is meant to capture.

In general, the juvenile justice system involves six steps: (1) intake, where the offender is referred to the juvenile justice system instead of being directed to other reform-oriented agencies like social services; (2) detention, where the state offender is either detained at a secure facility or released under care of a legal guardian; (3) petitioning, where the state decides to formally charge the minor or put forth a delinquency petition; (4) waiver, where the court can decide, before a judgment of delinquency, to transfer the offender to the adult criminal justice system; (5) adjudication, the hearing that determines the offender's involvement in the alleged crime; and (6) disposition, the decision by the judge as to how the court wishes to treat the offender's delinquency.

Because all of these processes require various interactions with the system and staff, many current approaches dealing with DMC under the new legislation are aimed at targeting the contact minorities have with police and schools at the intake stage. Because many of the referrals that place minority children in the juvenile justice system come from law enforcement, many of the recommendations for decreasing DMC have focused on local efforts like officer training, encouragement of community involvement, and increased conflict resolution in schools to prevent minority populations' placement in the juvenile justice system. The emphasis is now preventative as well as diagnostic. Instead of merely encouraging states to assess the status of DMC within their boundaries, the new amendments signal federal initiative toward preventing minorities from even entering the rank and file of the juvenile justice system.

In October 2007, the OJJDP unveiled its DMC Best Practices Database to assist various state and local jurisdictions in their efforts to decrease DMC. The DMC Best Practices Database is a fully searchable Website that provides jurisdictions with information and models that have shown to decrease DMC. According to the OJJDP Website, "the database organizes the DMC strategies into three categories corresponding to the different populations for which they are designed to impact: (1) direct services, which target at-risk or system-involved youths, their families, and communities; (2) training and technical assistance, which is geared to strategies for juvenile justice system, law enforcement, and related personnel; and (3) system change efforts, which strive to modify aspects of the juvenile justice system that may contribute to DMC."

A Historiographic Analysis of Race in Juvenile Justice

From its inception, juvenile justice has been conceptualized as an alternative justice system focusing primarily on the protection and rehabilitation of youth offenders, rather than the deterrence of crime and punishment for that crime. As conceptualized by progressive reformers, childhood is an era of human innocence and vulnerability. This assumption, however, came with some latent social Darwinist baggage. Because crime and criminality manifested itself as an aberration in children, the focus of the Progressive Era reformers was to attribute the criminal inclination of some children to the defects in their low-class status, or their racial and/or ethnic heritage. Historically, one of the earliest ideological perspectives of the juvenile justice system focused on the extent to which biological determinism (the view that genes determined mental, moral, and social capacities) predicted criminality and delinquency in children. While initially concerned by the overrepresentation of poor whites and the immigrant poor, the focus of juvenile justice became increasingly racialized. This shift made the juvenile justice system a state apparatus primarily conceptualized as a remedial social policy dedicated to dealing with the progeny of the "less than optimal populations" bent on reproducing their defective genes.

The social Darwinist inclination of the juvenile justice system led reforms to many of the foundational tenets of the eugenics movement in the early 20th century, specifically the idea that only the most fit human stock should be encouraged to reproduce. While this approach had a much more tempered effect on how adults were viewed in the criminal justice system, it resonated throughout the juvenile justice system and in large part determined which youths were amenable, morally impressionable, and worthwhile of rehabilitation. Following the Progressive Era assumption that most children are innocent, the juvenile justice system held that most children could be changed—socially adjusted beyond their delinquency—however, for those select "racialized" few, rehabilitation was simply not a worthwhile endeavor. The role the juvenile justice system played in assimilating the children of immigrants into mainstream, "white American" culture has been notable.

For those racial delinquents—the offspring of the unfit—the court envisioned itself as the benevolent guardian of these "neglected" and "unfortunate" racial and ethnic children. Since these children came from "unfit" parents, the juvenile justice courts determined that the best means of adjusting these children to the changing industrial world would be to replace their culturally defective families with the state. In this way, the court thought it necessary to expand the state's power to act as the parent patria or the super-parent for the culturally disadvantaged racial and ethnic children. While this in theory can be interpreted though an appeal to the altruism of the times, in reality, the parent patria doctrine was utilized and enforced as a mechanism of social control against raced populations. Some scholars have gone so far as to argue that the juvenile justice system's role as the parent patria was the most expansive and repressive aspect of the state regime concerning children and families. Because the system was organized around the social control of young racial and ethnic peoples, various state governments used the juvenile justice system as a way to assimilate eastern European immigrants and socially dominate young black males. In short, though the Progressive Era juvenile justice reformers viewed themselves as savers of children and the creators of a benign, nonpunitive, therapeutic enterprise, the doctrine of parent patria allowed the state to regulate and determine as acceptable various aspects of racial and ethnic peoples' lives.

From the Progressive era to the decades leading up to the civil rights era, the juvenile justice system was a key arena of social concerns for equality and the stage on which newly emergent racial policies were tested. While the paternalist focus of the court was not strictly scrutinized until the major social upheavals of the 1960s, the early 20th century saw the expansion of compassionate racial politics. For example, the 1920s and 1930s saw the Supreme Court interpret the Equal Protection Clause as a means to protect blacks from "southern justice," and provided a lens to better equalize the treatments of blacks and other minorities in the juvenile justice system, thus tempering some of the stark social Darwinist inclinations of the late 19th century. This trend continued into the *Brown v. Board* decade and the civil rights era as the U.S. Supreme Court began to call into question discriminatory criminal procedures as a part of the Warren Court's transformative doctrines. Unfortunately, the rights revolution of the 1960s was put to an abrupt halt in the 1970s, as the backlash to civil rights gains included a reasserting of the cultural inferiority theories that demanded the increased regulation of black families following the *Moynihan Report*. With the rising rates of crime, poverty, and the growth of welfare for racial and ethnic groups, political forces had fertile ground to begin linking crime, race, and delinquency to the natural degeneracy of minority children.

Bio-Underclass, Regulation, and "Other" Children

Recently, critical race scholars have begun to question the relevance of speaking about juvenile justice as separate from the core social motivations of racism in American society. Unlike the aforementioned scholars who evaluate race as a operating bias that individuals manifest at different levels of decision making and interactions with the racialized "other," critical race scholars have remarked on the ways that black children are constructed as social threats. Remarking on what she has called the "new bio-underclass" in her book *Killing the Black Body*, Dorothy Roberts claims that many Americans attribute the social pathologies under which many blacks suffer to their nature rather than their conditions. According to Roberts, "the powerful Western image of childhood innocence does not seem to benefit black children. Black children are born guilty. The new bio-underclass constitutes nothing but a menace to society—criminals, crackheads, and welfare cheats waiting to happen." This process of bio-determinism is a process of cultural degeneracy passed to black children in the womb. This dichotomous "othering" thereby robs the black child of "childhood," since blackness cannot be judged by degree.

Fueled by a media that paints crime as a problem belonging to blacks and Latinos, social problems have come to be viewed as caused by "something in" the people in these populations. This erroneous view has the effect of wedding the problem of poverty, and the rates of criminality that come along with it, to the very nature of black and Latino youths. An examination of the relationship these stereotypes have on children reveals that many white Americans view black and Latino youths as dangerous, criminal, and burdens on society. What these scholars emphasize when looking at the juvenile justice system is its similarity to larger patterns of racism in America, which has a history of racism, race discrimination, and the oppression of nonwhite groups. Critical race scholars claim that this history and the systemic nature of racism of American society reveal racial disparities in the juvenile justice system to be symptomatic of a larger ideological schema in the United States.

Insofar as whiteness is viewed as normal, positive, and human; and blackness is understood to represent something "other," negative, foreign, and inhuman; race disparities refer to the ways in which systems define, enforce, and legitimize the subordination of nonwhites. In this literature, whiteness is not simply a racial category, but also a privileged existence where whites are given certain benefits and safeguards simply on the basis of being white.

What these scholars emphasize is that inequality is not simply reflected in class status or discriminatory treatment, but by the ways that the United States legally and socially defines and values white life. By effect, whites are taken to be good and kind, whereas blacks are seen as evil and dangerous.

According to Kenneth Nunn's *The Child as Other*, "Blacks are the bearers of a dual otherness. They are other both due to their Africanness and their status as dependent, wild, and uncontrollable youths. As children of the other, they gain none of the positive benefits of childhood. They are viewed as threats, burdens, and competitors to deserving children. As children, they gain no protection from the ravages of racist oppression. They still carry the stigma associated with blackness in American culture." Whereas "childhood" for whites has been constructed as innocent and dependent on society for protection, black childhood is seen as dangerous and in need of social control. The contrast between these two notions of childhood is directly related to the ways in which society constructs and determines racial and ethnic identities (nonwhiteness). The culpability of white youths is determined and gauged by their age; but Pamela Smith, in an article titled "Reliance on the Kindness of Strangers: The Myth of Transracial Affinity Versus the Reality of Transracial Educational Pedism," notes,

> Age or the vulnerability of youth does not shield black children from the reach of racism. Instead, black children are just as much the victims of racism's long-reaching effects as are adults. Indeed, racism touches nearly every aspect of the child's life through discrimination, poverty, unemployment, economics, education, and the breakdown of the black family structure.

Rather than an abstract notion of difference, these scholars contend that "otherness," where the children of racial groups are constructed as "outside" of American society, concretely affects the life chances of these marginalized groups. This "otherness" severs the responsibility that America believes it has toward these "other" children. Instead of caring for these children, the United States views them as enemies. Kenneth Nunn continues in his analysis that "Motivated by a fear of the other, the juvenile justice system has always targeted other people's children." What these thinkers tend to highlight are the ways that different behaviors toward youths of color are in fact rooted in historical, systematic, and punitive sanctions against blackness and brownness. In his article "Throwaway Children: Conditions of Confinement and Incarceration," James Bell argues that "otherness" is not only imposed, but also internalized. He continues,

> There are assumptions about youths of color that contribute to their overrepresentation in the system. These beliefs hold that minority youths are prone to violence and criminal activity, they are not in school or working, and worst of all they expect to be incarcerated and therefore are not uncomfortable with being securely confined. Such assumptions reflection an expectation of failure that in turn is internalized by the young people who do in fact fail.

In this view, whereas white juvenile offenders are seen as acting out and socially defiant due to the effects of a negative environment, black and Latino offenders are seen as having deviant personalities, bad attitudes, and a general apathy toward social order. In short, "otherness" frames the ways that society and the people in society view whites committing crimes and blacks committing crimes.

There is a distinction between the discussion founded by critical race theorists and the differing positions that call for more piecemeal reforms within the juvenile justice system. These scholars argue that the foundations that support the need to punish black and brown youth offenders, instead of rehabilitating them like many of their white counterparts, stem from deeply rooted social practices that socialize many individuals from judges to law enforcement personnel that interact with youths of color to undertake racist actions toward them. The accounts of these scholars suggest that social inequalities are constructed upon the raced populations that must endure them.

Abolition and Juvenile Justice: A Still-Relevant Movement

In his infamous text, *Bad Kids: Race and the Transformation of the Juvenile Justice Court*, Barry C. Feld argues for the abolition of the juvenile justice system. For Feld, the last several decades of legislative judicial and administrative changes has made the juvenile justice system a second-class criminal court for young people. Whereas previous conceptualizations of juvenile justice focused on social welfare, albeit an overpaternalistic notion of social welfare; today, the political capital afforded to the policymakers willing to demonize raced youths have in many ways made juvenile justice a penal system. The at-large concerns that many Americans harbor about youth crimes like drugs, guns, and street violence encourage and reward legislators that pander to these widely held fears—encouraging the repression of youths, not their treatment. Recognizing the failure of the juvenile justice system in that it attempts to combine social welfare policy with criminal social policy, Feld advocates an integrated criminal court that would make "youthfulness" a special consideration. In his 1997 article "Abolish the Juvenile Court," Feld argues that "states should abolish juvenile courts' delinquency jurisdiction and formally recognize youthfulness as a mitigating factor in the sentencing of criminal offenders."

In Felds's view, the current juvenile justice system is fraught with deficiencies and is beyond repair. On the one hand, it has failed as a social welfare body because it simply lacks the resources and political support of public officials who in many ways are intolerant of its clients, namely poor, disadvantaged, minority youths. On the other hand, the juvenile justice system functions as a safety net for failed social policies and inadequate social services needed to serve poor minority populations. In this vein, the juvenile justice system intervenes in the lives of the racialized poor as a social control apparatus that provides comfort to whites and upper-class citizens who feel reassured when the children of "unruly populations" are under regulation. As Feld notes, there is a very real difference between a punitive juvenile justice system that condemns youths of color for their crimes and confines them away, and a system that condemns the criminal behavior of these youths and seeks to provide social services to remedy and help improve their life circumstances and conditions. On both fronts, Feld views the current juvenile justice system as a failure.

For some abolitionists, like Janet E. Ainsworth, the benefits come in the form of substantive rights gains from the enforcement of due process. While the *In re Gault* decision of 1967 guaranteed youth offenders "right to counsel," national studies have confirmed that this right is consistently waived by youth offenders. Even when counsel is made available to youths, it is often inadequate, leaving minority offenders who cannot afford private counsel in an extremely vulnerable position. For abolitionists like Feld, however, abolition of the juvenile court creates consistency in procedures and substantive protections, and eliminates the disparate racial treatment created by waiving black and Latinos to adult criminal courts. Because juveniles waived to adult criminal courts generally receive harsher punishments than their delinquent child-court counterparts, the racial disparity involved in waiving youths of color, particularly black males, makes abolition particularly relevant as a strategy to reduce DMC. Because get-tough and crackdown legislation has a disproportionate effect on minority youths, abolition is seen as a way to reduce the role racial bias has in sentencing through better counsel and the right to jury trials.

Scholarly Resistance: The Antiabolitionists

Many scholars have not embraced this thinking. In fact, in the conclusion of the authoritative work on racial disparity, *Our Children, Their Children*, special attention is given to the suggestion that racial disparities could be reduced or eliminated through abolition of the juvenile justice system. According to Kimberly Kempf-Leonard and Darnell Hawkins, "no children, whether generally perceived as 'ours' or 'theirs' will benefit if the attempted resolution of racial disparity involves ignoring race or ethnicity, or abolishing juvenile justice and returning to a single criminal justice system." For these scholars, many of the recent initiatives outlined by the federal government have inspired the nation to continue its efforts toward equality across racial, ethnic, and religious divides. The issue for these scholars is not a systemic reproduction of racism that cannot be cured, but rather an issue of responsiveness, accountability, and community involvement that will lead to, as Kempf-Leonard and Hawkins contend, "a racially and ethnically more equitable distribution of youths who understand what is expected of them and who have the skills to fill the citizenship roles expected of them."

Other antiabolitionists take the stance that Feld and Ainsworth are much too optimistic when looking at African American youths. John Kerbs, for example, points out that Feld merely asserts that youths will be given better counsel and procedural protection in criminal courts, without any real evidence of public counsel now. For African Americans specifically, this alternative is likely false. Whereas Kerbs acknowledges that juvenile courts do not live up to the due process mandates of *Gault*, he simply does not believe that the quality of urban public defenders is sufficient to guarantee the levels of protections Feld assumes to make criminal courts advantageous to black youths. Additionally, Kerb points out that Feld underestimates the disparate treatment of blacks in the criminal justice system. Because the War on Drugs legislation enables harsher penalties for drug-related offenses, black youths may actually face longer sentences in adult criminal courts than they would if they were in juvenile courts.

Pro: Support for the Theory of Racist Juvenile Justice

The growth of structural accounts of racism in American society has extended to the analysis of the juvenile justice system as a component of racial inequality and racist bias under the integrationist banner of the post-civil rights era. The scholars who contend that the juvenile justice system is racist make a threefold argument in support of their analysis concerning the racism against young nonwhites in the justice system.

First, there is the historical reality of how juvenile justice, as conceptualized by Progressives, has both treated and thought about black and Hispanic youths. While white youths have been the beneficiaries of the optimistic cause of rehabilitation, blacks and Hispanics have been thought of as being permanently "evil" and unaffected by rehabilitative treatment.

Second, more blacks and Hispanic youths are overrepresented at every level of the juvenile justice system. While some contemporary authors continue to maintain that the juvenile justice system is fair and colorblind, scholars who contend that the juvenile justice system is racist are able to point out the racist perceptions of those officers, administrators, and other individuals that impact juvenile incarceration. The cumulative evidence of studies like *Racial Disparities in Official Assessments of Juvenile Offenders: Attributional Stereotypes as Mediating Mechanisms* by George S. Bridge and Sara Steen, or *The Social Context of Race Differentials in Juvenile Justice Dispositions* by C. E. Frazier and colleagues, indicates that racism is an operational disposition in the sentencing and detainment of minority youths. Perhaps stated even more simply by Dorothy Roberts in her book *Shattered Bonds: the Color of Child Welfare*, "like every step in the juvenile justice process, this decision [to detain] is subject to unfettered discretion."

Last but not least, the third argument waged by authors who maintain the racism of the criminal justice system focuses on the relationship between the rise in the incarceration of black and Hispanic youths and the political and policy implications of whites' perceptions of minority crime and drug use. As argued by Jamie Fellner, "even though far more whites used both powder cocaine and crack cocaine than blacks, the image of the drug offender that has dominated media stories is of a black man slouching in an alley rather than a white man in his home." These public perceptions by whites thereby drive policies that demand the incarceration of blacks rather than whites whose usage continues without attention or criminal penalty.

Con: Rejection of the Theory of Racist Juvenile Justice

Building off the foundational work of William Wilbanks's 1987 book titled *The Myth of a Racist Criminal Justice System*, some authors maintain that while there are exceptions, the criminal justice system overall is fair, just, and not racially bias. These authors usually contend that while unfortunate, the juvenile justice system is working; since blacks and Hispanics are doing more crime, they are, in effect, doing more time. Under this view, the system of juvenile justice is not racist simply because it continues to identify criminals who happen to be of the same racial group. These authors maintain that it is the crime that is at issue, not the "racialized criminal" that is subject to the penalties of the justice system. Extending on the complex nature of enforcement in the *1999 Juvenile Offenders and Victims National Report*, Snyder and Sickmund maintain that rather than racism, it is the offense histories, behavior, and officer interaction involved with minority offenders that can affect detainment rates. Other scholars, like Joan McCord, editor of the collection titled *Violence and Childhood in the Inner City*, maintain that the issue of incarceration among young black and brown youths is an issue of poverty. These authors maintain that poverty and family environment is responsible for propelling nonwhite youths into the juvenile justice arena. A study in 2001 by Jens Ludwig and colleagues, titled *Urban Poverty and Juvenile Crime: Evidence From a Randomized Housing-Mobility Experiment*, found that moving at-risk minority children from areas of poverty decreased their violent behavior.

Conclusion

The truth of the matter concerning racial disparities in the juvenile justice system will not be arbitrated any time in the near future. For some, the idea that racism is at the heart of American society and can be seen through its repetitive assaults on black and Hispanic youths is too far fetched, while others will find the idea that racism is not the root cause of juvenile incarceration an excuse for a historically racist system. Either way, the evidence seems to suggest that a more rigorous structural critique could take into consideration the interrelationship of poverty and residential segregation on the enforcement of racial stereotypes. While it would be a piecemeal reform to suggest moving the racially targeted to less racially targeted areas, or dealing with family environment instead of attacking the system, it is nonetheless reform in a different sense. For academics and activists interested in the area of racial disparities, attention to the victims of these disparities may outweigh their agendas against the causes of racial disparities.

❖

See Also: 3. At-Risk Youth; 9. Juvenile Gangs and Delinquency; 10. Juvenile Offenders in Adult Courts; 12. Legal Representation; 14. Parental Responsibility Laws; 20. Treatment and Rehabilitation.

Further Readings

Ainsworth, J. "The Court's Effectiveness in Protecting the Rights of Juveniles in Delinquency Cases." *The Future of Children*, v.6/3 (1996).

Ainsworth, J. "Re-imagining Childhood and Re-Constructing the Legal Order: The Case for Abolishing the Juvenile Court." *North Carolina Law Review*, v.69 (1991).

Ainsworth, J. "Youth Justice in a Unified Court Response to Critics of Juvenile Court Abolition." *Boston College Law Review*, v.36 (1995).

Bell, J. "Throwaway Children: Conditions of Confinement and Incarceration." In *The Public Assault on American Children: Poverty, Violence, and Juvenile Justice*, edited by V. Polakow. New York: Teacher's College Press, 2000.

Bishop, D. "The Role of Race and Ethnicity in Juvenile Justice Processing." In *Our Children, Their Children*, edited by D. Hawkins and K. Kempf-Leonard. Chicago: University of Chicago Press, 2005.

Bray, T., L. Sample, and K. Kempf-Leonard. "Justice by Geography: Racial Disparity and Juvenile Courts." In *Our Children, Their Children*, edited by D. Hawkins and K. Kempf-Leonard. Chicago: University of Chicago Press, 2005.

Feld, B. C. "Abolish the Juvenile Court: Youthfulness, Criminal Responsibility and Sentencing Policy." *Journal of Criminal Law and Criminology*, v.88 (1998).

Feld, B. C. *Bad Kids: Race and the Transformation of the Juvenile Court.* New York: Oxford University Press, (1999).

Feld, B. C. "The Politics of Race and Juvenile Justice: The Due Process Revolution and the Conservative Reaction." *Justice Quarterly*, v.20/4 (2003).

Hawkins, D., and K. Kempf-Leonard, eds. *Our Children, Their Children.* Chicago: University of Chicago Press, 2005.

Kerbs, J. "(Un)Equal Justice: Juvenile Court Abolition and African Americans." *Annals of the American Academy of Political and Social Science*, v.564 (1999).

Michaelis, K. "School Violence: The Call for a Critical Theory of Juvenile Justice." *Brigham Young University Education and Law Journal* (2001).

Nunn, K. "The Child as Other: Race and Differential Treatment in the Juvenile Justice System." *DePaul Law Review*, v.51 (2002).

Piquero, A. "Disproportionate Minority Contact." *The Future of Children*, v.18 (2008).

Pope, C. E., and M. Leiber. "DMC: The Federal Initiative." In *Our Children, Their Children,* edited by D. Hawkins and K. Kempf-Leonard. Chicago: University of Chicago Press, 2005.

Roberts, D. *Killing the Black Body: Race, Reproduction, and the Meaning of Liberty.* New York: Vintage Books, 1997.

Smith, P. "Reliance on the Kindness of Strangers: The Myth of Transracial Affinity Versus the Realities of Transracial Educational Pedism." *Rutgers Law Review*, v.1 (1999).

16

Scared Straight Programs

William P. McCarty
University of Illinois, Chicago

Scared Straight and other similar programs involve taking at-risk kids or juvenile delinquents on organized tours of prison facilities. The tours often end with speeches or "rap sessions" with inmates, which can contain abrasive language, intimidation, and stories of the violent or sexual atrocities that can occur while someone is incarcerated. The participating youths are supposed to be "scared straight" through these interactions with prisoners and observations of the harsh conditions in prisons. The goal of such programs is deterrence, as proponents argue that witnessing the oppressive environment in prison will prevent the participants from committing future delinquent or criminal acts. Although Scared Straight and various slight derivations have existed in numerous states and even other countries, the most famous program originated at the Rahway State Prison in New Jersey in 1976. Originally titled the Juvenile Awareness Project, the program at Rahway was developed by a group of inmates known as the Lifers' Group, which was formed in 1975 and comprised of inmates serving sentences of 25 years or more. In a sincere effort to keep youths out of trouble, members of the Lifers' Group felt that exposing juveniles to the realities of prison life would dissuade participants from future offenses.

This particular program was the subject of a much-watched and critically acclaimed 1978 documentary called *Scared Straight!* which claimed that 80–90 percent of the youths involved in the Juvenile Awareness Project at Rahway ended up "going straight." Despite debate over the veracity of those figures, the high success rate catalyzed the formation of similar programs throughout the United States and abroad. Although the current popularity of such programs may not be as high as in the 1970s and 1980s, Scared Straight and other similar initiatives continue to be used today.

Scared Straight represents one of the numerous programs intended to decrease the prevalence of juvenile delinquency, which has long been a pressing issue among policymakers, criminal justice practitioners, and the general public. In 2008, for example, the Office of Juvenile Justice and Delinquency Prevention (OJJDP) found that juveniles accounted for 16 percent of all violent crime arrests and 26 percent of all property crime arrests. Beyond the statistics, stories of crimes committed by America's youth elicit shock, horror, and outrage among the entire citizenry. In 2009, for example, a 16-year-old boy, among others, was charged with the murder of a 14-year-old boy in Chicago. Even more horrific, this act was videotaped by one of the onlookers and shown on news broadcasts across the country. Given heinous examples such as this, as well as the overall prevalence of juvenile crime and delinquency, a thorough understanding of the initiatives intended to curb such behavior is essential as policymakers and practitioners continue to devise ways to steer young people away from these acts.

The original initiative at Rahway was called the Juvenile Awareness Project, while *Scared Straight!* refers to the title of the television documentary depicting that program. Over time, Scared Straight came to represent a broad term encompassing virtually all programs that immerse juveniles in a correctional institution for the purposes of intimidation, education, or information. Discussions on the topic follow that nomenclature by using Scared Straight to refer to both the documentary as well as the litany of programs that were based on the Juvenile Awareness Project at Rahway.

The History of the Juvenile Awareness Project

Although the Juvenile Awareness Project at the Rahway State Prison in New Jersey is widely considered as the origin of Scared Straight programming, it did not represent the first time prisoners were used as agents of change. During the 1960s, prisoner-initiated programs targeting youths existed in over 20 states. For example, the San Quentin Squires Program, often cited as the oldest juvenile awareness program in the United States, began in 1964. Formal evaluations of these early programs were minimal, and knowledge of their effectiveness was based on rudimentary measures, such as informal remarks and letters from participants.

In 1975, the Lifers' Group at Rahway State Prison was formed. Consisting of inmates whose sentences were 25 years or greater, the group's goals were noble, as they sought to counteract negative stereotypes of prisoners by becoming involved in worthwhile projects that helped the broader community. One of the top priorities for the Lifers' Group was getting involved in projects that helped keep youths out of trouble, which served as the impetus for the creation of the Juvenile Awareness Project in 1976. James O. Finckenauer has extensively detailed the process by which this program became a reality. The design of the Juvenile Awareness Project was based on educational prison tours done for college students. Even though the college tours were purely educational, the Lifers' Group believed that similar tours could provide deterrent effects for youths.

The actual implementation of such a program faced many roadblocks. First, the inmates needed permission of the superintendent of the prison to allow juveniles inside the institution. Second, they also needed cooperation from an outside official or agency to bring at-risk juveniles to the institution. The program appealed to many agencies and actors in the criminal justice system due to the prevailing get-tough mentality as well as an imbedded belief that something new or different needed to be done with juvenile delinquents. Referrals from judges, the police, and other agencies thus began, and the superintendent acquiesced to allowing juveniles into the prison. In 1976, the first group of youths entered the Rahway State Prison, and the Juvenile Awareness Project was born.

A Change in Tone

In its infancy, the Juvenile Awareness Project was concerned primarily with counseling juveniles. The participants would enter the prison after going through metal detectors, then interact with inmates either in groups or one-on-one. Discussions centered on the realities of prison and were often replete with foul and coarse language. The participants would tour the prison and the program would come to completion. Despite the presence of the strong and coarse language, the original intent was one of mentoring, as opposed to scaring or intimidating the participants. Over time, the tone became more confrontational, as the Lifers' felt like they were not getting through to the youngsters. The Lifers' also worried that adopting a more cordial tone would result in the participants romanticizing prison life, which was not the intended result. As a result, the tone of the Juvenile Awareness Project became more confrontational and adversarial, as the inmates sought to scare the participants straight.

Despite the change in tone, the Juvenile Awareness Project was highly regarded by criminal justice practitioners, the media, and the general public. Part of the popularity was due to the prevailing social climate. Crime was up, people were scared, and any program perceived to be tough on crime was popular with a large portion of the population.

The other part of the popularity was due to positive media accounts of the Juvenile Awareness Project. For example, on March 17, 1977, the *Bergen Record* reported that of the 600 offenders who had gone through the program, only nine had been arrested after completion. On April 17, 1977, the *Trenton Times-Advertiser* reported that only 14 of the 1,400 participants had gotten in trouble with the law (only five seriously) after completing the program at Rahway. These conclusions were based on data that were collected through questionnaires sent out by the Lifers' Group to parents or other groups who brought juveniles to Rahway. For example, the data cited in the aforementioned two articles as well as other positive media depictions were compiled from feedback from the various organizations that referred participants to the Juvenile Awareness Project. Those organizations provided feedback concerning how participants perceived the program as well as whether they were involved in any subsequent criminal or delinquent acts. The quality of these data has been brought into question, given that there was no uniform way of measuring these perceptions as well as subsequent delinquent or criminal behavior. Despite these possible methodological shortcomings, the early reaction to the Juvenile Awareness Project was mostly positive. Some concerns were expressed over the residual trauma that participants could experience, but the appeal of the Juvenile Awareness Project was unquestioned.

Aft first, the positive media coverage of the Juvenile Awareness Project existed mostly at a local level. This would escalate dramatically in 1978, when Roul Tunley's 1978 article, "Don't Let Them Take Me Back!" appeared in *Reader's Digest*. In great detail, the article described the Juvenile Awareness Project to the national audience. It described the realities of prison rape, solitary confinement, and other violence that were laid out in graphic terms by the inmates to the youthful participants. It described the fearful and pained reactions by the young participants when faced with these grim stories, detailing the palpable effect of the program as the students exited Rahway State Prison. The national scope of the *Reader's*

Digest piece caught the attention of Arnold Shapiro, who was the director of motion pictures and special projects for Golden West Television in Los Angeles. This interest ultimately resulted in the filming and airing of a documentary titled *Scared Straight!* that chronicled the Juvenile Awareness Project at Rahway and took the popularity of this program to another level.

The *Scared Straight!* Documentary

The appeal of the Juvenile Awareness Project to television producers was clear: the tacit tension between prisoners and juveniles that would make for compelling theater. The coarse language would both shock and amaze the audience. The documentary was an enormous success when it originally aired in Los Angeles on November 2, 1978. It was such a success that *Scared Straight!* aired nationally during the week of March 5, 1979. The film chronicled the stories of 17 youths, selected by the police, judges, counselors, and probation officers, who participated in the program at Rahway State Prison in New Jersey. All of the juveniles depicted in the film were between 15 and 17 years of age, and both males and females were included. The program began with the juveniles entering the prison through metal detectors. They were then marched through the maximum-security institution for a tour. As this tour unfolded, the participants were verbally accosted by inmates in the institution. Offensive language, references to sex and homosexuality, and other insults greeted the youths throughout the duration of the tour. Many of the juveniles were placed in cells in order to get a feel of what prison life was like. After the end of the tour, the group was brought into a large room where a "rap session" with inmates took place. This dialogue was fraught with colorful language, threats, insults, intimidation, and the basic message that if the juveniles continued their current behavior, they would end up in a horrible prison environment. The film showed many of the juveniles reacting with fear and apprehension as the inmates continued to berate and belittle the participants. Interviews with the young participants after the fact showed many of them expressing remorse for their behavior and promising to change their ways. The narrator, actor Peter Falk, claimed that 80–90 percent of the kids sent to the Juvenile Awareness Project end up going straight after going back to their communities.

A followup film, *Scared Straight! 20 Years Later* aired in 1999. Hosted by actor Danny Glover, this program tracked down virtually all of the participants and convicts that appeared in the original film. Almost all of the original participants were depicted as living crime-free lives. Interviews with many of the subjects highlighted the impact of the Juvenile Awareness Project on their decisions to live their lives free from crime. As a postscript, the film explains that 16 of the 17 participants in the original film (94 percent) were subsequently deterred from a life of crime.

Controversy

Given those amazing claims of the success, many states attempted to replicate this type of programming after the airing of the original *Scared Straight!* documentary. Approximately 38 states implemented programs based on the positive results cited in *Scared Straight!* For example, the Hawaii Stay Straight Program began in August 1979. Troubled youths were identified by police, courts, or school personnel. They were then taken to a maximum security prison to hear a two- to three-hour presentation by four to six inmates. Similar to the Rahway program, participants were searched before entering the prison environment. The presentation then took place in a cellar once used for solitary confinement. Unlike the Rahway program, scare tactics and intimidation were not used during the course of the presentation. Instead, the inmates would describe the events that led to their incarceration. Often, the inmates would then give advice to the participating youths about ways to live a life free from crime and delinquency. The stories and advice were presented in a more factual tone, as opposed to the more confrontational and adversarial tone at Rahway.

Congressional Inquiry

Despite the replication of such programs, concern was expressed about the premise of the Juvenile Awareness Project as well as the sweeping claims of success. On June 4, 1979, an oversight hearing took place before the House of Representatives, Subcommittee on Human Resources of the Committee on Education and Labor. The purpose of the hearing was to review and consider the Juvenile Awareness Project at the Rahway State Prison in New Jersey. Testimony was given both for and against the merits of the program, as well as the level of success it exhibited. For example, representatives of the National Center on Institutions and Alternatives (NCIA) testified that the grandiose claims of success cited in the *Scared Straight!* documentary were unprecedented and very difficult to believe. They testified that the 80–90 percent success rate cited in the film was not substantiated by any reputable data. They also took issue with the fact that many of the juveniles were not chronic offenders, as the documentary claimed. On the contrary, many in the group had minimal involvement with the law. Representatives of the NCIA worried that states would implement similar programs without proper planning, thought, or study. They cited one proposed program in California, which would mandate sending 15,000 teenagers on a multiple-day immersion program in a northern California prison.

The NCIA also questioned the authenticity of various scenes in the *Scared Straight!* documentary. For example, they referenced a scene in which the participants were shown entering the institution in a cocky and boisterous manner. This scene stood in stark contrast to one of the closing scenes, in which the participants left the institution in a very quiet, scared, and timid manner. In talking with the participants in the documentary, the NCIA discovered that the juveniles were instructed to behave in that manner before the respective scene was filmed. Given the concern over the veracity of the results and the authenticity of the documentary itself, the NCIA implored policymakers across the nation to eschew programs like Scared Straight, which promise simplistic solutions to complex problems.

James O. Finckenauer, who conducted the first systematic evaluation of the Juvenile Awareness Project, also delivered a statement at the hearing. His evaluation, undertaken in December 1977, examined how effective the program was at changing the juvenile's attitudes as well as deterring future delinquent acts. Using an experimental group of 46 juveniles who participated in the program and 35 juveniles who served as the control group, the evaluation indicated that the Juvenile Awareness Project did not significantly change the attitudes of the participants, and was also not effective in deterring future delinquent behavior.

Those involved with the *Scared Straight!* documentary defended their work during the congressional hearings. Arnold Shapiro, producer and director, stated that nothing in the film was inaccurate, irresponsible, or misleading. He also stood by the sweeping claims of success cited in the film. John Reynolds, executive vice president of Golden West Television, which produced the documentary, also testified that the events and terminology in *Scared Straight!* were accurate and honest.

Despite this controversy, numerous programs based on the Rahway model were developed. For example, the Wisconsin State Prison started a program called Project Aware that consisted of a group of adult prisoners meeting and confronting a group of institutionalized juvenile offenders.

The Showing How a Prison Experience Undermines People (SHAPE UP) program in Colorado was another replication of the Juvenile Awareness Project that focused more on counseling and less on intimidation than the original Juvenile Awareness Project. Although the popularity of these programs dissipated during the 1980s, a renewed interest in Scared Straight types of programming followed the release of *Scared Straight! 20 Years Later* in 1999. The impact of this film was not nearly the same as the original documentary, but Scared Straight programs still exist in the United States and abroad today. The philosophy of these modern programs remains the same, as they attempt to deter juveniles from future criminal or delinquent behavior through exposing and educating them about the harsh realities of prison life.

Pro: Advantages of Scared Straight Programs

Scared Straight programs became immensely popular since the airing of the *Scared Straight!* television documentary in 1979. The drive to replicate these programs was based initially on the level of success cited in the film. The documentary claimed that 80–90 percent of the participants remained law abiding for a period of three months after the program was completed. Beyond these early claims of success, proponents of Scared Straight often point to two basic reasons why this type of programming is advantageous. First, a large portion of the appeal of a Scared Straight program is based on its simplicity. The program itself does not take long; a typical Scared Straight program may last two to three hours. Second, this type of programming is also inexpensive. Overhead costs are minimal, as the key actors in the program, the inmates, receive nominal compensation (or nothing at all) for their participation.

Beyond this, Paul Klenowski and colleagues have found that Scared Straight programs can show promise when using less confrontational methods. Take, for example, Project Aware, a nonconfrontational juvenile awareness program in Mississippi. Project Aware involved civil discussions between prisoners and participants, devoid of the vulgarities, insults, and hostilities that characterized the Juvenile Awareness Project at Rahway. In their 1992 evaluation of this program, David Cook and Charles Spirrison found that Project Aware was effective in reducing the dropout rate and increasing school attendance for those who participated in the program. Programs using these less-confrontational methods place a greater emphasis on education, with inmates often stressing personal responsibility. The goal remains deterrence, and participants are still exposed to the realities of prison life, but the method of disseminating the information is less confrontational.

Scared Straight programs can also be advantageous for inmates. Robert L. Keller lent credence to these assertions through his interviews with 15 inmate counselors involved with the SHAPE UP program in Colorado that began in 1979. Many of the inmates felt useful as they conveyed their experiences to the youthful participants. Being involved in the program also elevated their status within the institution, which garnered additional respect from other inmates and guards. These factors may coalesce into improving the prisoner's overall self-concept and self-esteem.

Scared Straight programs also resonate positively with the general public because they place the fulcrum of responsibility directly on the individual. Blame is not transferred to the family or environment in which that juvenile lives on a daily basis. The juvenile is involved with the program because he or she made poor decisions, or is on the path toward making poor decisions. The impetus for individual change comes through seeing and hearing about the harsh realities of prison life; the individual is then supposed to react to those stimuli in a rational manner by changing course and making decisions that are not criminal or delinquent in nature. This premise is appealing to many people, which explains partially why Scared Straight programs are popular with the public.

Con: Disadvantages of Scared Straight Programs

While Scared Straight initiatives may be inexpensive and popular with the general public, detractors do not believe that these initiatives deter participants from future delinquent behavior. Skeptics argue that Scared Straight programs are ineffective deterrents because they simply make participants aware of the severity of the punishment. In order to be an effective deterrent, a program must make participants aware of the certainty of punishment. Simply having knowledge about the harsh realities of prison life may not be a sufficient deterrent, since participants might feel there is a low probability that they will end up in that environment.

Some research also supports this logic. Anthony Petrosino and colleagues have conducted an evaluation of Scared Straight and similar programs across the United States. Their review of nine programs, spanning over a quarter century and involving nearly 1,000 participants, indicates that Scared Straight and other similar initiatives are not effective crime prevention strategies. Further, evaluations of the nine programs for which data were available indicate that Scared Straight programs may actually increase the criminality of participants (experimental group) compared to nonparticipants (control group). This increase in criminality may be due to a variety of reasons. Some have speculated that young and impressionable participants in Scared Straight programs may find prison to be an appealing environment, given their lack of structure and belonging in their real lives. Others have speculated that the participants may look up to the prisoners, seeing them as representatives of the criminal lifestyle that may be romanticized by some films, television shows, or music. Finally, participating in a Scared Straight program may be a stigmatizing experience, which may elevate future criminal behavior.

The Panacea Phenomenon

Finckenauer and Patricia W. Gavin have evaluated and written extensively on Scared Straight and other similar programs. They have argued that the continued use of Scared Straight programming, even in the face of evidence countering its effectiveness, represents an example of what they call the "panacea phenomenon." In essence, the public and policymakers crave simple solutions to complex problems. Juvenile delinquency represents a complex problem. Its roots lie both inside and outside the juvenile, in the social, psychological, and physiological realms. A two- to three-hour tour of a prison facility, with or without intimidation from the inmates, may be inadequate to deal with such a complex issue. As a result, Paul Klenowski and his colleagues have argued that it is unreasonable to expect a program with such a small dosage of treatment to have any long-lasting deterrent effects for juvenile participants.

Additional concerns have been expressed over Scared Straight programming. First, skeptics have expressed apprehension about confrontational programs that attempt to intimidate and dehumanize participants, especially when they are juveniles. These skeptics point to the medical mantra that above all else, do no harm. They worry that even the slightest possibility of juveniles being emotionally harmed during the completion of the program makes Scared Straight too risky to pursue. Second, some skeptics have voiced concerns over how Scared Straight programs may portray prisoners as savages. They worry that this portrayal may have negative implications for both the prisoners themselves as well as how they are perceived by the general public.

Does the Program Work? Conflicting Answers

Reaching a definitive conclusion about the effectiveness of Scared Straight is made difficult by the litany of data that can be found both for and against this type of program. Skeptics argue that most of the positive data cited in the *Scared Straight!* documentary were anecdotal. The same skeptics argue that evaluations based on sound data and experimental methods indicate that Scared Straight programs are ineffective, if not hazardous ways of dealing with juvenile delinquency. Some of the minutia over the amount of success demonstrated by Scared Straight programming may have to do with the different lengths of time used in the various evaluations. No one can agree on the appropriate time period in which to evaluate the effectiveness of Scared Straight programming. Some have argued that evaluations should focus on short-term results. Proponents of that position argue that Scared Straight programming resonates immediately with the juvenile and, as a result, reductions in delinquent or criminal behavior are best detected over a short period of time after the program is completed. Others have argued that such programming may not have a discernible impact on crime or delinquency until a longer period of time has passed. Proponents of that position argue that the effects of Scared Straight are more gradual, as the program catalyzes youths to strengthen family ties and recommit to education. Regardless of the position, a clear picture of the effect of Scared Straight programming on crime and juvenile delinquency is made difficult, given the varying periods of followup found in the different evaluations.

Conflicting results may also be an artifact of researchers using different outcome or dependent variables. Some evaluations have focused on perceptive outcome measures. For example, a participant may be queried about the likelihood of committing a future offense after completing the program. Other evaluations have explored arrest data to determine whether Scared Straight programs work. Regardless of the measures used, a comprehensive understanding of the effectiveness of Scared Straight programs is made difficult by the various methods and approaches used in the evaluation studies. Despite these problems, this type of program still remains popular today. The original Juvenile Awareness Project, for example, has continued into the 21st century. The popularity of this premise has also seeped into other contexts. For example, as part of its business-ethics curriculum, some M.B.A. candidates at Pepperdine University have been taken to Nellis Federal Prison Camp outside of Las Vegas to meet with incarcerated white-collar criminals. The inmates describe the unpleasantries of prison life and implore the students to not let greed or temptation lead them to commit fraud or embezzlement.

See Also: 3. At-Risk Youth; 11. Juveniles in Adult Correctional Facilities; 20. Treatment and Rehabilitation.

Further Readings

Buckner, John C., and Meda Chesney-Lind. "Dramatic Cures for Juvenile Crime: An Evaluation of a Prisoner-Run Delinquency Prevention Program." *Criminal Justice and Behavior,* v.10/2 (June 1983).

Cavender, Gary. "Scared Straight—Ideology and the Media." In *Justice and the Media*, edited by R. Surette. Springfield, IL: Thomas, 1984.

Cook, David D., and Charles L. Spirrison. "Effects of a Prisoner-Operated Delinquency Deterrence Program: Mississippi's Project Aware." *Journal of Offender Rehabilitation*, v.17/3–4 (1992).

Dean, Douglas D. "The Impact of a Juvenile Awareness Program on Select Personality Traits of Male Clients." *Journal of Offender Counseling, Services and Rehabilitation*, v.6/3 (1982).

Finckenauer, James O. "Scared Crooked." *Psychology Today*, v.13/8 (1979).

Finckenauer, James O. *Scared Straight! and the Panacea Phenomenon*. Englewood Cliffs, NJ: Prentice-Hall, 1982.

Finckenauer, James O., and Patricia W. Gavin. *Scared Straight: The Panacea Phenomenon Revisited*. Prospect Heights, IL: Waveland Press, 1999.

Homant, Robert J., and Gregory Osowski. "The Politics of Juvenile Awareness Programs: A Case Study of JOLT." *Criminal Justice and Behavior*, v.9/1 (March 1982).

Keller, Robert L. "Some Unanticipated Positive Effects of a Juvenile Awareness Program on Adult Inmate Counselors." *International Journal of Offender Therapy and Comparative Criminology*, v.37/1 (1993).

Klenowski, Paul M., et al. "An Empirical Evaluation of Juvenile Awareness Programs in the United States: Can Juveniles Be 'Scared Straight'?" *Journal of Offender Rehabilitation*, v.49/4 (April 2010).

Lewis, Roy V. "Scared Straight—California Style: Evaluation of the San Quentin Squires Program." *Criminal Justice and Behavior*, v.10/2 (June 1983).

Martinson, Robert. "What Works? Questions and Answers About Prison Reform." *The Public Interest,* v.35 (Spring 1974).

McCord, Joan. "Cures That Harm: Unanticipated Outcomes of Crime Prevention Programs." *Annals of the American Academy of Political and Social Science,* v.587/1 (May 2003).

Tunley, Roul. "Don't Let Them Take Me Back." *Reader's Digest* (January 1978).

U.S. House. *Oversight on Scared Straight: Hearing Before the Subcommittee on Human Resources of the Committee on Education and Labor, House of Representatives, Ninety-Sixth Congress, First Session.* Washington, DC: U.S. Government Printing Office, 1979.

Petrosino, Anthony J., et al. "Scared Straight and Other Juvenile Awareness Programs for Preventing Juvenile Delinquency: A Systematic Review of the Randomized Experimental Evidence." *Annals of the American Academy of Political and Social Science,* v.589/41 (September 2003).

Petrosino, Anthony J., et al. "Well-Meaning Programs Can Have Harmful Effects! Lessons From Experiments Such as Scared Straight." *Crime and Delinquency,* v.46/3 (July 2000).

17

School Violence

Lyndsay N. Boggess
University of South Florida

Extreme acts of violence committed by children and young adults grab national headlines and the public eye. Violent school shootings, such as the tragedies in Jonesboro, Arkansas, Columbine high school in Littleton, Colorado, and at the Red Lake Indian Reservation, Minnesota, garner media, political, and public attention. These serious forms of violence are actually exceptionally rare at schools, but there are many more common forms of youth violence that do not involve firing a gun. These acts of violence, though not as high profile or attention grabbing, are no less significant. Youth violence, particularly violence on school grounds, is a continuum, ranging anywhere from bullying and teasing to more extreme homicides and school shootings. Managing and preventing more common forms of youth violence are equally important in remedying and reducing violence that interrupts America's educational goals.

School violence does not simply threaten students; it also impacts teachers and staff, parents, and anyone involved in the daily functioning of schools. One widely cited definition of school violence is a research-based perspective developed by the Center for the Prevention of School Violence that categorizes behaviors as violent if they violate one of three criteria. That is, school violence is any behavior that (1) goes against the school's educational mission, (2) violates the school's climate of respect, or (3) jeopardizes the school's ability to be free of aggression against persons or property, and free of drugs, weapons, disruptions, and disorder. This broad-scale definition of violence is useful in designing and implementing preventative strategies, but is too large an undertaking for a single discussion on school violence. Therefore, the definition of violence is here limited to interpersonal criminal acts or aggressive behaviors committed by elementary, middle school (junior high), and senior high school students that inhibit student development as well as harm the school climate. Though such school violence typically refers to violence against other students, it also encompasses acts against teachers, school staff, or other persons at the school.

Schools have historically been considered sanctuaries from the violence that occurs on the streets and in homes, and the vast majority of parents are not fearful for their children at school, but an epidemic rise in violence on school grounds in the 1990s brought considerable attention to the issue and the realization that schools are no longer safe havens from violent crime. After the Columbine shooting, a national Gallup poll revealed that two-thirds of Americans felt that a similar incident would be "very likely" or "somewhat likely" to occur in their neighborhood. At the same time, an increasing proportion of students began reporting feeling unsafe at school and when traveling to and from school, and one in five students stayed home from school because of violence-related fears. The causes of school violence are numerous—including psychological, social, and familial origins—and there is a vigorous debate about how to reduce and prevent future violence. Responses to violence tend toward the punitive "get tough" policies, but opponents argue in favor of early-intervention programs. Regardless, the scope and costs of school violence are vast.

The Scope of School Violence

There are a number of ways to measure school violence—self-report surveys, police arrest reports, and hospital admissions data, for example—but most methods reveal that students' fear of violence at school is not unfounded, and was particularly valid in the 1990s. At that time, youth violence in general was increasing, but particular attention was paid to the surge of violence occurring on school grounds. In 1995, three percent of students reported being a victim of violence, including rape or sexual assault, robbery, and aggravated or simple assault at school or on a school bus. Violent deaths on campus are rare; a Justice Policy Institute study estimates the odds of a student dying at school at approximately one in two million. Data collected by the Centers for Disease Control and Prevention

(CDC) show that between 1992 and June 1999, there were 218 school-associated homicides of youths 5–18 years of age; in 1992 alone, there were 34 youth homicides. More recently, evidence suggests that violence in schools is decreasing, and is no worse now than before the 1990s. The number of youth homicides at school dropped to 21 in 2007, and recent surveys show that the overall rate of student victimization has declined. Only four percent of students report having been victimized by violence or theft in 2007, compared to 10 percent in 1995. In the 2007–08 school year, 21 youths 5–18 years of age were murdered at school, on the way to or from school, or at a school-sponsored event. Overall, between the end of 1999 and June 2006, there were 127 student homicides at school, substantially lower than the prior 7.5 years. Schools, however, are still safer than society at large; fewer than one percent of elementary or secondary school-age homicide victims are killed on or around school grounds.

Data from the National Crime Victimization Survey (NCVS) shows that the annual rate of serious or violent victimization reported by students 12–18 years of age dropped dramatically in the 1999–2000 school year, and has continued to remain substantially lower than in the previous decade. The overall rate of violent crime victimization at school dropped to 1.3 percent from three percent in the 1990s. In a national sample of school safety administrators, only 20 percent of the respondents perceived violence in their district to be increasing. A smaller proportion of students reported being involved in a physical fight on school property in 2007 than they did in 1993. A recent survey of teachers shows not only a decrease in actual violence, but administrators and teachers also feel more confident now in their capacity to address the situation.

Students respond to school-associated homicides and the related publicity by bringing more weapons to campus, although as the overall rate of violence on campus has decreased, so has the percentage of students carrying a weapon, from nearly 12 percent in 1993 to about six percent in 2007. The majority of homicides on campus, however, are still the result of gunshot wounds, followed by stabbings and beatings. In a related finding, students report an increased fear of injury by a weapon at school: 10 percent of male high school students and 5.8 percent of female students reported being threatened or injured with a weapon on school campus in 2007, according to the Youth Risk Behavior Surveillance System (YRBSS) survey data compiled by the CDC. At the same time, the CDC reports an increasing percentage of students who stay home because they feel unsafe at or traveling to and from school.

Bullying

Victimization by bullies is often considered another form of school violence. Identifying bullying can be subjective, but most researchers, teachers, and prevention experts agree that bullying involves two primary components: repetition and an imbalance of power. That is, a person is a victim of bullying when he or she is repeatedly subjected to unwanted and negative actions by a person (or persons) against whom they are relatively defenseless. Bullying can take many forms, including being made fun of or insulted, social exclusion, pushing, shoving, or tripping, and the intentional destruction of property. The most common types of bullying are nonviolent and include name calling, insults, and spreading rumors. A new form of bullying that has garnered much attention recently is termed *cyber bullying,* which involves repetitious harassment between youths using a computer, the Internet, or a mobile device. More female students reported being a target of a cyber bully: two percent of male students compared to 5.3 percent of female students. Research suggests, and students report, that the majority of cyber bullying occurs outside the school environment, but more research needs to be done on this specialized form of bullying.

In 2007, 25 percent of schools reported having problems with school bullies; middle schools reported more bully problems than elementary or high schools. About 30 percent of male students and 33 percent of female students report being bullied. In general, schools that had more of a bully problem also reported more violent incidents overall. There is some indication, however, that despite increased attention to bullying, the frequency of bullying has been decreasing. In the 1999–2000 school year, 29.3 percent of schools reported weekly bullying disciplinary infractions, compared to 25 percent of schools 2007–08.

Violent Versus Nonviolent Crime

The majority of crime on school grounds is not violent. Data from the National Study of Delinquency Prevention in Schools (NSDPS) reveals that most school-associated crime consists of relatively minor property offenses such as theft or property damage; the most prevalent form of violence involved students hitting or threatening to hit another student. The YRBSS survey delivered biannually to a national sample of high school students shows that 12.4 percent of students had been in a physical altercation on school property at least once in the previous year. Overall, however, parents are not fearful of sending their children to school; Gallup polls since 2003 show that approximately 75 percent of parents do not fear their child's physical safety at school.

The amount of violent crime varies among schools, with some schools more susceptible to violence than others. Overall, public schools tend to have more problems with student discipline and violence. Violence is also more prevalent in middle schools than elementary or high schools. Some estimates suggest that middle-school students are twice as likely to be victims of violence as their high school counterparts, and that the typical offender at school is a seventh-grade male robbing or attacking a similar youth. There are several reasons for the discrepancy in rates of violence between junior and senior high schools. For one, students in middle school may be associating with people from different backgrounds or more distant communities for the first time. Second, middle-school students are typically entering an age where they have not yet learned socially acceptable behavior and are particularly susceptible to peer pressure. Third, the lower rates of violence in high school may be skewed because of high dropout rates, particularly in urban schools; the students most likely to have dropped out are also the students most likely to be violent or act out at school. Similarly, male students are more likely to be involved in school-related violence than females, as are students from lower-income households. Most school violence occurs during unstructured time before and after school, or in the hallways during class breaks.

The media often focuses on school shootings that occur in suburban or rural schools (such as Columbine or Jonesboro), but other serious forms of violence, such as assaults and robberies, are more common in urban schools. Students in the inner city are more likely to have brought a weapon to school or know someone who has. Discussions of the role of school environment and violence also cannot ignore the issue of gangs. Gang membership is a strong individual-level risk factor for violent behavior, but schools with greater gang membership are also more likely to have higher levels of violence overall. The National Center for Education Statistics (NCES) reports that gang violence is also more likely to be an urban school problem. In the 2007–08 school year, 13 percent of schools located in the city reported the presence of at least one gang compared to only nine percent of suburban schools and five percent of schools in more rural environments.

Causes of School Violence

For some time, violence has been considered one of the most important problems plaguing the United States. In the 1990s, violence was also considered to be the biggest problem in America's public schools. In order to develop successful strategies to address such an important issue, it is essential to consider the antecedents to school violence. Youth violence is a multifaceted problem, however, that can stem from individual psychological problems or personality disorders, characteristics of the school environment and the local neighborhood, and family characteristics, including a lack of parental control and discipline. Many school officials, educators, researchers, and parents would also agree that other societal factors such as media violence, cyber bullying, and easy access to weapons also contribute to school violence.

Psychological Factors

For some individual students, violent behavior can be a result of a psychological condition or personality disorder. Some studies attribute the violence as a reaction to bullying, teasing, or extreme duress experienced while at school. Violence as a means to exact revenge on other students is one of the most often-employed explanations for the violence at Columbine in 1999. Research has shown that students more prone to violence are those with low impulse control; substance abuse problems; or narcissistic, paranoid, or antisocial personality disorders. Other research suggests that anxiety, stress, and depression (which are also strongly tied to substance abuse), are also associated with behavioral problems in youths.

School Characteristics and Neighboring Factors

School-specific factors also contribute to the level of violence at school. In addition to public schools and schools located in urban communities, schools with a larger enrollment and a greater student-to-teacher ratio are typically associated with more problematic student behavior. In larger schools, there is less direct student supervision, which makes it difficult for teachers and administrators to identify potential problems. Likewise, increased anonymity among students and between teachers and students decreases students' sense of belonging. The NCES shows that for the 2007–08 school year, as student enrollment increased, the rate of violent incidents reported to the police also increased. Public schools with an enrollment of greater than 1,000 students average twice as many violent events as schools with enrollment between 500 and 999 pupils (the rate decreases even more when the enrollment drops to less than 300). Larger schools are typically also plagued with other correlates of youth violence, including higher drop-out rates, poverty, and more negative attitudes toward school. The same NCES study reveals a strong association between the percent of students eligible for a free or reduced-price lunch (an indicator of poverty) and levels of violence at school. In schools where fewer than 25 percent of students are in need of a subsidized lunch, the violent crime rate per 1,000 students is approximately 15 offenses, but when the percentage of low-income students surpasses 75 percent, the rate of violent incidents triples to 45.

In addition to school physical characteristics and location, other elements of school climate are related to varying levels of violence across campuses and classrooms. For example, schools with a generally positive atmosphere tend to have fewer discipline or school-avoidance problems. School management style is also strongly associated with different rates of violence, even among otherwise similar schools. Research has shown that schools that have clearly articulated and consistently and equitably enforced rules tend to have fewer discipline problems, as do schools where the teachers are perceived as tough but caring, respectful of the students, and genuinely concerned with student success. Students in schools with a more positive climate tend to feel a greater attachment to their school and a stronger desire to please teachers and school administrators.

Beyond the immediate school environment, characteristics of the neighborhood in which the school is located can also affect the level of violence at school. Because most public schools draw their students locally, schools are generally reflective of the local neighborhood, and violence in the community can intrude into the school. Some instances of violence on school grounds are perpetrated by local residents not affiliated with the school, and numerous incidents of student attacks occur when the student is in transit to or from campus. Characteristics that are associated with crime in communities, including poverty and racial/ethnic tension, are also likely associated with violence on school grounds.

Parental Influence

The general public believes that one of the largest causes of violence in school lies in a lack of parental discipline and control, a breakdown in family structure, and dysfunctional lifestyles. After the Columbine shootings, 92 percent of respondents believe that students' home life was extremely or very important in explaining the shootings. Students with parents involved in criminal behavior, illicit drug use, or abusive behavior are more likely to emulate those behaviors. Additionally, such parents are often physically and emotionally unavailable to their child.

Parental behavior or lack of discipline at home includes allowing unmonitored time to engage in violent video games, television programs, movies, or music lyrics. Some suggest that youths become desensitized to violence because of this, and may have trouble distinguishing between fantasy and reality. Empirical studies have been unable to find a direct link between viewing violence and violent behavior; however, some research suggests that media violence tends to increase aggression in the short term, but has not definitively been linked to violent behavior long term.

Technology and Guns

The widespread use of cell phones and the Internet, particularly social-networking Websites such as Facebook and MySpace, have introduced additional methods to tease and torment students through cyber bullying or cyber abuse. These new means to harass students are often cited, in addition to the teasing and bullying that happens on school grounds, as additional means to provoke students to violence.

Firearm violence poses a risk to children in the United States in general; in 2008, nearly 21,000 children and teenagers under 19 years of age were injured by a gun. Violence at school is worsened by the availability of handguns. Of the homicides at school between 1999 and 2006, 65 percent of the deaths were the result of gunshot wounds. An estimated 35 percent of homes with children under 18 have firearms in the house, though many students admit that they could acquire a gun without much effort. A study of school shootings in 2002 by the U.S. Secret Service found that about two-thirds (68 percent) of student attackers obtained the gun or guns used in their attack from their own home or from a relative, and according to the U.S. Department of Justice, between nine and 17 percent of high school students believe that it would be easy to obtain a weapon without alerting an adult. The majority of the general public also blame the ease of gun availability as partly responsible for school shootings; a 2001 Gallup poll showed that 77 percent of respondents think that the ease of obtaining a gun was an extremely or very important contributor to the Columbine tragedy. Evidence also suggests that students are carrying these weapons to school. According to the Center to Prevent Handgun Violence, 100,000 guns are brought to schools on a daily basis; other research shows that one out of every 18 high school students carried a gun with them to campus in 1991.

Regardless of the particular source of student violence, research suggests that there are several risk factors that can increase the probability that the student will engage in violent behavior. Risk factors vary at different points in the child's life; in the younger years, family-level factors play a more significant role, while peer group and neighborhood factors are more influential in the adolescent and teen years. In adolescence, three major risk factors for violence have been identified: (1) weak or nonexistent friendships with nondelinquent youths, (2) strong ties with antisocial and/or delinquent peers, and (3) gang membership. Other risk factors that indicate a potential for violence include a prior history of aggressive or violent behavior; drug or alcohol use; family dysfunction or violence; and poor grades, school attendance, or attitudes toward school. The risk factors are exacerbated if the child is from an impoverished or socially disorganized neighborhood. Risk factors are considered additive, and youths who display more predictors are typically considered more at risk for violent behavior.

The Cost of School Violence

Safety is expensive in schools. A sample of school safety administrators shows that 61 percent of the school districts surveyed spent more than $100,000 over two years on safety technology in their district; 40 percent of the sample spent more than $500,000. But the real cost of violence at school goes beyond financial obligations, such as insurance payments, medical bills, expenditures for substitute teachers, student counseling, and extra security. The price of violence includes the incalculable costs associated with individual injuries and death, and the hidden costs associated with school management. The aftermath of violence reverberates throughout the school environment and can affect the way that teachers teach and the ability of students to learn. A 2008 American Teacher Survey revealed that nine percent of teachers feel that violence is a significant impediment to learning for at least 25 percent of their students, particularly for students in urban environments; and 27 percent of teachers reported in the National Study of Delinquency Prevention that student behavior prevented them from teaching either "a fair amount" or a "great deal of the time." Students who are afraid at school may have difficulty concentrating on their work and may be more likely to stay home from school for reasons other than being ill; in this way, fear can consequently lead to students falling behind. Studies have shown that schools with higher rates of violence have lower test scores, reduced graduation rates, and a lower likelihood that a student will attend college. Jeffrey Grogger's study on neighborhoods and violence determined that even moderate levels of violence reduce the likelihood of graduating from high school by approximately five percent, and lower the likelihood of college attendance by nearly seven percent.

Solving the School Violence Problem

Mechanisms to reduce school violence can take either preventative or reactive means, or a combination of both measures. In some districts, school officials try to curb violent behavior at school by implementing programs or policies to reduce violence before it occurs. For example, the federal Safe and Drug-Free Schools and Communities Act (SDFSCA) of 1994 was a large-scale, violence-reduction strategy that sought to reduce youth violence and drug use in elementary and secondary schools. The SDFSCA supports early intervention programs that integrate health education, mentoring, and drug and alcohol rehabilitation with family services, as well as provide training for school personnel, family members, and the community. SDFSCA also supports law enforcement and neighborhood patrols to create and maintain "safe zones of passage" to ensure student safety traveling to and from school grounds. The installation of metal detectors, locker and property searches, and drug sweeps are other preventative measures to reduce school violence.

Other tactics, however, are more reactive, and aim to reduce school violence by punishing the offenders after the fact, and are designed to scare kids into good behavior. Reactive responses often include juvenile boot camps or shock incarceration programs (short-term prison programs run like military boot camps), and charges in adult court that could potentially lead to prison time. These "get tough" policies are intended to dissuade potentially violent students because the consequences of the punishment are so severe. Though most researchers, school officials, parents, and community members agree that there should be some element of preventative means taken to reduce school violence, there is disagreement about the use and effectiveness of more punitive measures applied to juveniles.

Pro: Benefits of Punitive Responses to School Violence

The most broadly implemented punitive response to student violence is the adoption of zero-tolerance policies. Zero-tolerance policies grew out of the reaction to high-profile violent events such as school shootings, and are generally defined as a mandated, predetermined consequence or punishment, without consideration of the situational context or mitigating circumstances such as student age or disciplinary history. Zero-tolerance policies, and other harsh disciplinary consequences, were designed for more severe violations such as aggressive behaviors and weapon possession, but are also applied to drugs and alcohol.

An example of a national zero-tolerance policy aimed at reducing school violence is the Gun-Free Schools Act of 1994, which mandated that schools expel any student who brings a firearm to school; the act was broadened by state or local laws to apply to any weapon. In November 2009, a California school district expelled a 16-year-old student for having unloaded shotguns in his truck. The student's vehicle was parked off campus at the time of the offense, but because schools are responsible for student safety to and from school, the zero-tolerance policy applied since the weapons were within 1,000 feet of the school. The California school district was operating under the legal doctrine of *in loco parentis* where school officials may act as parental figures.

Many schools have also made efforts to tighten security by implementing student identification cards, hiring security officers and using video surveillance, employing wide-scale locker and parking lot searches for contraband (sometimes in conjunction with canine detection), and installing metal detectors. In 2000, 66 percent of middle schools and 57 percent of high schools utilized at least one of these security or surveillance strategies, according to the NSDPS. These deterrent strategies have been effective in reducing the number of weapons brought to school. The percent of students bringing a weapon to school declined from 11.8 percent in 1993 to 5.9 percent in 2007, according to the YRBSS results; and a sample of New York City high school students showed that students were much less likely to carry a weapon to school if they attend a school with metal detectors. In part, the reduction of school-associated homicides can also be attributed to the deterrent effect of metal detectors and video monitoring. Researcher Robert Johnson shows that the number of guns confiscated in Chicago schools dropped dramatically after metal detectors were installed; and Crystal Garcia surveyed school safety administrators and found that over two-thirds considered video cameras and recorders as the most effective school safety technologies in the reduction of student disorder as well as property, violent, and drug offenses.

Zero-tolerance policies are popular among schools—approximately 75 percent of schools have adopted such guidelines—and they also have broad-scale public support. After the massacre at Virginia Tech, Gallup poll results demonstrated overarching endorsement of the installation of metal detectors

(61 percent favored) and the expulsion of students who exhibited violent tendencies in their behavior or their academic work (70 percent favored). School officials and parents alike believe that get-tough strategies make schools safer.

Con: Drawbacks of Punitive Responses to School Violence

Reactions against "get tough" policies such as zero tolerance include complaints that the policies are too punitive, ineffective, and inappropriately applied. Zero-tolerance policies have been criticized as being too rigid and overly harsh when, at the extreme, they are applied to trivial incidents such as students bringing aspirin, ibuprofen, or mouthwash to school, or to Halloween costumes with plastic guns or paper swords. In some instances, the children in violation of zero-tolerance have been referred to juvenile court or have faced adult charges. For example, in Palm Beach, Florida, a 14-year-old disabled student was charged with an adult felony after allegedly stealing $2 from another student. When punitive policies are applied to circumstances that many would consider unwarranted or excessive, the public perception is negative, and school administrators are blamed for not acting in the best interest of the student. The American Psychological Association reported finding no evidence that zero-tolerance policies reduced school violence or improved student behavior.

The American Bar Association and a number of other professional associations have adopted statements opposing zero-tolerance policies in schools because, in part, of the broad-scale application of the policies without consideration to the student's history or the circumstance of the offense.

There are deleterious effects of punitive, anticrime policies in school. Metal detectors in school can create a prison-like environment that is not conducive to learning, and simultaneously reinforces the idea that school is a dangerous place. Expelled and suspended youths often face serious challenges in the future and are at an increased risk of falling behind and dropping out. The CDC has found that youths who do not attend school regularly are more likely to carry weapons, use drugs or alcohol, or be involved in physical fights.

Evidence indicates that zero-tolerance policies are not equitably applied. A research study by the Civil Rights Project at Harvard University determined that the zero-tolerance policies have resulted in a disproportionately adverse effect on minority students. According to data from the Department of Education's Office of Civil Rights, African American students are suspended at a rate over twice that of white students. In one Phoenix, Arizona, school district, African Americans comprise only four percent of the student body, but are suspended or expelled at a rate 22 times greater than white students, and make up more suspension cases than white students (493 to 420). How to treat special needs' students further challenges the equitable application of zero-tolerance policies; in Maryland, special-education students make up 23 percent of the suspended youths, though they comprise only 13 percent of the total enrollment.

Opponents of get-tough, one-size-fits-all methods of punishment advocate for less severe penalties that apply a graduated system of sanctions that match punishment to offense and situational context. Some suggested alternatives to expulsion include (1) require a parent/guardian to attend school with the student for a portion of the day; (2) community service on school grounds; (3) in-school supervised suspension; or (4) transfer to an opportunity, alternative, or day school.

In lieu of punitive responses to misbehavior, other proactive, school-based interventions such as Life-Skills Training (LST), Promoting Alternative Thinking Strategies (PATHS), and the Olweus Bullying Prevention Program (BPP) have shown some positive impact on student behavior. Students themselves suggest that schools adopt bullying prevention programs, especially those that incorporate cyber bullying. The Center for the Study and Prevention of Youth Violence at the University of Colorado at Boulder has an extensive list of criteria for programs that strive to reduce student violence and behavioral problems. Model programs have shown evidence of a sustained deterrent effect on youth violence, delinquency, and drug use. These programs include early interventions that deal with emerging problems in both the academic realm as well as social, behavioral, and emotional issues. Though there are a variety of alternative violence prevention programs, successful programs generally promote social skills training and pro-social behaviors, and involve an element of counseling and supportive services, including facilitating positive parent and family interaction.

See Also: 2. Alternative Schools; 4. Boot Camps; 7. Group Homes.

Further Readings

Advancement Project and the Civil Rights Project. *Opportunities Suspended: The Devastating Consequences of Zero Tolerance and School Discipline Policies.* Cambridge, MA: Harvard University, 2000.

Agatston, Patricia W., Robin Kowalski, and Susan Limber. "Students' Perspectives on Cyber Bullying." *Journal of Adolescent Health* (2007). http://www.wct-law.com/CM/Custom/Students%27%20 Perspectives%20on%20Cyber%20Bullying.pdf (Accessed September 2010).

Almond, Lucinda, ed. *School Violence (Current Controversies)*. San Diego, CA: Greenhaven Press, 2007.

Binns, Katherine, and Dana Markow. V*iolence in America's Public Schools—Five Years Later: A Survey of Students, Teachers and Law Enforcement Officers*. New York: The Metropolitan Life Company, 1999.

Brooks, Kim, Vincent Schiraldi, and Jason Ziedenberg. "School House Hype: Two Years Later." Justice Policy Institute. (2000). http://www .justicepolicy.org/images/upload/00-04_REP_SchoolHouseHype2_JJ.pdf (Accessed September 2010).

Center for the Prevention of Youth Violence, Johns Hopkins Bloomberg School of Public Health. http://www.jhsph.edu/preventyouthviolence (Accessed September 2010).

Center for the Study and Prevention of Violence, University of Colorado at Boulder. http://www.colorado.edu/cspv/safeschools/index.html (Accessed September 2010).

Centers for Disease Control and Prevention. "School-Associated Student Homicides–United States, 1992–2006." *Morbidity and Mortality Weekly Report,* v.57/2 (January 18, 2008).

Centers for Disease Control and Prevention. "Source of Firearms Used by Students in School-Associated Violent Deaths–United States, 1992–1999." *Morbidity and Mortality Weekly Report,* v.52/09 (March 7, 2003).

Centers for Disease Control and Prevention. *Youth Risk Behavior Surveillance System (YRBSS)*. Washington, DC: CDC, 1993–2007.

Consortium to Prevent School Violence. http://www.ncsvprp.org.html (Accessed September 2010).

Cornell, Dewey G. *School Violence: Fear Versus Facts*. Mahawh, NJ: Lawrence Erlbaum Associates, 2006.

Elliott, Delbert S., Beatrix A. Hamburg, and Kirk R. Williams, eds. *Violence in American Schools*. Cambridge: Cambridge University Press, 1998.

Gallup. "Children and Violence." http://www.gallup.com/poll/1588 /Children-Violence.aspx (Accessed March 2010).

Garcia, Crystal. "School Safety Technology in America: Current Use and Perceived Effectiveness." *Criminal Justice Policy Review,* v.14 (2003).

Goldstein, Arnold, Beri Harootunian, and Jane Close Conoley. *Student Aggression: Prevention, Management, and Replacement Training.* New York: Guilford Publications, 1994.

Gottfredson, Denise. *Schools and Delinquency.* Cambridge: Cambridge University Press, 2000.

Grogger, Jeffrey. "Local Violence and Educational Attainment." *The Journal of Human Resources,* v.32 (1997).

Jimerson, Shane R., and Michael J. Furlong, eds. *Handbook of School Violence and School Safety: From Research to Practice.* Mahwah, NJ: Lawrence Earlbaum, 2006.

Johnson, Robert S. "Metal Detector Searches: An Effective Means to Help Keep Weapons Out of Schools." *Journal of Law and Education* (April 2000).

Langman, Peter. *Why Kids Kill: Inside the Mind of School Shooters.* New York: Palgrave Macmillan. 2009.

MetLife. "The MetLife Survey of the American Teacher: Past, Present and Future." (2008). http://www.metlife.com/assets/cao/contributions/found ation/american-teacher/MetLife_Teacher_Survey_2009_Part_1.pdf (Accessed February 2010).

National Youth Violence Prevention Resource Center. http://www.safe youth.org/scripts/index.asp (Accessed March 2010).

Neiman, Samantha, and Jill F. DeVoe. *Crime, Violence, Discipline, and Safety in U.S. Public Schools: Findings From the School Survey on Crime and Safety: 2007–08.* Washington, DC: National Center for Education Statistics, 2009.

Skiba, Russ. "Zero Tolerance, Zero Evidence: An Analysis of School Disciplinary Practice. Indiana Education Policy Center." http://www .indiana.edu/~safeschl/ztze.pdf (Accessed February 2010).

Thomas, R. Murray. *Violence in America's Schools: Understanding, Prevention, and Response.* Westport, CT: Praeger Publishers, 2006.

U.S. Department of Education. *Indicators of School Crime and Safety: 2009.* Washington, DC: U.S. Department of Education, 2009.

U.S. Department of Justice, Bureau of Justice Statistics. "Indicators of School Crime and Safety: 2009." http://bjs.ojp.usdoj.gov/content/pub /pdf/iscs09.pdf. (Accessed February 2010).

U.S. Department of Justice, Bureau of Justice Statistics. "National Crime Victimization Survey (NCVS), 1992–2005 and 2007." http://bjs.ojp.us doj.gov (Accessed February 2010).

18

Sentencing Options

Patricia E. Campie
National Center for Juvenile Justice

In the adult criminal justice system, the consequences that result from a finding or plea of criminal guilt are known as *sentencing options,* whereas in the juvenile justice system the consequences of adjudication (a finding of responsibility) are known as *disposition options.* This is just one of the many differences in language, function, and purpose of the two unique systems created to respond in age-appropriate ways to adult crime and juvenile delinquency. For purposes of clarity, the term *sentencing* is used to describe the disposition options currently available to youths adjudicated delinquent in juvenile justice systems across the United States.

Sentencing options in the juvenile system are meant to address the core principles of juvenile justice, which focus more on rehabilitation and competency development than sentences in the adult criminal justice system, which focus more on retribution and punishment. Because of this difference in purpose, the sentencing options in the juvenile justice system are ones that provide youth with opportunities to develop personal competencies, repair the harm to victims, and be accountable for their actions within a developmentally appropriate framework. These sentencing options have been heavily influenced by research on adolescent brain development and should be designed so that they are responsive to the unique needs of each youth according to his age, family situation, educational level, moral reasoning skills, and a host of other dynamic factors that influence the cessation of criminogenic behavior and support the development of pro-social skills.

The sentencing options available to juvenile offenders has primarily been left up to each state or local jurisdiction, depending on the manner in which specific delinquent and criminal offenses are defined, charged, and adjudicated at the local level. Some jurisdictions with informal or formal rules that allow truant and runaway-status youths to be processed through juvenile court would then have very different sentencing options for those youths, if adjudicated delinquent, than would jurisdictions where such status offenses are either informally or formally diverted out of the justice system completely. Likewise, jurisdictions vary in their treatment of juveniles who are determined to have committed a criminal act that is then charged and tried in an adult criminal court setting. Depending on how different jurisdictions handle these cases, very different sentencing options might be available for the very same criminal act. There was also variation in states sentencing youths to the most serious outcome—the sentence of death—until just recently, when the U.S. Supreme Court voided the constitutionality of condemning youths to death in its 2005 opinion in *Roper v. Simmon*. Even within states, the variability in sentencing options is quite distinct, with only very few states, such as Washington, using sentencing guidelines to standardize the sentencing process. The history of juvenile sentencing options has culminated in a variety of differing options currently available for juvenile offenders.

History of Juvenile Sentencing

The idea of sentencing a young person through the auspices of the juvenile court is fairly recent. It grew after the juvenile crime spike of the mid-1990s, which at the time seemed to suggest there was a coming wave of predator teenagers who were increasingly violent and in need of adult sanctions to punish their adult-like wrongdoing. When youths are sentenced, the options typically include some type of restitution; unsupervised or supervised probation; placement in a private or state-run residential facility; or, prior to sentencing, being tried as adults and subjected to the full range of sentencing options in the criminal justice system.

Between 1985 and 1994, there was a measurable increase (46 to 55 percent) in the number of delinquency cases that were formally handled by the juvenile court, which means that the case was either transferred to adult criminal court or a delinquency petition was filed in juvenile court. As recently as 2005, these percentages were not much different, with 56 percent of all cases handled formally. For some offenses, formal handling increased much more sharply during this time (61 percent of drug offenses formally handled in 1994, compared with 43 percent in 1985; and 62 percent of weapons cases formally processed in 1994, versus 45 percent in 1985). But in 2005, these numbers were down somewhat, with only 56 percent of drug cases and 58 percent of weapons cases handled in a formal manner.

Among those cases that are formally handled in the juvenile court, and for which a sentence is likely, the time between adjudication and sentencing is a key variable in determining the effectiveness of that sentence. While the constitutional guarantee of a speedy trial has never been applied to juvenile court proceedings for youths, case-processing research continues to show that the sooner a youth has his case disposed (or finalized) in court, the more effective the outcome of that disposition, whether it be engaging in community service, paying a fine, enrolling in a treatment program, or being sent to secure confinement in a juvenile correctional facility. Standards for timely case processing have been recommended by national juvenile justice organizations as well as the Office of Juvenile Justice and Delinquency Prevention (OJJDP) as no longer than 90 days for undetained youths and no more than 60 days for detained youths. When put into the context of a typical young person's life, that 60-day maximum is equivalent to one-fourth (25 percent) of their school year, so these time delays can negatively impact the young person from having a successful outcome when interacting with the juvenile court system. Between 1985 and 1994, the median time to disposition for delinquency cases increased 26 percent, from 43 to 54 days. Among jurisdictions with a total population larger than 400,000, youths experienced the lengthiest processing delays, with nearly one-half of all these cases taking more than 90 days to complete.

The 1990s: Probation

Like adult offenders, youths are typically ordered to sentences involving probation more than any other option. Between 1990 and 1999, the number of formal probation cases increased by 80 percent, and by 2005, this increase had reached 95 percent. Most of the increase in the use of probation during these two decades took place from 1985 to 1997, with the probation rate after this period remaining largely unchanged. Most probation cases included incidents involving drugs, public order, or person offenses, with probation used less often in cases of property crime. Nearly all demographic groups, except Asian and black youths (male or female) experienced this increase in the use of formal probation as a sentence in juvenile court, with the differences accounted for by type of offense. In 1999, juveniles were adjudicated delinquent in 66 percent of the 962,000 cases brought before a judge, and of those, 62 percent (398,200) were placed on formal probation. Less than a quarter (24 percent, or 5,200 cases) of these youths were placed in a residential facility, and 10 percent received other dispositions, such as referral to an outside agency, community service, or restitution. The remaining youths (~4 percent) were tried in adult criminal court, where the full range of sentencing options are available as defined by each state's criminal code.

The 2000s: Spike in Delinquency

Between 1985 and 2005 there were historic increases (83 percent) in the percentage of youths adjudicated delinquent. Even for relatively minor offenses such as public order/disorderly conduct offenses, from 1991 to 2005, youths in these cases experienced a 145 percent increase in being formally adjudicated as delinquent. Property offenses were the exception to this rule, with those offenses experiencing only a six percent increase overall during the 20 year period, and the most recent of those years (2005) experiencing a 25 percent decline in cases adjudicated delinquent. From 1985 to 2005, juveniles 15 years of age or younger were more likely to be adjudicated delinquent than were older juveniles, even when considering the severity of their offenses. Males continued to be adjudicated delinquent at a greater rate than their female counterparts. With regard to race, although most courts do not account for race/ethnicity data in an entirely accurate manner, the likelihood that a black youth would be adjudicated delinquent decreased from 58 percent in 1985 to 53 percent in 1995, as compared with white youths (66 percent in 1985 to 58 percent in 1995). However, these numbers increased in 2000, when 64 percent of black youths were adjudicated delinquent, followed by a decline to 62 percent in 2005.

In comparison, 68 percent of white youths brought before the juvenile court were adjudicated delinquent in 2005. The overall population of white youths is much greater than black youths in most jurisdictions, so the percentage of white youths adjudicated delinquent is taken from a much larger pool of youths in that community overall, while black youths adjudicated delinquent represent a larger proportion of the overall black population, which is much smaller, in these communities.

In many states, prosecutors play the pivotal role in determining whether youths will be handled in juvenile or adult court, similar to the adult criminal system, where prosecutorial discretion is perhaps the greatest determinant of how offenders enter the system (how they are charged) and what sentencing options then flow from those charges if the defendant's guilt is confirmed. Prosecutorial discretion, direct file, or prosecutorial waiver is a procedure that removes juvenile offenders from the jurisdiction of the juvenile court and transfers jurisdiction to the adult criminal court. In 2009, 15 states had prosecutorial discretion statutes impacting juveniles, with 11 of these states having reverse waiver provisions allowing a defendant to challenge the prosecutor's decision to file in criminal court. Despite the overall increase in formal filings from 1985 to 2005, the number of cases resulting in waiver to adult court has been quite variable over time, with a sharp increase in 1994 followed by a steep decrease that bottomed out in 2001.

Once an Adult, Always an Adult

As of May 2009, 34 jurisdictions had "once an adult, always an adult" provisions in their state statutes. These provisions typically mean that if a juvenile is ever convicted in adult criminal court, he will be tried in adult criminal court for any future offenses, no matter his age or the seriousness of the offense. Although these laws have been criticized and even challenged in court, case law remains clear that juveniles have neither a constitutional right, common-law right, nor a fundamental right to adjudication in juvenile court. Case handling as a juvenile is granted by the state legislature and, therefore, the legislature may restrict or qualify that right, as long as the classification process is not arbitrary or discriminatory.

The question of how many youths are actually transferred to adult court each year and tried as adults is not as clear. Early estimates of the juvenile transfer caseload projected that approximately one out of every 1,000 juvenile court cases were waived, or transferred, to adult court between 1990 and 1999, with this number increasing to an estimate of eight out of every 1,000 in 2005. These are cases where juvenile court judges are exercising their discretion to send these cases to the adult system. They do not account for cases involving juvenile defendants that begin in the adult system based on the use of prosecutorial discretion. Through 2008, all jurisdictions in the United States had some form of transfer mechanism for sending juveniles into the criminal court system.

Most of the cases waived by judges to adult court between 1990 and 1999 involved property crimes, while the use of this waiver decreased by 24 percent for black youths and increased by six percent for white youths, even though black youths were more likely than white youths to have their cases waived when cases involved crimes against a person. White youths were more likely to have their cases waived when the offense involved property crime. A study conducted in 2000, funded by the Office of Juvenile Justice and Delinquency Prevention (OJJDP), provided the first in-depth look at the practice of transferring juvenile cases to adult court. Previous studies in this regard suffered from a lack of parity between the types of cases being transferred to adult court and "similar" cases that were kept in the juvenile court system. The study found that judges usually agreed with prosecutorial decisions recommending waiver to the adult system, and that a youth did not necessarily need to have a lengthy juvenile court history in order to justify a transfer to criminal court. Offense severity was a prominent feature among the decision-making criteria used in two of the four study sites (South Carolina and Utah), with weapon use and victim injuries acting as key aggravators among person offenses waived to criminal court, even for first-time offenders. In Pennsylvania, the study found that more youths were being waived to criminal court in response to what was perceived to be a growing violent crime problem and a more persistent group of young offenders who had longer juvenile court histories, and for whom traditional juvenile court remedies seemed ineffectual.

Capital Punishment and Life Without Parole

Now that the juvenile death penalty has been voided by the *Roper* decision, life without parole is the most controversial sentencing option for youths, who have been as young as the age of 13 when given this lifelong sentence. Currently, 42 states allow the life without parole option for juveniles convicted in criminal court. A recent Supreme Court decision also issued a groundbreaking verdict on a life without parole case, which will have implications on life without parole sentences for crimes not involving a death.

The controversies arose around the types of cases and youths receiving the unusually harsh sentence of life without parole. Seven states currently have juveniles incarcerated under the life without parole sentence. Most states have the life without parole provision, but its use is rare and has only been implemented in seven states, making the punishment unusual under the terms of the Eighth Amendment. The Public Interest Law Center recently conducted an empirical study showing that in the United States, only 109 juveniles were serving life without parole sentences for nonhomicide crimes. Seventy-seven of these 109 youths were convicted and sentenced in Florida. Thirty-nine of the 47 states included in this study were shown to have no youths serving life without parole sentences for crimes other than murder. The rate at which Florida sentences youths to life without parole was found to be 19 times greater than any other state in the Union, and Florida is the only state that has used this sentence for youths as young as the age of 13 and for the crimes of burglary, battery, and carjacking. Further, the study suggests that this sentencing pattern unique to Florida disproportionately impacts youths of color, since 84 percent of those youths serving life without parole sentences for nonhomicide crimes were African American.

In one of these cases from Florida, a 17-year-old youth was sentenced to life without parole after violating the terms of probation by robbing a restaurant using a gun. The 2009 cases of *Graham v. Florida* and a companion case, *Sullivan v. Florida,* formed the basis for the first case accepted by the U.S. Supreme Court on the issue of whether the life without parole sentencing option for juveniles violated the Eighth Amendment's ban against cruel and unusual punishment. In the 2005 *Roper* decision, the High Court held that the Eighth Amendment banned the use of capital punishment for youths. Opponents of the life without parole laws argue that the same brain development research used to show that it is cruel to use the death penalty for youths, also applies to the use of life without parole laws for youths who do not commit homicides and who are under the age of 18 at the time of the crime.

In May 2010, the Supreme Court's decision on *Graham* (the Court declined to decide on the companion case), concluded that juveniles who committed crimes other than homicide may not be sentenced to life in prison without the possibility of parole. The ruling was the first time the Court excluded an entire class of offenders from a particular punishment outside the context of the death penalty.

Pro: Positive Sentencing Options

Sentencing Youths to Probation

The vast majority of juvenile offenders, who are also not likely to offend more than once, are being placed on probation where they can repair the harm to their community most effectively through restitution and community service and also receive appropriate services to address their criminogenic problems.

Many states (23) utilize a probation system that is administered in whole or in part through a state agency. In these states, the state probation system is administered by different types of agencies, from child welfare to adult corrections agencies. Seventeen states and the District of Columbia administer their probation services for youths through some form of locally controlled judicial entity. In 10 states, probation sentences are administered through the Administrative Office of the Courts, the state agency that oversees all courts in those states.

Probation departments that utilize dynamic risk needs assessments as the first step in a comprehensive case management process are more likely to experience greater success with youths completing their probation sentence fulfilling all the requirements of probation. And, in states like Pennsylvania, juvenile probation may also be responsible for ensuring that youths successfully re-enter the community after placement in a facility or residential program. In these cases, it's especially important that youths are properly screened when they first come to court to identify any immediate needs, followed by a more thorough assessment that can help prioritize these needs and create a plan for addressing them during the term of supervision imposed by the sentence of probation.

There is also a need for appropriate services and resources in the community/state to address these youths' needs; to be effective, these services must be based on programs that address criminogenic factors and are implemented with consistent practice by trained and qualified staff. Then, probation will need to check the progress being made toward addressing these needs, whether the youth is returned to the family or sent to placement, over the course of the probation term. Once the probation requirement has been satisfied, the juvenile's case is eligible to be closed by the juvenile court, at which time the juvenile court judge should review the youth's entire record, including the risk needs assessment results, progress made during probation, and goals achieved by the time of case closure. Using this probation case-management process, and ensuring that data are collected throughout the process to measure progress, provides the best chance for ensuring positive outcomes for the youth, the court, and the community overall.

Use of Judicial Discretion

Judicial discretion is a cornerstone of the juvenile court process because it allows judges to most fully consider the facts of the youth's offense, living situation, educational status, and any needs for treatment or interventions to address mental health, substance abuse, or trauma-related problems. In addition, more research is showing that many of the youths in the juvenile justice system currently have, have had, or will have, contact with the child welfare system or dependency court systems as well. Because of the complexity of the legal and personal situations that each youth presents to the juvenile court judge, the discretion to apply a wide range of consequences and sentences is an essential tool for ensuring the best possible outcomes for these youths and the communities in which they live. Judicial discretion with regard to juveniles waived to adult court provides the greatest amount of flexibility for considering the unique characteristics of the youth and his case than does prosecutorial discretion, which can often result in direct files that bypass judges altogether.

All jurisdictions in the United States but one allow juvenile court judges to apply discretion when sentencing youths who have been adjudicated delinquent. Only one state, Washington, uses a determinate juvenile sentencing practice where judges must consider the seriousness of the offense and the youth's criminal history within a grid of sentencing options. The Washington legislature recently changed sentencing laws as applied to youths tried as adults, after recognizing the growing body of scientific research demonstrating the substantial differences between youth and adult brain development. In Washington, youths waived to adult court by a judge are no longer subject to mandatory minimums within the adult sentencing structure. Youths who have their cases automatically filed or transferred to the adult system through prosecutorial discretion or statutory mandate are still eligible to be sentenced under Washington's adult mandatory minimums requirements.

Con: Negative Sentencing Options

Use of Formal Processing and Incapacitation

The increasing use of formal juvenile court processing, even for low-level offenses involving disruptions to public order, are too costly for handling youths who are unlikely to reoffend, and largely counterproductive for addressing the reasons why troubled youths are being disruptive in the community.

Although studies continue to show that youth outcomes are not improved when youths are formally processed in the juvenile justice system, public sentiment still remains high that the courts must respond formally whenever youth misbehavior is identified. Zero-tolerance policies in schools since the Columbine massacre are a good example of this practice, where even the mildest student behavioral problem prompts a response by police, who then take the youths off to juvenile court. A 2010 study by Christina Stahlkopf, Mike Males, and Daniel Macallair of California youth who had been committed to state correctional facilities showed that higher levels of incarceration failed to demonstrate reduced crime rates. The most comprehensive report on the effects of formal processing on reducing juvenile delinquency was released in early 2010 by The Campbell Collaboration, a group that undertakes systematic reviews of existing research studies. Their systematic review included 29 research studies analyzing the question of whether formal system processing reduces later youth delinquency. Findings showed that delinquency outcomes actually increased for youths who were formally processed by the juvenile justice system, even after controlling for seriousness of offense, prior offending behavior, and other predictors of future delinquency. Both of these recent reports have called on policymakers to take a serious look at alternatives to the use of formal processing and confinement to handle juvenile delinquency, since formal processing and confinement of youths (approximately $88,000/youth/year) are significantly more expensive than effective, evidence-based intervention alternatives, many of which have been demonstrated to produce positive youth outcomes.

Transfer to Adult Court

Juvenile transfer to adult court is a practice that is overly influenced by prosecutorial discretion, which is often influenced by public sentiment. Transfer also appears to be overused in a disproportionate manner against youths of color, especially when the crime involves a white victim—although data limitations tracking these youth transfers make this claim difficult to substantiate outside of a few jurisdictions.

There are a variety of mechanisms states use to move youths into the adult criminal justice system. Judges may be able to use their discretion to waive a youth into the adult system depending on offense severity and youth history. Prosecutors may be able to leverage their discretion to directly file charges against a youth in the criminal court, or the state may provide statutory rules that mandate which system youths are tried in, depending on the nature of the offense charged and/or other criteria. There are also mechanisms in some states to reverse course and have youths move back into the juvenile system for processing, and in some states, these decisions depend only on whether or not the youth had ever been tried as an adult previously. In these "once an adult always an adult" jurisdictions, youths are automatically under the jurisdiction of the adult system for any new offense. Basic data on how many youths are caught up in the adult system is surprisingly inconsistent, with as many as 12 states not able to report these numbers with any degree of certainty. Only 17 states have a fairly confident estimate of the number of youths in the adult system. Because of these data gaps, it has been difficult to build a large body of evidence to study the effects of juvenile transfer to the adult system. However, the studies that have been done fail to show that in most cases, treating youths as adults in the criminal justice system has a crime reduction effect, as intended by this "get-tough" approach to juvenile crime. In fact, some of these studies have found similar results to those studies on incapacitation in the juvenile system: re-offense likelihood increases when youths are confined.

Conclusion

Although public sentiment seems to be squarely behind the idea that youths who "do adult crime should do adult time," there is no reliable research to suggest that youths are less likely to offend in the future because they are dealt with more punitively. Adolescent brain research continues to suggest that most youths are not neurologically mature until the age of 24, so in addition to having no criminological research available to support a deterrent effect based on treating youths like adults, the scientific literature would seem to suggest that adult responses to juvenile crime would have limited utility for impacting adolescent decision making.

The juvenile justice system is based on principles of rehabilitation and competency development. Although the administration of juvenile justice is decidedly local in flavor, depending on statutory law and other factors, these basic principles provide the underpinnings for the unique sentencing options that predominate for juveniles. Similar to adults, most juveniles are sentenced to some form of restitution, community service, or probation for first-time and minor offenses. For more serious crimes or for repeat offenses, juveniles may be sentenced to spend time in a residential facility, where they will be required to complete a series of activities toward building their skill sets and achieving competency in core areas that support the development of pro-social behaviors and, as a result, act to deter or reduce reoffending behavior.

❖

See Also: 6. Death Penalty for Juvenile Offenders; 8. Juvenile Detention Facilities; 10. Juvenile Offenders in Adult Courts; 11. Juveniles in Adult Correctional Facilities; 15. Racial Disparities.

Further Readings

Advancement Project. "Opportunities Suspended: The Devastating Consequences of Zero Tolerance and School Discipline." Cambridge, MA: Harvard University, 2000.

Annino, Paolo G., David W. Rasmussen, and Chelsea Boehme Rice. *Juvenile Life Without Parole for Non-Homicide Offenses: Florida Compared to the Nation.* Tallahassee, FL: Public Interest Law Center (2009).

Butts, Jeffrey. *Delays in Juvenile Court Processing of Delinquency Cases OJJDP Fact Sheet #60.* Washington, DC: Office of Juvenile Justice and Delinquency Prevention, March 1997.

Butts, Jeffrey. *Juvenile Court Processing of Delinquency Cases, 1985–1994, OJJDP Fact Sheet #57.* Washington, DC: Office of Juvenile Justice and Delinquency Prevention, March 1997.

Drake, Elizabeth. *Evidence-Based Juvenile Offender Programs: Program Description, Quality Assurance and Cost.* Olympia, WA: Washington State Institute for Public Policy, 2007.

Griffin, Patrick. *Different From Adults: An Updated Analysis of Juvenile Transfer and Blended Sentencing Laws, With Recommendations for Reform.* Pittsburgh, PA: National Center for Juvenile Justice. 2008.

Henning, Kristin. "The Case Against Juvenile Life Without Parole: Good Policy and Good Law." *FindLaw* (October 26, 2009).

Griffin, Patrick, and Melanie King. "National Overviews." *State Juvenile Justice Profiles.* Pittsburgh, PA: National Center for Juvenile Justice, 2006.

Puzzanchera, Charles M. *Delinquency Cases Waived to Juvenile Courts, 1990 to 1999, OJJDP Fact Sheet #04.* Washington, DC: Office of Juvenile Justice and Delinquency Prevention, 2003.

Puzzanchera, Charles, and Melissa Sickmund. *Juvenile Court Statistics, 2005.* Pittsburgh, PA: National Center for Juvenile Justice, 2008.

Redding, R. "Juvenile Transfer Laws: An Effective Deterrent to Delinquency?" *OJJDP Juvenile Justice Bulletin* (August 2008).

Roper v. Simmons, 543 U.S. 551 (2005).

Snyder, H., M. Sickmund, and E. Poe-Yamagata. *Juvenile Transfers to Criminal Court in the 1990s: Lessons Learned From Four Studies.*

Washington, DC: U.S. Department of Justice, Office of Justice Programs, Office of Juvenile Justice and Delinquency Prevention, 2000.

Stahl, Anne L. *Delinquency Cases in Juvenile Courts, 1999, OJJDP Fact Sheet #02*. Washington, DC: Office of Juvenile Justice and Delinquency Prevention, 2003.

Stahlkopf, Christina, Mike Males, and Daniel Macallair. "Testing Incapacitation Theory." *Crime and Delinquency,* v.56/2 (2010)

Steinberg, L. "Should the Science of Adolescent Brain Development Inform Public Policy?" *American Psychologist*, v.64 (2009).

Steinberg, Laurence, and Alex R. Piquero. "Manipulating Public Opinion About Trying Juveniles as Adults: An Experimental Study." *Crime and Delinquency,* v.56 (2009).

Szymanski, Linda. "Direct File, Prosecutor Discretion, Prosecutorial Waiver (2001 Update)." *NCJJ Snapshot,* v.7/4 (April 2002).

Szymanski, Linda. "Once and Adult Always an Adult (2009 Update)." *NCJJ Snapshot,* v.4/5 (May 2009).

Torbet, P. *Building Pennsylvania's Comprehensive Aftercare Model: Probation Case Management Essentials for Youth in Placement.* Pittsburgh, PA: National Center for Juvenile Justice, 2008.

19

Serious and Violent Juvenile Offenders

Norman A. White
Saint Louis University

Serious and violent juvenile offenders are a significant problem. Their offending has a substantial impact on the communities in which they live, the juvenile and criminal justice systems, and the research community. Scholars and practitioners have devoted considerable resources to identifying the characteristics of serious violent juveniles. Research shows that there is an intersection of three classes of offenders: serious, violent, and chronic. Serious offenders are individuals who have committed serious acts of delinquency that include all violent offenses, serious property offenses, and drug trafficking. Violent offenders are those criminal acts against persons included in the Uniform Crime Report, a summary-based federal reporting system with data gathered from the city, county, state, and other geographic levels. They include homicide, aggravated assault, robbery, arson, kidnapping, and sexual assault or rape. Chronic offenders are individuals who begin their involvement in criminal offending at an early age and commit the lion's share of the criminal acts recorded each year. Approximately one-third of chronic offenders participate in violent behavior.

While the discussion of serious and violent juveniles is important, the intersection between these juveniles and chronic offenders leads to a sizeable sharing of risk factors, making it difficult to disentangle. The intersection of these groups can lead to substantial errors in criminal justice processing. National concern with and study of the development of serious violent juvenile offending has its roots in postwar society. Chronic offending also plays a role in the study of serious and violent juveniles. While there are positive aspects of identifying and responding to serious and violent juveniles, the negative implications of targeting serious and violent juveniles also remain a challenge.

Historical Developments

Concern with serious violent juvenile offending has been fueled in part by M. E. Wolfgang, R. M. Figlio, and T. Sellin's now-classic study, *Delinquency in a Birth Cohort*. They found that out of 9,450 boys born and raised in Philadelphia 1945–63, 3,475 engaged in delinquent acts resulting in 10,214 arrests, and that 6.4 percent of the entire sample committed more than 50 percent of all delinquent acts. Wolfgang and his colleagues coined the term *chronic offenders* to describe this group. Chronic offenders exhibit an early onset of arrests, a high frequency of offending, and a progression to engage in more serious offenses as they age. Many eventually engage in violent crime. These findings have been replicated in the United States and abroad using self-reports and official data.

Another study contributing to the attention given to serious violent juvenile offending was the work of Albert Blumstein and his colleagues. Their research on criminal careers and career criminals identified several dimensions that comprised a criminal career including onset, duration, escalation, and termination. This seminal work on criminal careers raised several important questions. Did offenders exhibit offense specialization during their career? Were there crime-specific trajectories (i.e., violence) that could be followed from onset to conclusion? Was a criminal career characterized by learning a specific trade that led to crimes committed in areas of expertise? As a result of the Blumstein study, little evidence suggests that specialization exists among offenders regarding the type of offense, and there are no crime-specific trajectories that can be followed. However, the interest in the chronic offender or career criminal has been of critical importance to the study of serious juvenile violence. These high-rate offenders, while at risk to engage in violent acts, are more likely to engage in nonviolent acts as a dimension of their cafeteria-style offending.

Chronic and serious juvenile violent offending is studied utilizing official records (arrests or convictions) and self-reports. Official records of arrests and convictions are helpful in understanding which behavior comes to the attention of police or is sanctioned in court. However, a significant number of delinquent and violent acts go undetected by police, representing hidden delinquency. Given the infrequency of arrest for violence, the use of official data alone results in a significant proportion of violent offenders going uncounted. It is precisely because of the relatively low base rate of violent offending, the low arrest rate of violent offenders, and the importance placed on serious violent offenders that the inclusion of chronic offending is important in a discussion of the serious and violent offending. The inclusion of the highly active "serious and violent few" who commit the lion's share of criminal acts provides a larger population from which to conduct research.

Criminological theory for much of the 20th century focused on social forces and their influence on delinquency and violence. The sociological orientation, an outgrowth of the Chicago School that placed the causes of crime in the social arena, had diminished the willingness to focus on individuals and their behavior. These socially derived models proposed that crime and violence was related to social inequality or disadvantage (social structure); later, social processes connected individuals to criminal others. This theoretical perspective diminished the focus on individuals that had driven much of criminological theory in the 19th century. Research on chronic offenders, career criminals, and serious and violent juvenile offenders necessitated a return to examining individual trajectories.

Risk and Violence

How do serious violent offenders differ from others who engage in delinquency and violence? This question has led to the development of theoretical models that provide taxonomies for articulating differing trajectories and etiologies. Among these are Patterson and colleagues' coercion model, Moffitt's dual taxonomy, and Loeber and associates' pathway model. These developmental or life-course perspectives suggest that the seeds to more serious offending in adolescents are sown in the early, formative years of life. They all suggest that offenders who begin early (younger than 12) differ from those who begin later, and there is concurrence that individuals who begin offending at an early age are at heightened risk for serious violent and chronic offending. Current research shows that age of onset is one of the most robust predictors of chronicity and seriousness of offending. The role early onset plays as a predictor of life-course offending and serious violence is significant for both males and females.

The research on the life course of delinquent and violent offending shows that risk resides in five domains of life: individual, family, school, peer, and community. Experiencing risk in any one of these domains can have a toll on an individual's ability to thrive, and experiencing risk across domains substantially increases the likelihood of engaging in delinquency. Further, the more risk experienced across the five domains, the greater the likelihood of engaging in problem behavior such as violence.

The dominance of the theoretical perspective of the Chicago School influenced a significant amount of research focusing on the social forces in urban areas. Research generated in that tradition provides substantial evidence supporting the role of peers, family, communities, and schools in the occurrence of serious and violent crime. Earlier research identified individual risk factors for delinquency and violence; little attention had been paid to that area in the mid-20th century. The focus on the individual domain was renewed when the attention turned to delinquent trajectories.

Individual Risk

Although family, friends, schools, and communities may greatly affect negative life trajectories, individuals can experience these risks and remain free from trouble. Serious, violent, or chronic offenders exhibit a great deal of individual risk in comparison to the nonchronic or nonviolent offender. Individual risk factors such as birth complications, hyperactivity, attention problems, impulsiveness, risk-taking, and aggression have been examined in relation to violence. Youths whose mothers experienced complications related to childbirth may experience parental rejection. Research shows that maternal rejection due to birth complications is related to serious violent offending in comparison to those with less serious violence and later onset of offending. Others report that minor physical abnormalities due to complications in prenatal development were also predictive of violence at 20–22 years of age. Even before one takes their first breath, risk may be developing, which could have lifelong negative implications.

In addition to the experiences of birth, research shows that diagnoses of attention deficit disorder (ADD) and attention deficit hyperactivity disorder (ADHD) in youth are robust predictors of violence in adolescence and adulthood. Research shows that the impact of childhood hyperactivity is greater for assault than for robbery. The study of youth attention problems further shows that attention problems identified at the age of eight, 10, 14, and 16 were significantly associated with self-reports of violence.

The effect of these early attention problems is significantly related to self-reported violence at the age of 18 and arrests for violence at the age of 26.

Another factor among individual characteristics that is predictive of later violence is impulsive behavior. There is a relationship between impulsivity and risk-taking at 8–10 and 12–14 years of age, and violent juvenile (age 18) and adult (age 26) offending. Risk-taking, another form of impulsive behavior, measured at 14 and 16 years of age, is related to self-reported violence at the age of 18.

Research on violent offending shows that there is substantial evidence and a great deal of continuity between early aggressive behavior and later violence. Aggression in childhood (12<) is significantly associated with self-reported violence at 12–18 years of age. Aggression observed by teachers in first grade is predictive of violence at the age of 20 for males and females. Similarly, teacher ratings of aggression in adolescence (age 10–16) are predictive of official records of violence at the age of 26.

Brain chemistry has been examined in the effort to understand violent behavior. Chemicals found in the brain, such as serotonin, influence an individual's sense of well being, affecting impulse control, regulation, and general social functioning. Substantial evidence shows that low levels of serotonin are predictive of aggression and violence. Serotonin is a significant regulator of anger, fear, insecurity, and depression. Inability to control or appropriately respond to these emotional states or moods can increase the likelihood of violent behavior.

Overall, risk in a variety of areas that measure individual functioning reflect significant associations with later serious violent offending. Risk factors associated with genetic makeup or measured at birth, in childhood, and pre-adolescence, have long-term effects on individual involvement in serious violence. These variables are also shared with chronic offending, reflecting a parallel pathway for many serious violent offenders. Life-course research focusing on individual differences helps explain how youths living in similar environments differ in their involvement in delinquency and violence. Extant research on serious violent juvenile offending shows that variables from the individual domain play a key role in explaining these offending differences.

System Response

Efforts to identify chronic and serious violent juvenile offenders have run parallel to changes within the juvenile justice system, holding juveniles more accountable for their actions. Since the late 1970s, accountability has been tied to substantially more punitive methods of dealing with criminal offenders and juvenile offenders in particular. Every U.S. state has developed mechanisms to remove or waive youths who engage in more serious offending from the juvenile court. The stage for this was set by several important Supreme Court cases: *Kent v. United States, In re Gault,* and *In re Winship.* The *Kent* case required that any youth being removed from juvenile court jurisdiction be given a formal hearing and be represented by a lawyer. This ruling was limited to cases of waiver of jurisdiction. The *Gault* decision furthered this ruling by requiring that any youth who was subject to lose their liberty due to a legal proceeding should be given a notice of charges, be given legal counsel, and be able to depose their accusers. The *Winship* case went one step further and shifted the burden of proof from the civil standard of the preponderance of the evidence to beyond a reasonable doubt. All of these cases represented seed changes in juvenile justice, marking a watershed period that moved juvenile court proceedings in the direction of the more adversarial adult criminal court.

Important court decisions opened the door for refinement of processes related to waiving youths out of the jurisdiction of the juvenile court and exposing them to adult penalties for "adult" behaviors of serious criminal offenses. Hence, waiver meant accountability in a period when accountability and personal responsibility were deemed important. Waivers took several approaches: legislative, prosecutorial, and judicial. Legislative waiver of jurisdiction meant that certain youth offenders were removed from the juvenile court's jurisdiction and were no longer considered delinquent. Ultimately, they were classified as adults and processed in adult criminal courts, no longer enjoying the protections of the juvenile court.

Prosecutorial waiver allows the prosecutor to have dual jurisdiction and the discretion to charge the offender as an adult or a juvenile. The prosecution reviews the case and the youth's history to assess the appropriate systemic handling of the case. These waivers are also referred to as *direct file.* The direct filing allows the prosecutor to act without a hearing, sending cases forward without judicial review or a formal waiver hearing. Florida allows for direct file, and many questions have been raised regarding their processing of juveniles.

A third type involves placing the authority for retention or removal from the juvenile system in the hands of the juvenile court judge, who assesses whether a youth is amenable to the services and protections of the juvenile system. If the judge's assessment indicates that a youth can no longer benefit from the juvenile court's services, he or she can waive them. Missouri follows a system of judicial waiver wherein the juvenile court judge holds a hearing to certify a youth as an adult, and once the youth has been certified for the presenting offense, he is permanently removed from the juvenile system.

The shift toward a more adversarial and punitive juvenile system has made identification of the serious violent juvenile offender all the more important. Although a relatively small number of youths are transferred each year from the juvenile to the adult systems, it is important to accurately classify youths based upon the risk for future serious and violent offending.

To summarize, a convergence of factors contributed to research focusing on the serious violent juvenile offender. Scholarly research identified a population of youths who accounted for much of the offending among juvenile offenders. Within that population, a significant number also engaged in serious and violent offending. This serious and violent few who represent only five to 10 percent of the juvenile population have driven research and policy.

Pro: Benefits of Predicting Serious Offenders

It is important to seek out explanations for serious juvenile offending. The juvenile justice system, as with most publicly funded services, operates with limited resources. Not all youths who commit delinquent acts are in need of long-term treatment. This is evident from the development of diversion programming that has developed in the family or juvenile court. Some youths may do just as well through diversion processes, wherein they receive needed services outside the jurisdiction of the court. But in reality, some youths need intervention provided by the justice system. The question is, which youths and which system?

The identification of serious violent juvenile offenders allows for needed resources to be invested in youths who are significant community problems—youths whose behaviors are substantially harmful to themselves, their communities, and most certainly to their victims. A central question asks which youths are the best investments, which allows for separating those with lifelong patterns of behavior from the one-time offenders who may have gotten involved in an act of violence circumstantially. For example, a youth might be involved in a fight that becomes deadly or results in serious injury. Some commit a single act of violence in a lifetime, and others make it part of their behavioral repertoire. Those engaged in delinquency for a relatively short period of time or for a single event may be more likely to benefit from juvenile case processing or diversion than the long-term offender who has a criminal career.

Research on serious violent offenders can also help identify risk factors that may be ameliorated and life-altering. It is possible that trajectories can be altered at points in life courses where individuals are susceptible to change. Patterns of past experiences become evident that are similar for many youths who become serious or violent offenders. In an actuarial view, there is a sense that all things being equal, patterns of offending become predictable. Although prediction is not very successful, given the limits on existing resources, every effort to make cost-beneficial decisions is worthwhile.

Con: Drawbacks of Predicting Serious Offenders

While predictive models may help identify individuals whose backgrounds place them at increased risk for exhibiting violent behavior, prediction of future dangerousness is difficult. The search for the serious violent juvenile offender is admirable and worthwhile; however, the problem lies in the fact that the academic identification of risk has practical implications in the lives of young offenders who come in contact with the justice system. There has been a convergence of academic research, policy, and practice in the juvenile justice system. Instruments used to assess risk are also used to predict dangerousness, and the door opens wide for both false positive and false negative identification. Some youths whose profiles suggest that they are at increased risk for violent behavior may never commit another serious or violent act. Others who do not fit the risk profile may be in the early stages of their careers, and later will cross the line and commit more serious and violent acts.

The implications for serious violent juvenile offenders are that juvenile justice policy has been fueled by voices calling for serious responses to youth violence. These policies include more punitive sentences, treatment of children as adults, and the incapacitation of some youths based on perceived risk for future dangerousness. The calls for accountability can eliminate future hopes, given rates of recidivism among offending populations. As Sampson and Laub have described the consequences of justice system involvement, these youths are likely to experience a cumulative disadvantage that becomes a burden for life. The search for the serious violent juvenile offender can contribute to a widening of the net for the juvenile court population. Individuals whose life circumstances immerse them in risk can be mistaken for the most dangerous of the population because their profiles are similar.

There has been a significant social implication connected to the outgrowth of juvenile and criminal justice policy that is intended to target serious violent offenders. One problem is the longstanding pattern of disproportionate minority contact with the justice system. Young African American males are overrepresented in both arrest and victimization statistics for serious and violent crime. A more punitive justice philosophy that is geared toward serious and violent offenders has contributed to what Jerome Miller has described as a mission to "search and destroy" young urban African American males, resulting in large numbers of youths with criminal or juvenile records. This has led to the United States leading the industrialized world in imprisoning its citizens.

While it is not unreasonable to believe that violent offenders should be arrested and prosecuted to the fullest extent of the law, many young people have been subject to exposure to the adult criminal system because of waiver processes. For example, according to Jeffrey Fagan, in 1996 alone, 210,000–260,000 youths were subject to the adult court system. Noted criminologist Donna Bishop maintains that one in 10 youths arrested each year will wind up being processed through the adult system. Many of these youths have not committed a violent offense; rather, they have been labeled as not amenable to treatment. As a result of youthful mistakes, these youths are no longer free from lifetime harm. They cannot return to their youth and are not truly adults.

Conclusion

The problem of serious violent juvenile offenders needs to be reckoned with by both local communities and the juvenile and criminal justice system. On the research agenda since the 1980s, the presence of chronic offenders and career criminals in offending populations has increased the scholarly examination of life trajectories that include violent offending. The research on serious violent juvenile offending shows that many of the social characteristics that predict chronic offending also predict youth violence. Serious offenders are likely to begin early, thereby experiencing a host of environmental risks in the areas of family, peers, community, and schools. Furthermore, they are likely to exhibit individual risk that, when coupled with environmental factors, make them more likely to engage in serious and violent behavior.

Serious violent offenders are a problem for their communities. They also represent a problem for their peers, both from the standpoint of their victimization of them to their having shaped justice policy that can have an impact on their nonviolent peers. Today, sweeping reforms use a broad brush to paint many more offenders, making them accountable for crimes that may be a single delinquent action. Legislative and justice system efforts to target youths who are more violent and less amenable to treatment from the juvenile court contribute to greater exposure to serious punishment for youthful indiscretions. Instead of catching only the serious violent juvenile, there has been a widening of the net, and less serious, nonviolent offenders are also in jeopardy of adult treatment and punishment.

See Also: 3. At-Risk Youth; 9. Juvenile Gangs and Delinquency; 10. Juvenile Offenders in Adult Courts; 11. Juveniles in Adult Correctional Facilities; 15. Racial Disparities; 20. Treatment and Rehabilitation.

Further Readings

Capaldi, D., and G. Patterson. "Can Violent Offenders Be Distinguished From Frequent Offenders: Prediction From Childhood to Adolescence." *Journal of Research in Crime and Delinquency,* v.33/2 (1996).

Farrington, D. P. "Early Predictors of Adolescent and Adult Violence." *Violence and Victims* (1989).

Feld, B. "Bad Kids: Race and the Transformation of the Juvenile Court." London: Oxford University Press, 1999.

Loeber, R., and D. F. Hay. "Key Issues in the Development of Aggression and Violence From Childhood to Adulthood." *Annual Review of Psychiatry,* v.48 (1996).

Loeber, R., and D. P . Farrington, eds. *Serious and Violent Juvenile Offenders: Risk Factors and Successful Interventions.* Thousand Oaks, CA: Sage, 1998.

Miller, J. *Search and Destroy: African-American Males in the Criminal Justice System.* Cambridge: Cambridge University Press, 1996.

Patterson, G., J. B. Reid, and T. Dishion. *Antisocial Boys: A Social Interactional Approach.* Eugene, OR: Castalia, 1992.

Piquero, A., D. P. Farrington, and A. Blumstein. "The Criminal Career Paradigm." In *Crime and Justice*, edited by M. Tonry. Chicago: University of Chicago Press, 2003.

Raine, A., P. Brennan, and S. Mednick. "Interaction Between Birth Complications and Early Material Rejection in Predisposing Individuals to Adult Violence: Specificity to Serious, Early-Onset Violence." *The American Journal of Psychiatry*, v.154/9 (1997).

Retz, M., P. Retz-Junginger, T. Supprian, J. Thome, and M. Rosler. "Association of Serotonin Transporter Promotor Gene Polymorphism With Violence: Relation With Personality Disorders, Impulsivity, and Childhood ADHD PsychoPathology." *Behavioral Sciences and the Law* (2004).

Stattin, H., and D. Magnusson. "Onset of Official Delinquency." *British Journal of Criminology*, v.35 (1989).

Tolan, P. H., and P. Thomas. "The Implications of Age of Onset for Delinquency Risk II: Longitudinal Data." *Journal of Abnormal Child Psychology*, v.15/1 (1995).

Vaughn, M. G., M. DeLisi, K. M. Beaver, and J. P. Wright. "DAT1 and 5HTT Are Associated With Pathological Criminal Behavior in a Nationally Representative Sample of Youth." *Criminal Justice and Behavior*, v.36 (2009).

Wolfgang, M. E., R. M. Figlio, and T. Sellin. *Delinquency in a Birth Cohort*. Chicago: University of Chicago Press, 1987.

20

Treatment and Rehabilitation

Phillip M. Lyons
Sam Houston State University

The first juvenile court was established through the state's parens patriae authority 1899 in Cook County, Illinois, to correct wayward youths and set them on the right path. This responsibility of the juvenile court to provide treatment and rehabilitation services was articulated by the U.S. Supreme Court in the watershed case of *Kent v. United States*:

> The Juvenile Court is theoretically engaged in determining the needs of the child and of society rather than adjudicating criminal conduct. The objectives are to provide measures of guidance and rehabilitation for the child and protection for society, not to fix criminal responsibility, guilt and punishment.

In that same case, the Court lamented the system's abject failure in this regard in observing, "There is evidence, in fact, that there may be grounds for concern that the child receives the worst of both worlds: that he gets neither the protections accorded to adults nor the solicitous care and regenerative treatment postulated for children." The juvenile court system was established more than 100 years ago to focus on "guidance and rehabilitation" of youths and was vested with an obligation to facilitate their "solicitous care and regenerative treatment." Half a century later, it wasn't working.

However abysmal the realization of treatment and rehabilitation goals by the juvenile justice system 50 years ago, there is reason to think the picture has worsened. This is so because of the explicit rejection of rehabilitation ideals that has subsequently occurred. Notwithstanding the view articulated in *Kent*, in the past three decades, transfers of juveniles to adult court have increased by about 75 percent, as noted by R. E. Redding in 2006. About half of the states have adopted blended sentencing approaches that allow for the imposition of adult punishments on children who remain subject to juvenile court jurisdiction.

The juvenile justice system's departure from treatment and rehabilitation ideals was part of a broader move in that direction that had its genesis in the adult system. Fueled by the "nothing works" sentiment of the time, the criminal justice system retreated rapidly from what the U.S. Supreme Court called the "outmoded rehabilitation model" in *Mistretta v. U.S.* (1989). The public policy responses to the "nothing works" conclusion were regrettable because the underlying premise, as it turns out, was wrong.

Evolution of Treatment and Rehabilitation Approaches

Treatment of Youths in General

Developing informed policy around treatment and rehabilitation depends on understanding the underlying problems. That understanding, in turn, depends on knowledge about the treatment needs of children and youths more broadly, as opposed to a narrow view of the treatment needs of youths involved in the juvenile justice system. This is so because, according to G. B. Melton, P. M. Lyons, and W. J. Spaulding in *No Place to Go: The Civil Commitment of Minors* (1988), "Even a cursory examination of children's mental health needs requires consideration of multiple systems whose boundaries are often blurred." Consequently, examining the mental health needs of children and youths in general is a useful starting point for exploring the treatment needs of youths involved in the justice sector.

Many of the mental health issues of children and youths are similar to those of their older counterparts, although the developmental demands of successfully transitioning into adulthood compound the problems experienced by youths. Those mental health issues generally involve problems of thought, mood, behavior, or some combination of these. Because chronic, disabling mental health problems often manifest first in late adolescence or early adulthood, some young people experiencing disturbances in thought or mood are simply beginning what will be a long and difficult, lifelong struggle with serious mental illness. Milder disturbances in thought or mood are likely to be the result of more transient problems that likely will improve with little treatment, according to researchers such as B. J. Blinder, W. M. Young, K. R. Fineman, and S. J. Miller. Although problems in thought and mood are not uncommon for persons of this age, behavior problems are most likely to be associated with youths involved in the juvenile justice system.

Treatment of Youths in the Justice Sector

Upward of 75 percent of youths involved in the juvenile justice system have a diagnosable mental disorder involving disordered mood, thought, or behavior, as noted by J. Cocozza and K. Skowyra in 2000. Unlike young people receiving treatment for thought or mood disorders, those engaged in treatment for behavior disorders are typically coerced into such treatment by juvenile justice officials or others. They are not troubled by their problems; rather, they are troubling to others. A key consideration in this regard, therefore, is how to treat these youths in order to minimize the extent to which they cause problems for others.

For those youths under supervision of the juvenile justice system, this means providing treatment and rehabilitation services oriented toward minimizing recidivism as well as treatment and rehabilitation of youths who are beginning to experience serious disturbances in thought or mood and who are accessing services through the juvenile justice system, as opposed to the education, child protection, or child specialty mental health systems.

Minority youths historically have been much more likely to receive services through juvenile justice systems than have their white counterparts, as researched by C. Barber, A. Rosenblatt, L. Harris, and C. Attkisson in 1992. Drawing conclusions from their study of hospital and correctional admissions in *Vulnerabilities to Delinquency* (1981), D. O. Lewis and S. S. Shanok flatly concluded, "In brief, violent, disturbed adolescent blacks were incarcerated; violent, disturbed whites were hospitalized. Even when black children were initially considered to be psychiatrically disturbed and were hospitalized, they often subsequently were transferred to corrections."

In sharp contrast to the available evidence on the effectiveness of punishment at reducing recidivism, rehabilitative treatments have been shown to be generally effective. Drug courts, for example, which traditionally have had a strong treatment emphasis, have been shown to reduce recidivism whether in the community or the prison setting. Drug treatment programs other than drug courts have been associated with lower rates of recidivism, as have work, education, and vocational programs and relapse prevention programs. Some of these studies did not involve youthful offenders directly, and one of these reported small benefits of treatment on recidivism for the adult offenders studied. These findings raise questions as to whether treatment is likely to be more effective for youthful offenders than older ones—questions that should be answered before a more thorough examination of juvenile treatment efficacy.

Culpability or Treatment Amenability: Youths Versus Adults

The treatment and rehabilitation rationale of the first juvenile courts rested not only on the assumption that youthful offenders should be helped, but also that they could be helped. As L. Steinberg and E. Cauffman observed in 1999: "In sum, the juvenile court presumes that offenders are immature, in three different senses of the word: their development is incomplete; their judgment is callow; and their character is still malleable. The adult court, in contrast, presumes that defendants are mature: competent, culpable, and unlikely to change." Cauffman and Steinberg also observed that, in comparison with their older adult counterparts, adolescents were "less responsible, more myopic, and less temperate."

The past few decades have yielded impressive insights into the functioning of the human brain, which may illuminate some of the differences between how adults and juveniles think. Particularly noteworthy findings relate to the development of the frontal lobes of the brain, the region that is responsible for executive functions such as impulse control, planning, metacognition, concentration, attention, self-monitoring, and decision making. The ability to act in one's own self-interest is also associated with frontal lobe functioning. Results of numerous studies of brain scans and other techniques for mapping brain function provide convergent evidence that the frontal lobe region of the brain continues to develop into the 20s, long after maturation has ceased in other regions of the brain.

How to Treat

The questions pertaining to treatment and rehabilitation do not end once a decision is made that treatment is appropriate and the specific problems or issues to be treated are identified. Different problems or issues require different interventions. Moreover, not all interventions are equally effective, even in addressing the same problem. The last couple of decades have seen mental health treatment providers and scholars move toward identifying those treatments that work well (and those that do not) in order to ensure that the maximum benefit of treatment is realized. The movement in mental health toward the identification and promotion of these so-called empirically supported treatments (ESTs) has been paralleled by movement toward evidence-based corrections; that is, discovering and employing what works in corrections, according to research by D. L. MacKenzie in 2000. The studies of what works have yielded promising results.

Interpersonal skills training, for example, has shown some promise for reducing recidivism among children and young adults, according to research by M. W. Lipsey and F. T. Wilson in 1998. The most effective approaches, however, seem to be cognitive-behavioral programs, which are intended to address the dysfunctional thinking of offenders, and have shown considerable evidence of effectiveness. This type of intervention is so effective it led P. Gendreau, C. Goggin, F. Cullen, and D. Andrews to summarize the findings of their 2001 meta-analysis of treatment efficacy as follows: "In summary, the addition of this body of evidence to the "what works" debate leads to the inescapable conclusion that, when it comes to reducing individual offender recidivism, the 'only game in town' is appropriate cognitive-behavioral treatments which embody known principles of effective intervention."

Two other, closely related approaches have also been shown to be effective, particularly in community settings. Multisystemic Therapy (MST) and Functional Family Therapy (FFT) have been identified as model programs by the Center for the Study and Prevention of Violence's Blueprints program. MST is an intervention approach targeting multiple facets of youths' lives across multiple service sectors that is effective in reducing delinquency, substance abuse, and the deleterious effects of emotional disturbance. FFT also targets youths at high risk for recidivism by employing a team approach in multiple settings. It, too, has been shown to be effective, according to several researchers, including J. Alexander in 1998. Although there are a number of specific approaches with demonstrated efficacy in addressing particular problems, the answers to the question "what works" have also led to broader conclusions.

Principles of Effective Treatment

Whether the treatment at issue is interpersonal skills training, some type of cognitive–behavioral intervention, multisystemic treatment, or functional family treatment it should be focused on criminogenic needs. This treatment emphasis on dynamic risk factors is one of three principles for effective treatment programming advanced by Andrews and colleagues in 1990. Another they identify as "responsivity," but essentially involves relying on ESTs and evidence-based correctional practices. The third principle urges focusing resources and efforts on those at greatest risk for recidivism or escalation of their delinquency, largely because they are also the most responsive to treatment.

Whom to Treat

Within the juvenile justice system, the distinction between those who are likely to benefit from treatment and those who are not is an important one, in large part because it has implications for striking the balance between punishment and treatment. The efforts to draw the distinction are complicated by the fact that the need for rehabilitative treatment is highly variable across people and within people across time. The variability in treatment need is acutely problematic for adolescents. According to Steinberg and Scott in 2003, developmental differences between adolescents and adults undermine the ability to make reliable predictions about how they will behave in the future. This is so for a variety of reasons, including: (1) not all people have the same problems, (2) not all people with problems have them to the same degree, and (3) not all problems are equally amenable to treatment.

Efforts at identifying good treatment candidates and poor treatment candidates are further complicated by the ubiquitous nature of delinquency. According to Piquero, Brezina, and Turner in 2005, about 90 percent of adolescents engage in at least one delinquent act. However, contemporary research suggests that there are two very different trajectories for those who engage in delinquent acts, each with different prognoses and treatment strategies. Terry Moffitt has identified life course–persistent delinquents as those whose delinquency begins early and persists across much of the lifespan, whereas adolescence-limited delinquents begin to engage in delinquent acts later than their life course–persistent counterparts and stop much sooner. For this latter group, their delinquency trajectory begins in adolescence, peaks during the teen years, and then falls sharply in late adolescence. Support for Moffitt's conceptualization of delinquency has been found with males, the group at highest risk for delinquency, community samples, and populations at risk for delinquency.

Pro: Arguments in Support of Treatment

The move away from treatment and rehabilitation has been a move toward punishment and incapacitation. To the extent the clamor for more punishment and less treatment is rational, it likely is grounded in specific deterrence theory, which supposes that errant behavior decreases in proportion to the severity of the consequences of that behavior, according to J. Andenaes in 1968. The public and some policymakers believe strongly in the deterrent value of incarceration. This belief and resulting policy decisions have little underlying empirical support—an unfortunate truism for correctional policies related to treatment in general, as D. L. MacKenzie relates in 2000.

Studies of the effectiveness of punishment in the form of incarceration have led to the conclusion that it simply does not work to reduce recidivism—specifically, research by R. L. Akers and C. S. Sellers 2004, and Cullen and colleagues in 2002. Some studies suggest that prison actually increases recidivism, such as findings by J. R. Petersilia, S. Turner, and J. E. Peterson for the RAND group in 1986, perhaps through the weakening of social bonds, as found by R. J. Sampson and J. H. Laub in 1993. These results pertaining to the relative ineffectiveness of punishments seem robust, as the findings generalize beyond samples from the United States and apply to boot camps as well as incarceration. Moreover, even where there has been evidence of the effectiveness of incarceration on deterrence, efficiency may be called into question. T. Fabelo, for example, in 1995 reported that a 30 percent increase in incarceration rates led to a five percent decrease in crime. The available evidence in support of incarceration suggests that deterrence is only likely to work with those already at low risk and where relatively harsh prison conditions are involved.

Treatment Does Work

In their review of meta-analyses of the relative efficacies of treatment versus sanctions, Lipsey and Cullen in 2007 found that sanctions, at best, yielded modest reductions in recidivism and, at worst, increases in recidivism; whereas studies of treatment consistently showed its effectiveness.

They found that the worst mean treatment effect sizes for treatment were better than the best effect sizes for sanctions. Of course, not all treatments are equally efficacious. Recent research shows that treatment to reduce recidivism can be effective if it targets criminogenic factors, relies on approaches that build skills, and is directed at those at highest risk for recidivism.

Con: Arguments Against Treatment

Proponents of treatment amenability and the effectiveness of punishment, from the vantage point of the clinical psychologist, focuses on the effect of these interventions on the person whose behavior is targeted, namely the youthful offender. Although this is one important consideration in American justice systems—both juvenile and adult—it is only one. As A. Gruber observed in 2010: "In criminal law circles, the accepted wisdom is that there are two and only two true justifications of punishment: retributivism and utilitarianism. The multitude of moral claims about punishment may thus be reduced to two propositions: (1) punishment should be imposed because defendants deserve it, and (2) punishment should be imposed because it makes society safer."

This conclusion—that treatment works—really focuses only on the latter proposition, namely, that punishment should be imposed because it makes society safer. The conclusion is largely silent as to the first proposition, that "defendants deserve it." Attention to desert renders treatment efficacy irrelevant and changes the questions from focusing on what we do for and with youthful offenders, to what we do to them.

Although it is somewhat gauche to state openly, humans feel compelled to hurt the people who hurt them. This observation is not discernible only through introspection; "empirical studies confirm a nearly universal human intuition that serious wrongdoing deserves punishment," stated P. H. Robinson and R. Kurzban in 2007. This principle has been embodied in the doctrine of *lex talionis,* which has its genesis in the Book of Deuteronomy and is defined thus in *Black's Law Dictionary* (2009): "the law of retaliation, under which punishment should be in kind—an eye for an eye, a tooth for a tooth, and so on." More recently, the classic moral philosopher John Rawls, said,

> What we may call the retributive view is that punishment is justified on the grounds that wrongdoing merits punishment. It is morally fitting that a person who does wrong should suffer in proportion to his wrongdoing. That a criminal should be punished follows from

his guilt, and the severity of the appropriate punishment depends on the depravity of his act. The state of affairs where a wrongdoer suffers punishment is morally better than the state of affairs where he does not; and it is better irrespective of any of the consequences of punishing him.

Although the suggestion that the severity of punishment should "depend on the depravity of [the] act" seems straightforward enough, determination of desert as a function of blameworthiness is extremely difficult, even under the best of circumstances. The difficulty is exacerbated where, as here, extenuating circumstances—in this case, youth—may partially exculpate wrongdoing. Fortunately (or not), blameworthiness is not the only criterion for determining desert.

Distributive Justice

An alternative approach to determining desert is one that focuses on distributive justice. A. Gruber notes, "The distributive theory of criminal law holds that an offender ought to be punished, not because he is culpable or because punishment increases net security, but because punishment appropriately distributes pleasure and pain between the offender and victim." Punishment of this variety is oriented toward improving the welfare of the victim of the crime. This facet of distributive criminal justice distinguishes it from the Rawlsian approach.

In response to increasing juvenile crime rates in the 1990s, systemic responses to juveniles became not only more punitive and oriented toward the welfare of victims, but also less rehabilitative and focused on the needs of youthful offenders. The very name of the recently introduced Juvenile Justice Accountability and Improvement Act of 2009 makes it clear that juvenile offender accountability should is a primary objective of lawmakers.

Despite the juvenile justice system's early laudable emphasis on offender treatment and rehabilitation, it is a justice system nonetheless, and the dictates of justice increasingly demand that offenders be held to account. Unfortunately, these dual goals of treatment and accountability are sometimes at odds with one another, and may lead to confusion of approach, as noted by P. M. Lyons in 2002. The things people do to make other people suffer should be different from the things that are done to make people better.

Issues of distributive criminal justice, blameworthiness, criminal culpability, and retribution are beyond the scope of a work on treatment and rehabilitation. Moreover, such concerns are more properly addressed on deontological, moral, philosophical, or other grounds, whereas treatment and rehabilitation are more properly addressed on empirical grounds. The point of this argument is not to strike the balance on the fulcrum of desert, but rather, to point out that such a fulcrum exists and that reasonable people will seek the tipping point.

The Future of Treatment and Rehabilitation

The future of treatment and rehabilitation should be bright. The movements toward empirically supported mental health treatments and evidence-based practices in corrections have demonstrated that many approaches work not only to reduce recidivism, but also to address the mental health needs of children who happen to be accessing services through the juvenile justice system as opposed to one of the other youth-serving systems. Appropriate assessment techniques should allow system personnel to target those persons most at risk. Once identified, known criminogenic needs can be addressed through approaches that are known to work. Although it has taken a century, the treatment and rehabilitation ideals that prompted the establishment of the juvenile court in the first place are finally within reach.

See Also: 3. At-Risk Youth; 4. Boot Camps; 8. Juvenile Detention Facilities; 10. Juvenile Offenders in Adult Courts; 11. Juveniles in Adult Correctional Facilities; 15. Racial Disparities; 19. Serious and Violent Juvenile Offenders.

Further Readings

Aguilar, B., L. A. Sroufe, B. Egeland, and E. Carlson. "Distinguishing the Early-Onset/Persistent and Adolescence-Onset Antisocial Behavior Types: From Birth to 16 Years." *Development and Psychopathology,* v.12 (2000).

Akers, R. L., and C. S. Sellers. *Criminological Theories: Introduction, Evaluation, and Application.* Los Angeles: Roxbury, 2004.

Alexander, J., C. Barton, D. Gordon, J. Grotpeter, K. Hansson, R. Harrison, S. Mears, S. Mihalic, B. Parsons, C. Pugh, S. Schulman, H. Waldron, and T. Sexton. "Functional Family Therapy: Blueprints for Violence Prevention: Book Three." In *Blueprints for Violence Prevention Series*, edited by D. S. Elliott. Boulder, CO: Center for the Study and Prevention of Violence, Institute of Behavioral Science, University of Colorado, 1998.

Allen, F. A. *The Decline of the Rehabilitative Ideal*. New Haven, CT: Yale University Press, 1981.

Andenaes, J. "Does Punishment Deter Crime?" *Criminal Law Quarterly*, v.11 (1968).

Andrews, D. A., I. Zinger, R. D. Hoge, J. Bonta, P. Gendreau, and F. T. Cullen. "Does Correctional Treatment Work? A Clinically Relevant and Psychologically Informed Meta-Analysis." *Criminology*, v.28, (1990).

Barber, C. C., A. Rosenblatt, L. Harris, and C. C. Attkisson. "Use of Mental Health Services Among Severely Emotionally Disturbed Children and Adolescents in San Francisco." *Journal of Child and Family Studies*, v.1 (1992).

Blinder, B. J., W. M. Young, K. R. Fineman, and S. J. Miller. "The Children's Psychiatric Hospital Unit in the Community: I. Concept And Development." *American Journal of Psychiatry*, v.135 (1978).

Bloom, R. B., and L. R. Hopewell. "Psychiatric Hospitalization of Adolescents and Successful Mainstream Reentry." *Exceptional Children*, v.48 (1982).

Blumstein, A. "Final Thoughts: An Overview of the Symposium and Some Next Steps." *Annals of the American Academy of Political and Social Science*, v.602 (2005).

Burns, B. J., K. Hoagwood, and P. J. Mrazek. "Effective Treatment for Mental Disorders in Children And Adolescents." *Clinical Child and Family Psychology Review*, v.2 (1999).

Center for Substance Abuse Prevention. *Strengthening America's Families: Model Family Programs for Substance Abuse and Delinquency Prevention*. Salt Lake City, UT: Department of Health Promotion and Education, 2000.

Christopher, R. L. "Deterring Retributivism: The Injustice of 'Just' Punishment." *Northwestern University Law Review*, v.96 (2002).

Chung, I., K. G. Hill, J. D. Hawkins, L. D. Gilchrist, and D. S. Nagin. "Childhood Predictors of Offense Trajectories." *Journal of Research in Crime and Delinquency*, v.39 (2002).

Cocozza, J., and K. Skowyra. "Youth With Mental Health Disorders: Issues and Emerging Responses." *Office of Juvenile Justice and Delinquency Prevention Journal*, v.7/1 (2000).

Cullen, F. T., and P. Gendreau. "Assessing Correctional Rehabilitation: Policy, Practice, and Prospects." In *NIJ Criminal Justice 2000: Changes in Decision Making and Discretion in the Criminal Justice System*, edited by J. Horney. Washington, DC: U.S. Department of Justice, National Institute of Justice, 2000.

Cullen, F. T., and K. E. Gilbert. *Reaffirming Rehabilitation.* Cincinnati, OH: Anderson, 1982.

Cullen, F. T., T. C. Pratt, S. L. Micelli, and M. M. Moon. "Dangerous Liaison? Rational Choice Theory as the Basis for Correctional Intervention." In *Rational Choice and Criminal Behavior: Recent Research and Future Challenges,* edited by A. R. Piquero and S. G. Tibbets. New York: Routledge, 2002.

Damasio, A. R., and S. W. Anderson. "The Frontal Lobes." In *Clinical Neuropsychology,* edited by Kenneth M. Heilman and Edward Valenstein. New York: Oxford University Press, 2003.

DeJong, C. "Survival Analysis and Specific Deterrence: Integrating Theoretical and Empirical Models of Recidivism." *Criminology,* v.35 (1997).

Dowden, C., D. Antonowicz, and D. A. Andrews. "The Effectiveness of Relapse Prevention With Offenders: A Meta-Analysis." *International Journal of Offender Therapy and Comparative Criminology,* v.47 (2003).

Fabelo, T. *Testing the Case for More Incarceration in Texas: The Record So Far.* Austin, TX: Criminal Justice Policy Council, State of Texas, 1995.

Fombonne, E., G. Wostear, V. Cooper, R. Harrington, and M. Rutter. "The Maudsley Long-Term Follow-Up of Child and Adolescent Depression: 1. Psychiatric Outcomes in Adulthood, and 2. Suicidality, Criminality and Social Dysfunction in Adulthood." *British Journal of Psychiatry,* v.179 (2001).

Gendreau, P., C. Goggin, and F. Cullen. *The Effects of Prison Sentences on Recidivism.* Ottowa, ON: Solicitor General Canada, 1999.

Gendreau, P., C. Goggin, F. T. Cullen, and D. Andrews. "The Effects of Community Sanctions and Incarceration on Recidivism." In *Compendium 2000 on Effective Correctional Programming: Volume 1,* edited by L. L. Montiuk and R. C. Serin. Ottawa, Ontario, Canada: Correctional Service Canada, 2001.

Gruber, A. "A Distributive Theory of Criminal Law." *William and Mary Law Review,* v.52 (2010).

Hobbs, N. *The Troubled and Troubling Child: Reeducation in Mental Health, Education, and Human Services Programs for Children and Youth.* San Francisco: Jossey-Bass, 1982.

Hudspeth, W. J., and K. Pribram. "Psychophysiological Indices of Cerebral Maturation." *International Journal of Psychophysiology,* v.12 (1992).

Jackson-Beeck, M., I. M. Schwartz, and A. Rutherford. *Trends and Issues in Juvenile Confinement for Psychiatric and Chemical Dependency Treatment in the U.S., England, and Wales.* Minneapolis: University of Minnesota, Center for the Study of Youth Policy, 1987.

Katz, L. "Criminal Law." In *A Companion to Philosophy of Law and Legal Theory,* edited by D. Patterson. Victoria, Australia: Blackwell, 1996.

Kent v. U.S., 383 U.S. 541; 86 S. Ct. 1045; 16 L. Ed. 2d 84 (1966).

Knapp, M., P. McCrone, E. Fombonne, J. Beecham, and G. Wostear. "The Madsley Long-Term Follow-Up of Child and Adolescent Depression: 3. Impact Of Comorbid Conduct Disorder on Service Use and Costs in Adulthood." *British Journal of Psychiatry,* v.180 (2002).

Landenberger, N. A., and M. W. Lipsey. "The Positive Effects of Cognitive-Behavioral Programs for Offenders: A Meta-Analysis of Factors Associated With Effective Treatment." *Journal of Experimental Criminology,* v.1 (2005).

Lewis, D. O. and S. S. Shanok. "Racial Factors Influencing the Diagnosis, Disposition, and Treatment of Deviant Adolescents." In *Vulnerabilities to Delinquency,* edited by D. O. Lewis. New York: Spectrum, 1981.

Lipsey, M. W. "Juvenile Delinquency Treatment: A Meta-Analytic Inquiry Into the Variability of Effects." In *Meta-Analysis for Explanation: A Casebook,* edited by Thomas D. Cook, Harris Cooper, David S. Cordray, Heidi Hartmann, Larry V. Hedges, Richard J. Light, Thomas A. Lewis, and Frederick Mosteller. New York: Russell Sage, 1992.

Lipsey, M. W., and F. T. Cullen. "The Effectiveness of Correctional Rehabilitation: A Review of Systematic Reviews." *Annual Review of Law and Social Science,* v.3 (2007).

Lipsey, M. W., and D. B. Wilson. "Effective Intervention for Serious Juvenile Offenders: A Synthesis of Research." In *Serious and Violent Juvenile Offenders: Risk Factors and Successful Interventions,* edited by R. Loeber and D. P. Farrington. Thousand Oaks, CA: Sage, 1998.

Lipton, D. S., R. Martinson, and J. Wilks. *The Effectiveness of Correctional Treatment: A Survey of Treatment Evaluation Studies.* New York: Praeger, 1975.

Lyons, P. M., Jr. *Deviation From Progressive Sanctions Guidelines in Juvenile Justice: What Does it Mean?* Testimony before the Texas Senate Jurisprudence Committee (April 25, 2002).

MacKenzie, D. L. "Corrections and Sentencing in the 21st Century: Evidence-Based Corrections and Sentencing." *Prison Journal,* v.81 (2001).

MacKenzie, D. L. "Evidence-Based Corrections: Identifying What Works." *Crime and Delinquency,* v.46 (2000).

MacKenzie, D. L., D. B. Wilson, and S. B. Kider. (2001). "Effects of Correctional Boot Camps on Offending." *The Annals of the American Academy of Political and Social Science,* v.578 (2001).

Melton, G. B., P. M. Lyons Jr., and W. J. Spaulding. *No Place to Go: The Civil Commitment of Minors.* Lincoln, NE: University of Nebraska Press, 1998.

Mesulum, M. "Behavioral Neuroanatomy: Large-Scale Networks, Association Cortex, Frontal Syndromes, the Limbic System, and Hemispheric Specializations." In *Principles of Behavioral and Cognitive Neurology,* edited by M. Marsel Mesulam. New York: Oxford University Press, 2000.

Mistretta v. U.S., 488 U.S. 361; 109 S. Ct. 647; 102 L. Ed. 2d 714 (1989).

Mitchell, O., D. B. Wilson, and D. L. MacKenzie. "Does Incarceration-Based Drug Treatment Reduce Recidivism? A Meta-Analytic Synthesis of the Research." *Journal of Experimental Criminology,* v.3 (2007).

Moffitt, T. E., A. Caspi, H. Harrington, and B. J. Milne. "Males on the Life-Course-Persistent and Adolescence-Limited Antisocial Pathways: Follow-Up at Age 26 Years." *Development and Psychopathology,* v.14 (2002).

Morris, N. *The Future of Imprisonment.* Chicago: University of Chicago Press, 1974.

National Institutes of Health. *Preventing Violence and Related Health-Risking Social Behaviors in Adolescents: An NIH State-of-the-Science Conference.* Bethesda, MD: NIH, 2004.

O'Donohue, W., J. A. Buchanan, and J. E. Fisher. "Characteristics of Empirically Supported Treatments." *Journal of Psychotherapy Research and Practice,* v.9 (2000).

Osgood, D. W., E. M. Foster, C. Flanagan, and G. R. Ruth, eds. *On Your Own Without a Net: The Transition to Adulthood for Vulnerable Populations.* Chicago: University of Chicago Press, 2005.

Petersilia, J. R., S. Turner, and J. E. Peterson. *Probation in California: Implications for Crime and Offender Recidivism.* Santa Monica, CA: RAND, 1986.

President's New Freedom Commission on Mental Health. *Achieving the Promise: Transforming Mental Health Care in America—Final Report.* Rockville, MD: DHHS, 2003.

Rawls, J. "Two Concepts of Rules." *The Philosophical Review,* v.64 (1955).

Redding, R. E. "Adult Punishment for Juvenile Offenders: Does it Reduce Crime?" In *Handbook of Children, Culture, and Violence,* edited by Nancy E. Dowd, Dorothy G. Singer, and Robin F. Wilson. Thousand Oaks, CA: Sage, 2006.

Redding, R. E., and J. C. Howell. "Blended Sentencing in American Juvenile Courts." In *The Changing Borders of Juvenile Justice,* edited by Jeffrey Fagan and Franklin Zimring. Chicago: University of Chicago Press, 2000.

Robinson, P. H., and R. Kurzban. "Concordance and Conflict in Intuitions of Justice." *Minnesota Law Review,* v.91 (2007).

Sampson, R. J., and J. H. Laub. *Crime in the Making: Pathways and Turning Points Through Life.* Cambridge, MA: Harvard University Press, 1993.

Silver, S. E., A. J. Duchnowski, K. B. Kutash, R. M. Friedman, M. Eisen, M. E. Prange, N. A. Brandenburg, and P. E. Greenbaum. "A Comparison of Children With Serious Emotional Disturbance Served in Residential and School Settings." *Journal of Child and Family Studies,* v.1 (1992).

Simic, M., and E. Fombonne. "Depressive Conduct Disorder: Symptom Patterns and Correlates in Referred Children and Adolescents." *Journal of Affective Disorders,* v.62 (2001).

Steinberg, L., and E. Cauffman. "The Elephant in the Courtroom: A Developmental Perspective on the Adjudication of Youthful Offenders." *Virginia Journal of Social Policy and Law,* v.6 (1999).

Thatcher, R. W., R. A. Walker, and S. Giudice. "Human Cerebral Hemispheres Develop at Different Rates and Ages." *Science,* v.236 (1987).

U.S. Department of Health and Human Services. *Mental Health: A Report of the Surgeon General.* Rockville, MD: HHS, 1999.

U.S. Public Health Service. *Youth Violence: A Report of the Surgeon General.* Washington, DC: U.S. Public Health Service, 2001.

U.S. Senate. *Senate Report No. 98-225* Washington, DC (1983).

Velez, L. A. "Rethink How We Punish Juveniles." *Atlanta Journal and Constitution* (August 18, 2010).

Wilson, D. B., C. A. Gallagher, and D. L. MacKenzie. "A Meta-Analysis of Corrections-Based Education, Vocation, and Work Programs for Adult Offenders." *Journal of Research in Crime and Delinquency,* v.37 (2000).

Wilson, D. B., D. L. MacKenzie, and F. N. Mitchell. "The Effects of Correctional Boot Camps on Offending." (2005). The Campbell Collaboration. http://www.campbellcollaboration.org (Accessed November 2010).

Wilson, D., O. Mitchell, and D. L. MacKenzie. "A Systematic Review of Drug Court Effects on Recidivism." *Journal of Experimental Criminology,* v.2 (2006).

Index

Index note: Chapter titles and their page numbers are in **boldface**.

About the General Editor

William J. Chambliss is professor of sociology at The George Washington University. He has written and edited more than 25 books and numerous articles for professional journals in sociology, criminology, and law. His work integrating the study of crime with the creation and implementation of criminal law has been a central theme in his writings and research. His articles on the historical development of vagrancy laws, the legal process as it affects different social classes and racial groups, and his attempt to introduce the study of state-organized crimes into the mainstream of social science research have punctuated his career.

He is the recipient of numerous awards and honors including a Doctorate of Laws Honoris Causa, University of Guelph, Guelph, Ontario, Canada, 1999; the 2009 Lifetime Achievement Award, Sociology of Law, American Sociological Association; the 2009 Lifetime Achievement Award, Law and Society, Society for the Study of Social Problems; the 2001 Edwin H. Sutherland Award, American Society of Criminology; the 1995 Major Achievement Award, American Society of Criminology; the 1986. Distinguished Leadership in Criminal Justice, Bruce Smith, Sr. Award, Academy of Criminal Justice Sciences; and the 1985 Lifetime Achievement Award, Criminology, American Sociological Association.

Professor Chambliss is a past president of the American Society of Criminology and past president of the Society for the Study of Social Problems. His current research covers a range of lifetime interests in international drug-control policy, class, race, gender and criminal justice and the history of piracy on the high seas.